Masks and Staffs

Integration and Conflict Studies

Published in association with the Max Planck Institute for Social Anthropology, Halle/Saale

Series Editor:
Günther Schlee, *Director at the Max Planck Institute for Social Anthropology*

Editorial Board:
Brian Donahoe, *Max Planck Institute for Social Anthropology*
John Eidson, *Max Planck Institute for Social Anthropology*
Peter Finke, *University of Zurich*
Joachim Görlich, *Max Planck Institute for Social Anthropology*
Jacqueline Knörr, *Max Planck Institute for Social Anthropology*
Bettina Mann, *Max Planck Institute for Social Anthropology*
Stephen Reyna, *Max Planck Institute for Social Anthropology*

Assisted by:
Cornelia Schnepel and Viktoria Zeng,
Max Planck Institute for Social Anthropology

The objective of the Max Planck Institute for Social Anthropology is to advance anthropological fieldwork and enhance theory building. "Integration" and "conflict," the central themes of this series, are major concerns of the contemporary social sciences and of significant interest to the general public. They have also been among the main research areas of the institute since its foundation. Bringing together international experts, *Integration and Conflict Studies* includes both monographs and edited volumes, and offers a forum for studies that contribute to a better understanding of processes of identification and inter-group relations.

For full volume listing, please see page 251.

Masks and Staffs

Identity Politics in the Cameroon Grassfields

Michaela Pelican

berghahn
NEW YORK • OXFORD
www.berghahnbooks.com

First published in 2015 by
Berghahn Books
www.berghahnbooks.com

© 2015, 2017 Michaela Pelican
First paperback edition published in 2017

All rights reserved. Except for the quotation of short passages
for the purposes of criticism and review, no part of this book
may be reproduced in any form or by any means, electronic or
mechanical, including photocopying, recording, or any information
storage and retrieval system now known or to be invented,
without written permission of the publisher.

Library of Congress Cataloging-in-Publication Data
Pelican, Michaela, author. Masks and staffs : identity politics in the Cameroon Grassfields / Michaela Pelican.
   pages cm. -- (Integration and conflict studies ; volume 11)
   ISBN 978-1-78238-728-2 (hardback : alk. paper) — ISBN 978-1-78533-514-3 (paperback) — ISBN 978-1-78238-729-9 (ebook)
   1. Ethnicity--Cameroon. 2. Ethnic conflict--Cameroon. 3. Ethnic relations--Political aspects. 4. Cameroon--Ethnic relations. I. Title. II. Series: Integration and conflict studies ; v. 11.
   DT570.P45 2015
   305.80096711--dc23
                                                              2015006531

British Library Cataloguing in Publication Data
A catalogue record for this book is available from the British Library

ISBN 978-1-78238-728-2 (hardback)
ISBN 978-1-78533-514-3 (paperback)
ISBN 978-1-78238-729-9 (ebook)

for Stefan

Contents

List of Figures and Tables	viii
Acknowledgements	x
Notes on Transliteration	xi
List of Abbreviations	xii
Introduction	1
1 Setting the Scene: Cultural Difference and Political Rivalry in Times of Transition	23
2 The Power of the *Fon*: Nchaney Political History	48
3 From Pastoral Society to Indigenous People: Mbororo Identity Politics	76
4 A Shift to Economic Competition? Farmer–Herder Conflict and Cattle Theft in the Misaje Area	109
5 On Being Hausa: Consolidation of the Hausa Ethnic Category in the Grassfields	135
6 Grassfielder by Birth, Muslim by Choice: Religious and Ethnic Conversion	161
7 The Murder of Mr X: Legal Pluralism and Conflict Management in the Early 2000s	184
Epilogue	210
Glossary	215
References	219
Index	235

Figures and Tables

Figures

I.1	A working model of ethnic and cultural categories relevant for this study	13
I.2	Administrative structure of the North West Region	14
I.3	Research area	15
I.4	The central area of Misaje town	17
1.1	Painting of Mbororo *kariya* versus Nchaney *nggumba ju-ju*	26
2.1	Shey Sale and Fon Michael, 1968	56
2.2	Administrative induction of Fon Richard, 1998	57
2.3	The Nchaney polity and neighbouring chiefdoms	60
2.4	Layers of Nchaney identity	72
3.1	Aku and Jaafun migration to northwest Cameroon	81
3.2	Spatial distribution of Jaafun and Aku in the North West Region	86
3.3	Early Mbororo grazier in the Cameroon Grassfields, 1930s	87
3.4	Historical Sabga rulers	97
3.5	Grassfields and Mbororo rulers, 1993	98
4.1	The enactment of farmer–herder conflict, 2001	124
5.1	Current Hausa settlements in the North West Region	136
5.2	Hausa long-distance trade between Nigeria and the Grassfields	142
5.3	Donkey caravan, 1930s	143

Tables

I.1	Population statistics, Misaje Sub-Division, 1999/2000	16
2.1	Name-list of Nchaney *fon*s	54
4.1	Cattle-herding statistics for the Misaje area, 2000/2001	117
6.1	Comparing religious and ethnic conversion in the Grassfields and northern Cameroon	179
7.1	Elwert's field of four poles	185

7.2 Schematic illustration of legal forums operative in northwest
     Cameroon   189
7.3 Forum shopping in the murder conflict   202

Acknowledgements

I wish to express my profound gratitude to the many people and academic institutions that have made this book possible. First and foremost my appreciation goes to interlocutors and friends in Cameroon for welcoming me in their midst and sharing their experiences with me. Among them were the members of my research team, Haruna Kadiri, Jonathan Ngeh, Talatu Yusufa, the late Bebi Halima, the late Jerome Bah and my hosts and long-term friends Jeinabu Nyapendo and Patrick Nji. I also thank the current and former members of MBOSCUDA and Ballotiral for their continuous support and comradeship.

Moreover, the realization of this study would not have been possible without the stimulating intellectual environment and the generous support of the Max Planck Institute for Social Anthropology in Halle/Saale. I thank its director Günther Schlee and all my former colleagues for inspiring discussions and their collegiality, as well as for administrative support. Likewise, I thank Burkhard Schnepel of the University of Halle-Wittenberg and Glenn Bowman of the University of Kent for their critical feedback. The book further benefited from stimulating comments of Cameroonist scholars and the readers of Berghahn. It also includes findings from subsequent research carried out at the Department of Anthropology, University of Zurich, as well as insights derived from being a member and co-director of the University of Cologne Forum 'Ethnicity as a Political Resource: Perspectives from Africa, Latin America, Asia and Europe'. I thank Cornelia Schnepel for her editorial assistance and appreciate the support provided by the Max Planck Institute of Social Anthropology and the University of Cologne in the book's concluding phase. My special thanks go to my family and friends, to Billy MacKinnon for his vital input and support, and to Patrick La Barre for his enduring encouragement.

Notes on Transliteration

As this study is set in a multi-ethnic and multilingual region, local terms are drawn from a variety of languages, including Fulfulde, Hausa, various Grassfields languages and Pidgin English, the *lingua franca* of anglophone Cameroon. In terms of transliteration, I have tried to combine correct linguistic principles with pragmatic modifications to facilitate their reading. For this purpose, I have drawn on the dictionaries of Noye (1989) and Tourneux and Dairou (1999) for Fulfulde, as well as Awde (1996) and Herms (1987) for Hausa. With regard to Grassfields languages and Pidgin English, I use my own transliterations. The terms are written in a way that allows the average English-speaking reader to pronounce them approximately as they should sound.

The following basic rules apply:
B   indicates an implosive 'b', as in FulBe
D   indicates an implosive 'd', as in *arDo*

Abbreviations

APESS	Association pour la Promotion de l'Elevage au Sahel et en Savane (international NGO)
BECUDA	Bessa Cultural and Development Association (regional NGO)
CFA	Communauté Financière Africaine (the CFA franc is the currency used in many parts of West and Central Africa)
CONAC	Commission Nationale Anti-Corruption (government body)
CPDM	Cameroon People's Democratic Movement (political party) also known as 'Chop People Dem Moni' in Pidgin English, meaning 'the party that eats people's money'
DO	Divisional officer (administrative head of a sub-division)
ECOSOC	Economic and Social Council (United Nations organ)
GERDDES	Groupe d'Etudes et de Recherche en Démocratie, Développement Economique et Sociale (group of Cameroonian scientists)
IMF	International Monetary Fund
MBOSCUDA	Mbororo Social and Cultural Development Association (national NGO)
MELA	Misaje Area Elite Association (regional NGO)
NGO	non-governmental organization
NOWEFA	North West Fons' Association (NGO with political aspirations, superseded by NOWEFU)
NOWEFCO	North West Fons' Conference (NGO with political aspirations, superseded by NOWEFU)
NOWEFU	North West Fons' Union (NGO with political aspirations)
NUDP	National Union for Democracy and Progress (political party)
SDF	Social Democratic Front (political party) also known as 'Suffer Don Finish' in Pidgin English, meaning 'the end of suffering'

SIRDEP	Society for Initiatives in Rural Development and Environmental Protection (national NGO)
SODELCO	Société de Développement d'Elevage et du Commerce (national NGO)
SODEPA	Société de Développement et d'Exploitation des Productions Animales (parastatal enterprise)
UN	United Nations

Introduction

Cameroon, October 1997. Conflict emerges over the obligation to abstain from wearing caps or headscarves during the investiture ceremonies of a new Grassfields chief. While starting off as a minor disagreement over religious and cultural difference, the issue soon evolves into a near-violent clash that threatens to undermine the social coexistence of Grassfielders, Mbororo and Hausa. Two factions face each other in a symbolic stand-off with staffs, masks and guns to hand. Imminent violence is obviated by the intervention of state authority; the crisis is diffused. Eventually, the parties reconcile and agree to ignore the matter.

July 2001. The decapitated body of a local Grassfielder is found by a riverbank. Circumstantial evidence regarding the culprit points to an influential and wealthy Mbororo man, whose relationship with the local Grassfields community has been coloured by competition over access to land. While legal prosecution takes its course, the local Grassfielders' elite association takes up the issue and elevates it from an individual to an ethnic conflict. Their attempts to mobilize Grassfielders against Mbororo and to influence legal procedure through political lobbying both fail. Eventually, the case is put off without judgement, and social relations gradually revert to normal.

The two incidents above constitute the vertices of this book. They both occurred in Misaje, a small town in the anglophone northwest of Cameroon – also known as the Cameroon Grassfields – and took place just four years apart. What is remarkable about them? First, both incidents were perceived as conflicts over religious and cultural difference, and framed in ethnic terms. Second, while the first conflict had a rather confrontational, nearly violent character, the actors in the later conflict opted for procedural approaches, namely litigation and lobbying. Both conflicts are representative of their time. The 1990s represent the heyday of Cameroon's democratization, which was accompanied by an increased propensity for militancy and violence, both on the part of the population and the government. Concurrently, the country's economy dwindled owing to structural adjustment programmes and the devaluation of the CFA franc in 1994. The subsequent decade witnessed the rise of global discourses of human and minority rights, with a significant impact on people's self-understanding and political strategies. During both decades, emphasis was placed on ethnic over national identity, thus engendering an ethnicization of national and local politics.

This book investigates the role of ethnicity in conflict situations, and considers the mechanisms that promote peaceful cohabitation and integration in an ethnically and culturally heterogeneous environment. It looks at transformations in conflict strategies, placing individual and group strategies in the context of national and international political discourse.

Philip Burnham opens his book *The Politics of Cultural Difference in Northern Cameroon* (1996) with a description of two incidents of ethnic violence in Meiganga that took place in the early 1990s and culminated in some hundred dead. He places these events in the context of the country's political transition, and points out that compared to the large-scale massacres in Rwanda, Somalia and Liberia – or more recently in Sudan, Côte d'Ivoire and Congo-Kinshasa – they were rather unremarkable. However, less impressed by numbers than by the unexpected nature of these events, Burnham engages with interethnic relations in north central Cameroon and the social processes and cultural logics that may contribute to ethnic conflict. He concludes with a rather gloomy projection of increasing political instability, disorder and violence – a scenario that, luckily, has not materialized. This study tries to answer the question of why Burnham's prediction has been vitiated by recent history, and to delineate the factors that account for integration and the avoidance of ethnic violence in a political environment that nonetheless accentuates ethnic and cultural difference.

In a topical book, Peter Geschiere (2009) investigates the current salience of discourses of autochthony in various parts of Africa and Europe. He places the growing obsession with local belonging in the context of globalization, and argues that, in Africa, democratization and decentralization have contributed to the emergence of a politics of belonging, thus undermining national citizenship in favour of ethnic and regional identities. This book takes up Geschiere's suggestions, and explores the ways in which individuals and collectives in northwest Cameroon apply and experiment with concepts of ethnicity, autochthony, indigeneity and similar notions of belonging in order to substantiate their claims vis-à-vis each other, the state and international organizations. While this study acknowledges variation and creativity in the use of these concepts, it also considers the limits of their applicability, as illustrated in the failed mobilization of Grassfielders against Mbororo in the above-mentioned murder conflict. In studying multiple ethnic categories and changing political strategies, it asks: Do all ethnicities entail the same potential for political mobilization? And if not, how can we account for variation?

This leads us to another aspect of identity and belonging, namely its emotional capacity and visceral quality which, as Geschiere rightly points out, cannot fully be explained by historical deconstruction. We may thus draw on the work of Nicolas Argenti (2007), who analyses the embodiment of historical memory in the Cameroon Grassfields. With his focus on ritual, performance and masking as sites of contention between youths and elders, women and men, Argenti illustrates how the historical experience of marginalization, subjection and enslavement is embodied, relived and subverted. Taking into account the discursive silence regarding slavery and forced labour in Cameroon, Argenti's findings are even more compelling. In a similar vein, this book engages with both the performative and discursive sides of ethnicity. The performative and embodied dimensions of belonging are exemplified in the symbolic stand-off between Grassfields masks and Mbororo staffs in the investiture conflict, introduced above. In retrospect, interlocutors expressed bewilderment and discomfort with the confrontational character of ethnic coexistence at that time. We thus ask: How do we account for the social energy in performance? What are the conditions and mechanisms that trigger the emotional capacity of ethnicity?

On the discursive side, the book examines ethnic stereotypes, their historical roots and the conditions of their perpetuation. Here, tacit knowledge resulting from accumulated group histories and vestigial memories is a crucial factor in shaping social interaction and the perception of conflict. In this regard, we will question why farmer–herder conflict – a long-standing and pertinent issue widely addressed in research and policy across West Africa – continues to be perceived and framed in ethnic terms, despite economic diversification and alternative lines of conflict.

Starting off with the analysis of a near-violent altercation over cultural difference and political rivalry, and closing with a law case over occult murder and land issues, this book investigates both confrontational and integrative dimensions of ethnic and social coexistence, as well as collective histories in the Cameroon Grassfields. It does so by focusing on a particular political moment in history – Cameroon's democratic transition – that was shaped by a virulent politics of belonging and the subsequent traction of global rights discourse. In this sense, ethnicity is here highlighted as a salient feature of inclusion and exclusion whose particular momentum is contingent upon historical and political circumstances. Concurrently, this book argues against an easy correlation of ethnicity and conflict, and advocates thorough ethnographic and historically informed analyses of specific conflict situations.

The book takes as a case study a small town in the Cameroon Grassfields, a region that since the colonial period has enjoyed considerable attention by historians and anthropologists. Much of the literature has concentrated on the political and economic organization of Grassfields societies, with a focus on the formation and development of Grassfields polities and their interrelations. Leading scholars in this field, such as Igor Kopytoff and Jean-Pierre Warnier, have long emphasized the heterogeneous and composite nature of Grassfields societies, as reflected, for example, in Kopytoff's classical essay on 'the internal African frontier' (Kopytoff 1987). Recently, Warnier (2007) has outlined the ways in which, in the Mankon chiefdom, territorialization and locality were produced by a governmentality of containers. That is, both the chief and the chiefdom were treated as fragile containers whose bounds needed to be secured against leaking their precious contents, namely, ancestral substances and viable subjects. Conversely, unwanted social elements – Warnier figuratively calls them 'the royal excrement' – were expelled via the slave trade. Moreover, loyalty and adherence to the chiefdom were generated via control over sexuality and reproduction, a political technique internalized by means of strict moral standards. Eventually, the governmentality of containers crumbled in the first half of the twentieth century due to the chiefdom's opening up to external influences; these included the adoption of Christian ideas about love and marriage, the migration of young men to cities, their unrestrained access to commodity resources as well as the disintegration of sexuality and social reproduction. Today, the power of Grassfields chiefs no longer rests on their intrinsic connection with ancestral substances but on having access to state resources, procuring development projects and guiding cultural associations.

Following the arguments of Kopytoff and Warnier, I maintain that, up to today, territorialization and the production of locality are central to notions of ethnicity and belonging in the Grassfields. Furthermore, I argue that Grassfields societies have the capacity and techniques to accommodate not only Grassfields 'others' but outsiders in general, both historically and contemporarily. The very presence of Mbororo and Hausa throughout the Cameroon Grassfields is demonstrative of this capacity, and a feature generally understudied.

As I will demonstrate in detail, Mbororo compliance with the political authority of Grassfields chiefdoms has long supported their regional integration. It is only in the wake of Cameroon's political liberalization and the subsequent traction of international rights discourses that Mbororo individuals openly questioned their marginal position in the local and national power hierarchy. They thus initiated a vivid and ongoing debate over Mbororo identity and struggles for political recognition. As I will argue, the Mbororo case in particular illustrates the potential of ethnicity as a political resource, a discursive space and a source of social transformation.

Hausa presence in the Grassfields is a subject largely neglected in the scholarship on the region. This book argues that, while having historical roots in long-distance trade between northern Nigeria and Cameroon, today's Hausa population may be understood as a residual category composed of individuals who for structural or personal reasons have opted out of their original community, be it as a result of migration, intermarriage or religious conversion. It includes Muslim migrants from northern Cameroon and Nigeria, as well as Grassfielders who converted to Islam and settled Mbororo, all of whom congregate in specific neighbourhoods and assume a sedentary Muslim identity. The Hausa category thus serves as an example illustrating the composite, contextual and flexible character of ethnic identities in the Grassfields, as well as the complex and multiple liabilities that come with it. By integrating Grassfields societies, Mbororo and Hausa in the same study, this is the first book to focus on their very coexistence and identity politics in this region.

Naming and Claiming Identities

This study contends that in the Cameroon Grassfields ethnic awareness and the recognition of cultural difference are critical factors that shape the self-understanding of individuals and collectives, as well as their interaction with each other and the state. Ethnicity or ethnicities are here understood very broadly as instances of identity and difference. Furthermore, ethnicity is seen as essentially relational and processual.

In considering ethnicities in the Grassfields, this book takes a historical approach as promoted, among others, by John Comaroff (1995) and Carola Lentz (1998). Both authors convincingly argue that a single, abstract theory of ethnicity is impracticable, as processes leading to the creation of ethnicities are historically and regionally specific. Moreover, a historical perspective helps to avoid the fruitless controversy between primordialist and constructionist approaches, and shows that ethnic identities are neither fixed nor wholly invented.

Fredrik Barth is often seen as the leading figure of modern theories of ethnicity. In a frequently cited piece, Barth (1969) suggests focusing on group boundaries as the primary locus of defining ethnic identities and difference. Furthermore, he interprets ethnicity as a specific form of social identity, constructed under particular historical and political circumstances, and based on self-ascriptions and ascriptions by others. In a later contribution, Barth (1994) recommends modelling processes of ethnic identification on three interpenetrating levels: the micro level of individual action and experience; the median level of entrepreneurship, leadership and rhetoric; and the macro level of state policies.

In line with Barth's propositions, this book examines the emergence, transformation and political articulation of ethnic identities in the Cameroon Grassfields by focusing on historical and contemporary encounters with political or cultural 'others', as well as with colonial and postcolonial governments. It pays special attention to gendered perspectives on collective histories, and inquires if the individuals and collectives under study hold distinct emic conceptions of ethnicity, and how this affects inter-group relations. Inspired by the work of Eric Hobsbawm and Terence Ranger (1983), the study engages with the question of the extent to which ethnic identities in the Grassfields are colonial constructs. Hobsbawm and Ranger's approach has been taken further by Adam Kuper (2003, 2005), who suggests that recent policies of the United Nations that involve classifying selected groups as 'indigenous peoples' has led to the creation of 'neo-colonial' categories and identities. The interplay of global discourses, national policies and local strategies of identification and representation is a central theme explored throughout this book.

Another take on ethnicity vital to this study is the instrumentalist approach of Abner Cohen (1969, 1974). In his work on immigrant Hausa communities in southern Nigeria, Cohen shows that, in the multi-ethnic and urban environment of Ibadan, ethnicity constitutes an important form of political and economic capital, and is the key condition to individuals' participation in trading activities. Furthermore, among Hausa immigrants in Ibadan, internal status differences are largely ignored, and ethnic boundaries are kept flexible and permeable. It is on the basis of these and related findings that Cohen understands ethnicity as essentially political and instrumental.

Cohen's findings are instructive for my analysis of strategies of inclusion and exclusion among Hausa and Mbororo. While both count as immigrant and minority groups in the Cameroon Grassfields, they differ considerably in their ethnic self-understanding and degree of political mobilization. How can this be explained? Here we may do well to consider circumstantial factors, such as group size. As Günther Schlee (2008) has argued, the economies of group size and social position are crucial in determining strategies of inclusion and exclusion. For example, whereas for members of small, marginal groups it can be advantageous to integrate strangers and bond with others so as to gain political weight, leaders of larger, economically powerful groups generally benefit from excluding newcomers in order to limit the sharing of profits. This book will investigate if these and similar considerations account for different strategies of inclusion and exclusion among the groups under study.

Moreover, in examining instances of political mobilization, this study draws on the radically constructionist perspective of Roger Brubaker. Brubaker (2004) outlines the pitfalls of 'groupism'; that is, the tendency to treat ethnic groups as substantial entities to which interests and agency can be attributed. Rather, he argues, we should disentangle 'ethnicity' and 'groups', and study both as instances of social processes and perspectives on the world. Moreover, he calls on analysts to recognize organizations and individuals as the protagonists of conflict, and to be sensitive to acts of framing and narrative encoding that not only interpret but constitute conflict as ethnic. Similarly, this book argues for paying attention to the possibility of different and changing degrees of 'groupness', and to the role of individual and collective actors in the politicization of ethnicity.

Integration and Conflict: A Two-Way Street

I take as a starting point the Cameroon Grassfields as the overarching unit that all inhabitants and population groups consider themselves part of. The way individuals and collectives relate to each other can take varying forms, which depend on the different rhetorics of inclusion and exclusion used at different moments in time, in different situations or concurrently. Moreover, these relations are seen as embedded in and shaped by the interplay of integration and conflict. Integration is here defined as a process whereby individuals or collectives become part of an overarching unit or systemic connection (Schlee 2003). Conflict, on the other hand, is conceived in Georg Elwert's terms as 'an action based upon the perception of partially incompatible interests or intentions between two or more persons' (Elwert 2001: 2542), an action that does not necessarily involve violence.

In popular understanding, integration and conflict are perceived as two opposite poles of social relations. Integration is often associated with sameness or coherence, while conflict is associated with difference. As Schlee (2008) and other anthropologists have argued, this view is far too simple. There are many ways for individuals and collectives to be integrated into overarching units, be it through assimilation to a dominant culture, the coexistence of distinct groups or via antagonistic relations. Furthermore, as many recent and past conflicts have proved, a low level of difference does not guarantee peaceful coexistence.

The situation examined in this book may provide a case in support of Schlee's model of integration through difference (Schlee 2001). While the different population groups have occupied quite separate but complementary economic and ecological niches, current trends towards political engagement and economic diversification have led them to emerge from their niches. The study thus investigates the effect of economic transformation on the sociopolitical fabric of the Grassfields. It considers whether economic diversification promotes mutual understanding and social integration, or rather engenders competition and conflict. Placing these developments in a national perspective, it asks to what extent the country's economic crisis has advanced an ethnicization of competition.

Similarly, as sameness and integration do not necessarily correspond, conflict cannot be seen as an entirely negative force. This approach was put forward by scholars of the Manchester School, who perceived conflict as part and parcel of social relations. As Max Gluckman (1955) argued, actors are embedded in a web of individual and group allegiances that, on the one hand, promote minor confrontations while, on the other, reducing the potential for violent conflict. Furthermore, such minor confrontations are seen as contributing to social cohesion. Victor Turner (1967, 1974) further elaborated on Gluckman's approach by focusing on the processual and performative dimensions of conflict. He introduced the model of the social drama to study the phases and symbolism of conflict.

Building on Gluckman and Turner, this book critically examines the way in which the two conflicts introduced at the beginning may be interpreted as part of an uneven integration process. It also asks how bloodshed may have impacted on social coexistence, drawing on earlier experiences. And what are the symbolic meanings of the masks and staffs exerted in the investiture conflict? Complementary to the two major altercations mentioned above are minor and less dramatic events, which, as shall be shown, are equally significant in understanding interethnic relations and social cohesion in the Cameroon Grassfields.

As I stated earlier with regard to Burnham's thesis, this book aims at delineating the factors that promote integration and the avoidance of violence. While difference and conflict have been outlined as possibly integrative factors, we will also consider relations that transcend or challenge ethnic boundaries. A classical and controversially discussed example is the concept of cross-cutting ties. It was introduced by Gluckman (1955) to denote allegiances that unite individuals across 'tribal' or social units. Drawing examples from Evans-Pritchard's study of the Nuer (Evans-Pritchard 1940), Gluckman came to the conclusion that cross-cutting ties contribute to social cohesion because they inhibit violent conflict and the destruction of the wider social order. His thesis of the de-escalating propensity of cross-cutting ties was criticized by later scholars, whose studies did not support Gluckman's argument. In his study of violent conflict within Tauade society in Papua New Guinea, Hallpike (1977) came to the conclusion that cross-cutting ties do not necessarily contribute to social cohesion, but may serve as channels of vengeance and evasion. Meanwhile, Schlee (1997, 2000, 2004) has examined clan relations among pastoral groups in northern Kenya. In his reading there is no correlation between the existence of cross-cutting ties and the prevention or escalation of conflict. However, he found that interethnic clan relations help to overcome the consequences of violent conflict. As these divergent findings suggest, cross-cutting ties in themselves have no general effect, but used as raw material for political rhetoric, they may promote either social cohesion or violent conflict.

This study picks up on this debate and examines the relevance of cross-cutting ties in view of ethnic coexistence in the Grassfields. More specifically, it looks at economic allegiances as well as social and religious ties that result from intermarriage and religious conversion. In the Cameroon Grassfields, conversion from local African religions and/or Christianity to Islam is relatively infrequent, but it is a common feature in northern Cameroon, where religious conversion also entails ethnic conversion. Several authors have analysed the correlation of these processes, as well as converts' individual motivations. It is the aim of this book to extend this discussion to the Cameroon Grassfields, and to consider the factors that may account for different outcomes in the country's two regions.

Give and Take in Conflict Strategies

Current anthropological conflict theory builds on the findings of the Manchester School but takes a more differentiated approach, distinguishing different types of conflict with different impacts on social relations. Elwert (2001, 2004, 2005), for example, orders the multitude of concepts used to describe conflict in a field defined by four poles: destruction, warring, procedure and avoidance. These poles differ from one another in that they are characterized by greater or lesser degrees of violence, and stronger or weaker degrees of embedding. Elwert defines embedding as follows: 'the ensemble of moral values, proper norms, and institutional arrangements which set limits to a specific type of action and make simultaneously the outcome of these actions calculable' (Elwert 2001: 2543).

In his model, it is the degree of embedding in social action, rather than violence, that determines the integrative or dissociative propensity of conflict. Elwert's conflict theory is useful to analyse local approaches to conflict management as studied in this book. While procedure in his model – as the most embedded and least violent strategy – seems most effective and integrative, the situation on the ground may prove otherwise. In the murder conflict, for example, procedure – in this case litigation and lobbying – produced no satisfactory solution, but aggravated existing resentments. We may ask: What are the necessary conditions for a successful outcome of procedure? Are they attainable under Cameroon's current political and legal framework? And how effective are local applications of global concepts, such as human, minority and indigenous rights?

In the same way as this book critically engages with Elwert's category of procedure, it also pays attention to the strategy he terms 'avoidance'. In his model, avoidance is characterized by weak social embedding and a low potential for violence, while being prone to relapse into destruction. Yet avoidance strategies may be more common and stable than Elwert suggests. In the African context, several authors have reported conflict strategies that could be grouped under the heading of avoidance.

This study suggests looking at avoidance in terms of functional indifference. By functional indifference, I refer to a strategy that opts for overlooking difference and rivalry for the sake of continued coexistence. For example, in the case of the investiture conflict, the opposing parties eventually resorted to leaving the issue of wearing caps or headscarves unresolved and consciously ignored the possibility of near-violent escalation.

Finally, this book highlights compromise as part and parcel of conflict resolution. In Elwert's model, compromise, understood as a process of negotiation that involves mutual concession, may fall under the heading of procedure. I argue, however, that probably all forms of conflict resolution, with the exception of the total annihilation of one or more of the rival parties, entail a certain degree of give and take. Thus, while procedure with its focus on negotiation seems to encourage reconciliation, it may also go hand in hand with avoidance. This study aims at determining the role of compromise in conflict strategies in the Cameroon Grassfields, while taking into account political discourses that may, in fact, promote confrontation.

Ethnicity – Conflict – Compromise: The Book's Central Arguments

This study considers the phenomenon of ethnicity, its individual histories, meanings and instrumentalities, its role in conflict and most importantly its scope for compromise. It provides a case in support of the model of integration through difference developed by Schlee (2001). The locale of the study is limited quite strictly to the Cameroon Grassfields, but it also considers the issue of ethnicity within a national and, indeed, global context.

Here, difference is broadly understood in terms of ethnicity, culture and religion, but also embraces the distinctions of gender, age and class. The book examines how difference is sustained and amplified, and in which situations it may be minimized. It argues that ethnic distinctions do not evolve exclusively from competition and conflict over local resources. In turn, it contends that difference is politicized and validated by government initiative, and the interventions of the global development establishment.

The book shows that, at this particular moment in history and in a particular place, conflict is generally perceived in ethnic terms. How can this ethnicization of conflict be explained? As I argue, there are both instrumental and emotive dimensions. Moreover, one should not underestimate the effect of accumulated group histories, reflected in popular stereotypes and embodied practice. The book argues that, under conditions of stress, historical memory – however vestigial – may contribute to a hardening of ethnic lines of conflict where in fact few exist in everyday conduct and affairs. Conversely, individual and collective actors may seek to exacerbate and enhance ethnic distinctions in pursuit of economic and political self-interest.

Finally, the book engages with strategies of local conflict management that are inspired by national and international political discourses. It highlights the transition from more confrontational to more processual solutions, and argues that while the latter promise a decline of violence, they also engender new potential for conflict. The possibility of recourse to conflict mediation via superordinate frameworks reduces incentives for locally negotiated understanding and integration.

Research Methodology

This book is based on nearly five years of residence in northwest Cameroon, carried out between 1991 and 2014. While the main bulk of the material was collected during fourteen months of fieldwork from 2000 to 2002, subsequent revisits confirmed the continuing relevance of my findings and their theoretical validity.

My interest in the Grassfields goes back to the early 1990s, when I first came to Cameroon to teach in a secondary school. My stay took place in a period of political instability and civil unrest, set off by the country's democratization and economic crisis. When I returned in 1996 – this time to carry out anthropological fieldwork – the situation had calmed down somewhat, and Cameroonian politics had taken a new turn. This was the heyday of the politics of belonging and the sudden growth of ethnic and regional elite associations. My third, lengthy stay in Cameroon took place from 2000 to 2002. At this time, local activities were governed by the latest trends in international development policy, in particular the discourse on human and minority rights. A few years later, the United Nations concept of 'indigenous peoples' gained ground in Cameroon, with the Mbororo – along with other population groups – achieving international recognition. Since 2007, I have been following these developments and have also paid attention to new forms of social and physical mobility. This book attempts to make sense of the transformations in the lives of individuals and collectives that I have witnessed and closely followed over the past two decades.

During my main fieldwork from 2000 to 2002, I was assisted by a group of young women and men of Grassfields, Mbororo and Hausa background. They contributed their own ideas and initiatives, making my research an interactive endeavour. What is more, they made it fun. As my focus was on both the discursive and performative dimensions of ethnicity, much information was gained from informal conversations and local gossip, as well as formal interviews.[1] In addition to standard methods of ethnographic research, we applied approaches drawn from visual and theatre anthropology, such as video documentation and the analysis of locally performed role playing.[2]

In this study, varying methods of representation are used. In describing and analysing the two major conflicts introduced above, I have applied the extended case method of the Manchester School. Other procedures, such as the reconstruction of group histories and the analysis of relations transcending ethnic boundaries, cannot be carried out with reference to a single case study; they are better approached from multiple angles. In general, the book aims at integrating both narrative and visual data, and pursuing a multivocal approach.

The Field Site

The book's regional focus is on the anglophone northwest of Cameroon, which, together with the francophone West Region, constitutes the Cameroon Grassfields. The country looks back on a triple colonial history: initially administered by the Germans, it was split in 1919 and placed under the mandate of the French and British colonial powers. At independence (1960/61), the two parts reunited to form contemporary Cameroon, which comprises eight francophone and two anglophone administrative regions.[3]

The Cameroon Grassfields form both a geographical and cultural unit. They are located in the Western Highlands, at an altitude of 1,000 to 3,000 metres. The landscape is varied and includes mountain ranges, grass-covered plateaus, wooded valleys, plains, volcanic lakes and numerous rivers. Thanks to their high altitude, the Grassfields have a relatively pleasant climate, with an annual rainfall of 2,000 millimetres and a moderate dry season of four to five months (November to March). The soil is fertile, owing partly to its volcanic origins, and supports both agriculture and animal husbandry.

Today, as in the past, the Grassfields are renowned for their chiefdoms, masquerades, linguistic diversity and agricultural production, features that have been widely explored in the scholarship on the region. Grassfields societies are predominantly Christian or adherents of local African religions. They engage in subsistence agriculture and complementary activities, such as small-scale animal husbandry and the sale of food and cash crops. Furthermore, the region has been characterized by a high degree of mobility. In the pre-colonial period, mobility was promoted by inter-chiefdom relations and individuals' participation in a complex system of short- and long-distance trade (Nkwi 1987; Warnier 1985). During the colonial and postcolonial period, labour migration to coastal plantations and urban centres in the country's south became common practice (Ardener et al. 1960; Warnier 1993). Another factor that contributed to the region's ethnic diversification was the arrival of Mbororo and Hausa in the early twentieth century. While the Mbororo are agro-pastoralists and entered the area in the 1910s in search of fresh pastures for their cattle, the first Hausa immigrants were traders involved in long-distance commerce between the Cameroon Grassfields and urban centres in northern Nigeria and northern Cameroon. Both Mbororo and Hausa are generally Muslims and differ in their economic and socio-political organization from their Grassfields neighbours.

At the heart of this study is Misaje, a small town and its environs at the northern fringes of the Cameroon Grassfields. The toponym Misaje refers to the town as well as the administrative unit of Misaje Sub-Division; both are covered in this study. Its inhabitants identify themselves with reference to an array of ethnic and cultural categories, detailed in the figure below (Figure I.1). This is a working model; its purpose is to provide the reader with an overview of the ethnonyms central to this study. As an abstraction, it is necessarily static and reductionist, and it cannot fully account for the flexible and overlapping ways in which informants identify themselves and others. Alternative models will be introduced in subsequent chapters.[4]

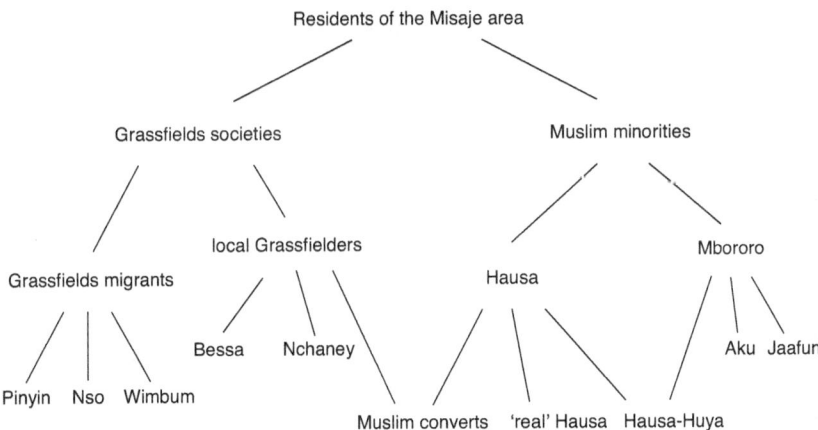

Figure I.1: A working model of ethnic and cultural categories relevant for this study. Source: Author's fieldwork.

The Misaje Area and Misaje Town

The North West Region is divided administratively into seven divisions. The Misaje area is part of the Donga-Mantung Division in the northeast of the region, which shares an international border with Nigeria (see Figure I.2).

14 *Masks and Staffs*

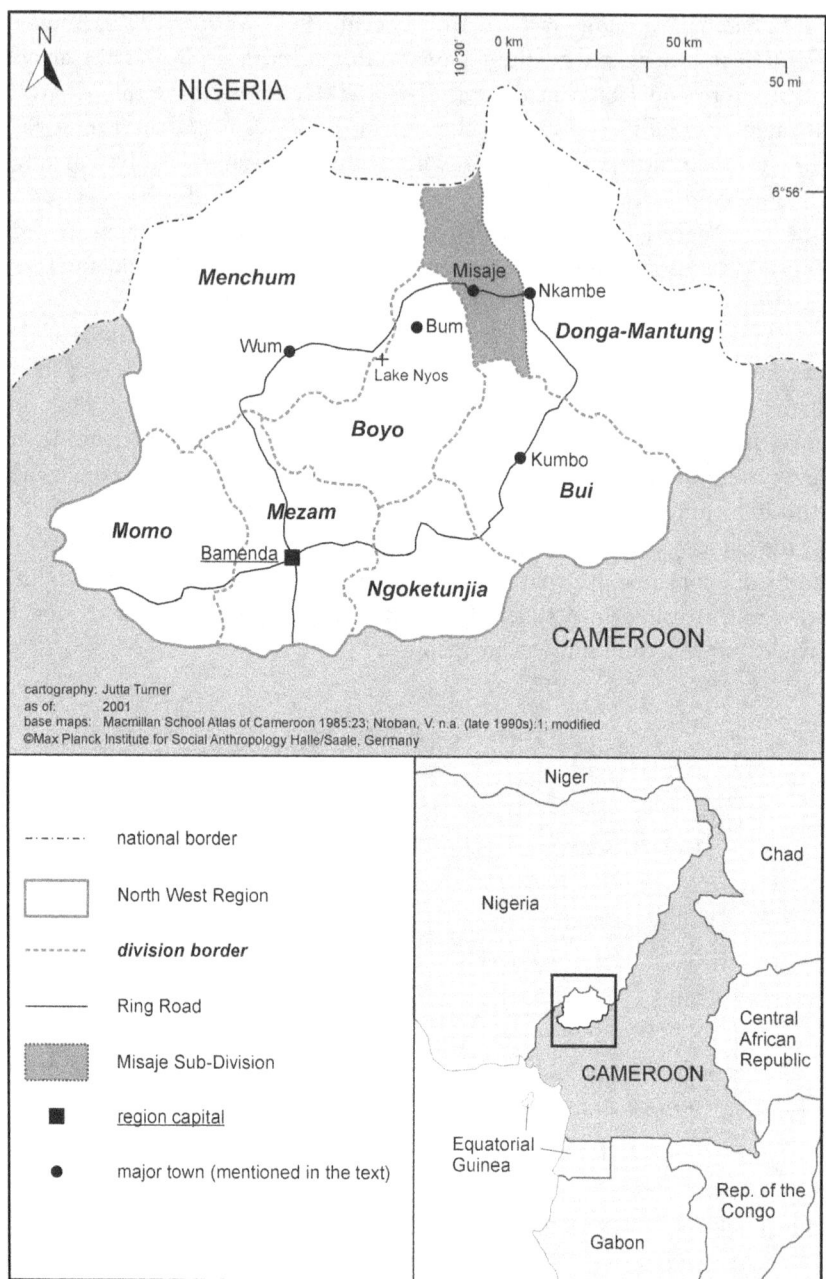

Figure I.2: Administrative structure of the North West Region. Reproduced by kind permission of the Max Planck Institute for Social Anthropology, Halle.

Introduction 15

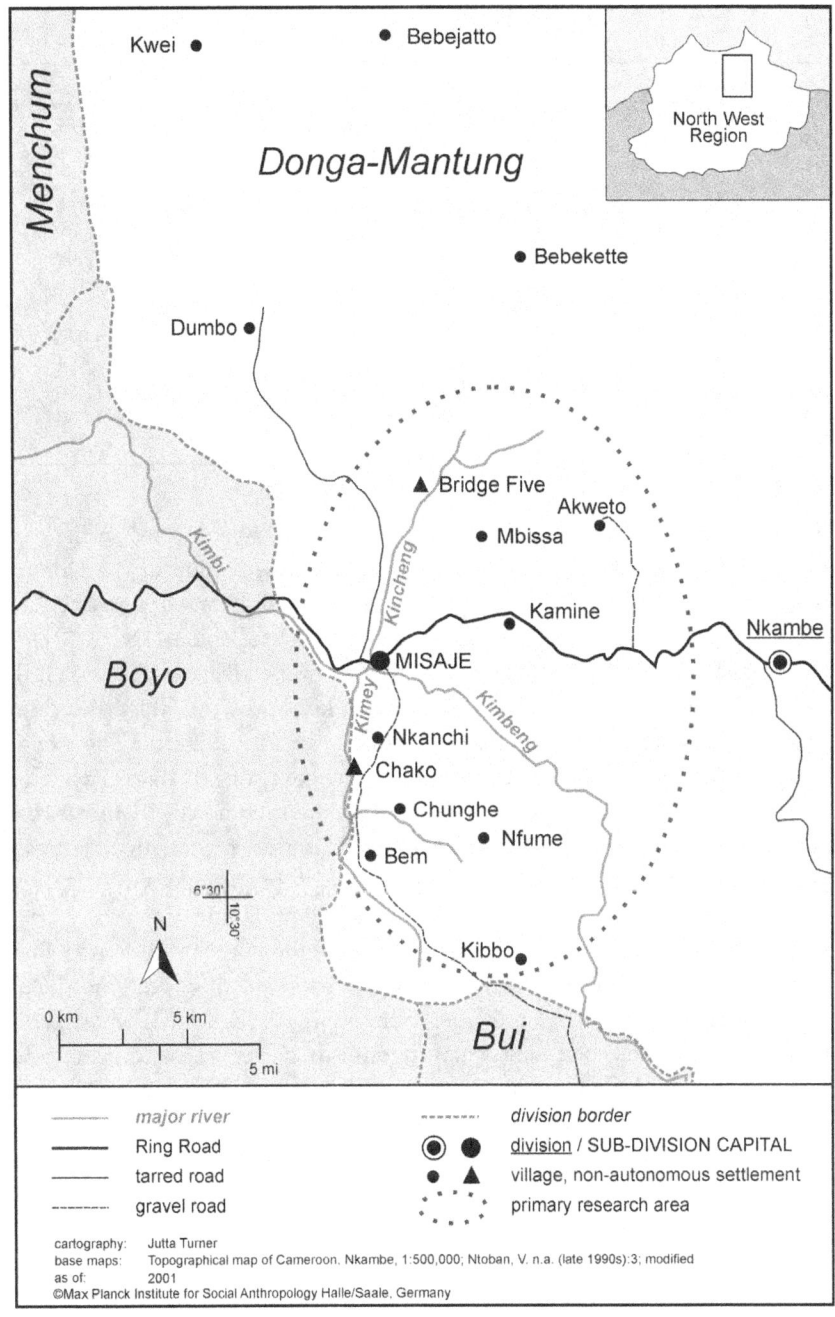

Figure I.3: Research area. Reproduced by kind permission of the Max Planck Institute for Social Anthropology, Halle.

Table I.1: Population statistics, Misaje Sub-Division, 1999/2000. Source: Divisional Office, Misaje, 2001.

Local Grassfields Groups	Villages	Population
Nchaney	Nkanchi	10,887
	Bem	1,378
	Kibbo	935
	Chunghe	818
	Nfume	2,489
Bessa	Mbissa	1,502
	Kamine	3,179
	Akweto	3,420
Kemezung	Dumbo	4,976
	Kwei	524
Bebe	Bebekette	1,384
	Bebejatto	1,760
Total		33,252

The divisional capital is Nkambe, the nearest large town, located to the east of Misaje. In 1993, the Misaje area was made a sub-division of the Donga-Mantung Division. By 2000, it measured 750 square kilometres and had an estimated population of slightly more than 33,000 (see Table I.1).

The Misaje Sub-Division contains a total of twelve villages (see Figure I.3). Each village is headed by a chief or sub-chief, known by the Grassfields term *fon*, who is in charge of the village territory and its inhabitants.[5] The twelve villages belong to four independent polities that constitute distinct Grassfields societies. In addition, there are a number of non-autonomous settlements that count as quarters of the main villages. For historical reasons, Misaje town counts as a quarter of Nkanchi, the head village of the Nchaney ethnic group.

Population statistics in Cameroon generally omit ethnicity as a valid category of distinction. Hence, it is difficult to assess the numbers associated with different ethnic categories. I would estimate, however, that local Grassfields societies account for at least 60 per cent of Misaje Sub-Division's inhabitants, while Mbororo pastoralists may amount to 25 per cent, and Hausa and migrants from within the Grassfields to 5 to 10 per cent. Compared to averages in the North West Region of 5 to 15 per cent for Mbororo and less than 1 per cent for Hausa (Boutrais 1996: 548, 636), the proportion of Mbororo, Hausa and Grassfields migrants in Misaje Sub-Division is relatively high. This is partly due to the attraction of Misaje town and Dumbo as centres of commerce and cattle trade.

During my research I focused on the southern half of Misaje Sub-Division, equivalent to the territory of the Nchaney and Bessa chiefdoms. Special attention was paid to Misaje town and its immediate surroundings (Figure I.4).

Figure I.4: The central area of Misaje town. Photograph by Michaela Pelican, 2001.

Misaje town is not a 'traditional village' with a long-standing history; it is a place of contested claims and multiple origins, dating back only as far as the colonial period. It is located near the Nigerian border and along the Ring Road, the main infrastructural axis of the North West Region. In 2000 its population amounted to approximately 7,000 people; it is an agglomeration of various ethnic and occupational groups, mainly attracted by economic opportunities.

From the very start, Misaje has had a multi-ethnic character. In the nineteenth century, the area now occupied by Misaje town was used as a hunting ground by inhabitants of nearby villages. The first families to take up residence and cultivate farms in the area were from Nkanchi. In the 1920s, Mbororo pastoralists began to settle in the nearby highlands. Most probably, they were responsible for coining the name Misaje, which eventually became the established toponym. According to current folk etymology, Misaje is a derivate of *mai saje*, a Hausa term meaning 'master of the beard'. This nickname is said to have been given to a prominent Bessa businessman who operated a rest house for traders and travellers. His business was frequented by Hausa traders and Mbororo herdsmen, and soon the hamlet was popularly known as 'the place of *mai saje*' – in short, Misaje.[6]

During the 1930s, the British colonial administration decided to set up a customary court and a native authority area of the same dimensions as the current Misaje Sub-Division.⁷ A few years later, they asked early Hausa settlers, first established at Nkanchi, to transfer to Misaje town. More settlers were to join in the course of the construction of the Ring Road in the late 1940s and 1950s. Workers were recruited from surrounding villages and throughout the Grassfields; some took up permanent residence and engaged in farming and business activities. Around the same period, a second group of Mbororo pastoralists entered the region and were encouraged by the British administration to settle in the grassy lowlands of the Misaje Native Authority Area. Consequently, the cattle business flourished and attracted Hausa and Grassfields traders. The people of Pinyin, a village in the southwest of the North West Region, were particularly involved in cattle trade, and a few established themselves in Misaje.

All these developments turned Misaje town into a conglomeration of people from inside and outside the region and supported its economic growth. In the early 1970s, Fon Michael, then chief of Nkanchi, transferred his palace to Misaje. In 1975, the Société de Développement et d'Exploitation des Productions Animales (SODEPA), a major parastatal enterprise that produces breeding stock and beef for the national market, was opened in Dumbo (Boutrais 1990: 82–87). While its establishment caused the displacement of many Mbororo families, the ranch attracted technicians and business people from all over Cameroon and contributed to improving the region's economy and infrastructure.

By the late 1970s and early 1980s, Misaje had developed into a small town with a flourishing economy. Conversely, the area experienced a major downturn in the second half of the 1980s. In 1986, Lake Nyos – a volcanic lake to the west of Misaje – produced an eruption of toxic gas, after which approximately 1,700 people and thousands of cattle died (Leenhardt 1995; Shanklin 1988). While the emissions did not reach as far as Misaje town, the incident seriously affected business operations in the northern part of the North West Region. Many migrants and business people decided to return to their home areas, due to the loss of capital and customers, or in fear of further deadly eruptions.⁸ In the late 1980s the town's economic stagnation and the decrease in population were further reinforced by the nationwide economic depression.

In the 1990s, Misaje town, like most places in the North West Region, experienced vicious party-political struggles and the divisive effects of the politics of belonging. At the same time, it benefited from administrative changes, in particular the creation of Misaje Sub-Division in 1993, which resulted in gradual improvement in the town's infrastructure. Further developments characterizing Misaje in the 1990s and 2000s will be explored in subsequent chapters.

Book Outline

The vertices of this book are the two conflicts sketched at the beginning of this chapter. The people involved in these conflicts will be introduced in a series of chapters focusing on their collective histories and emic conceptions of ethnicity. Two further chapters will be concerned with ethnic coexistence and the negotiation of ethnic boundaries.

Chapter 1 opens with the case study of the critical altercation that occurred in 1997 during the investiture ceremonies of a local Grassfields chief, and which resulted in a polarization of Misaje's population along lines of ethnic and cultural difference. The chapter analyses the conflict in its socio-political context and symbolic dimensions, and provides insight into local strategies of conflict management pertinent in the 1990s.

Chapter 2 recounts the emergence and expansion of the Nchaney chiefdom on the basis of local and colonial accounts. It outlines historical transformations in Nchaney self-understanding in the context of encounters with Grassfields and cultural 'others', as well as the colonial and postcolonial government. The Nchaney here typify Grassfields societies in general, with whom they share similarities in their historical development and socio-political organization.

Chapter 3 describes the establishment of Mbororo pastoralists in the Grassfields, specifically in the Misaje area. It focuses on alterations in their self-understanding in the course of their historical migration and subsequent sedentarization. It also sheds light on the recent politicization of Mbororo identity in response to Cameroon's political liberalization and global rights discourse.

Chapter 4 focuses on the complementary and competitive potentials of economic relations between Nchaney and Mbororo. It describes the effects of economic diversification on intra-ethnic and interethnic relations, and addresses two issues of public contention: farmer–herder conflict and cattle theft.

Chapter 5 engages with the historical origins of the Hausa ethnic category in the Cameroon Grassfields, and the factors that have contributed to its lasting consolidation in this region. It pays attention to gendered and subethnic perspectives, and highlights interrelations between Hausa, Mbororo and Grassfields societies, which also impact on Hausa strategies of political participation and representation vis-à-vis the government.

Chapter 6 focuses on the processes of religious and ethnic conversion in the Grassfields, and relates them to similar phenomena in northern Cameroon. Furthermore, it conveys individual perspectives on managing multiple identities and liabilities, and examines the circumstances under which ensuing cross-cutting ties may be used to support or undermine social cohesion in Misaje.

Chapter 7 describes the conflict resulting from the murder in 2001, briefly sketched above. The case brings together issues of occult aggression and conflicting land claims. Furthermore, the chapter analyses the arguments of the prosecutor and defendant, and highlights the process of ethnic framing. It also illustrates current approaches to conflict resolution, and considers individual and collective strategies of managing Cameroon's plural legal system.

The Epilogue provides an update on recent developments in Mbororo identity politics. It concludes by qualifying the potential of ethnicity for political mobilization, and anticipates possible transformations in conflict idioms.

Notes

1 With the exception of historical and public figures (politicians, community leaders, eminent elders), the names of interlocutors have been changed. All quotations from interviews have been translated into English; only key terms are indicated in their original language.
2 Two short videos of role playing with reference to farmer–herder conflict and milk sales are accessible via the virtual archive of the Max Planck Institute for Social Anthropology in Halle/Saale. These are: M. Pelican. 2002. *Farmer–Herder Conflict: Role Play of the Ballotiral Staff* (Nkambe, 29 January 2001). Video clip, 2.46 mins, with English subtitles. File name: Conflict_RolePlay.mpeg; and M. Pelican. 2002. *Sippoygo (Selling Milk): Role Play of the Mbororo Women's Group of Chako* (Chako, 8 April 2001). Video clip, 4.27 mins, with English subtitles. File name: MilkSales_RolePlay.mpeg.
3 Until recently, these administrative units were named provinces. In 2008, the government changed the terminology from provinces to regions as part of its decentralization measures.
4 It is important to note that I treat ethnic groups and identities as ideal types in Max Weber's sense (Weber 1949). I am aware of the difficulties entailed in deriving ideal types from ethnographic material. Hence, when I write of 'the Nchaney', 'the Bessa', 'the Mbororo' or 'the Hausa', it signifies an abstraction for the sake of comparison of ideal types. It should not be mistaken for a naive interpretation of the Misaje community as being composed of distinct ethnic groups; rather, such terms refer to groupings of individuals whose identities are practical constructs (Bourdieu 1990) and modelled in interaction with each other.
5 *Fon* (also spelled *foyn* or *mfon*) is the generic term and title for 'chief' in most Grassfields languages and dialects. It has entered Pidgin English and administrative English, and occasionally Grassfields chiefdoms are referred to as 'fondoms'. The term *fon* is also common in academic writings on the Cameroon Grassfields.
6 A concurrent version to this etymology was reported to M.D.W. Jeffreys during his administrative tour in the late 1930s (Jeffreys 1951: 112).
7 The court was first installed at Bridge Five, a place in Bessa territory that was considered a central location between Dumbo, Nkanchi and Akweto, the three major settlements of the planned native authority area. The British later realized that the place was too

remote and relocated the court to Misaje, which at that time was still a minor settlement. Consequently, Misaje became the centre of the area and attracted more settlers.
8 In 2001, an international scientific project was set up to 'de-gas' the lake, and today Lake Nyos it is under steady surveillance (Jones 2010).

1

Setting the Scene
Cultural Difference and Political Rivalry in Times of Transition

Several months into my fieldwork, two Hausa women friends mentioned a conflict that had occurred in 1997 during the investiture ceremonies of the current head of the Nchaney chiefdom. Up to then, interlocutors had described ethnic relations between Grassfielders, Mbororo and Hausa as relatively unproblematic, though overshadowed by farmer–herder disputes. Yet, as it soon turned out, this incident – which henceforth will be referred to as 'the investiture conflict' – had nearly caused a breakdown of ethnic coexistence in the Misaje area. The conflict was framed as an altercation over religious and cultural difference that opposed the Nchaney palace hierarchy to the Muslim community, with Mbororo and Hausa conflated in the latter category.

I began to investigate the investiture conflict by addressing the topic in conversations with Grassfielders, Mbororo and Hausa elders, youths, women and government administrators. Most were aware of the incident, and were able to recount the happenings in varying detail. As it had occurred prior to my research, I was unable to observe the conflict directly. Thus the following narrative is a composite version based on the retrospective accounts of eighteen interlocutors. While I focus in the description of the conflict on the events of three days, the analysis spans a period from the early 1990s to 2002.

The Course of Events

The dramatis personae in this case study are both individuals and collectives, and will be introduced in the course of the story. The historical context is the 1990s, a period characterized by political turmoil and socio-economic instability.

In 1996, Fon Michael, head of the Nchaney chiefdom, died. As is common in Grassfields chiefdoms, succession rites took more than a year. They culminated in the ceremonial investiture of Fon Michael's son and chosen heir, Richard, in October 1997. The investiture ceremonies lasted for two weeks, and included general feasting, cultural performances and courtesy visits of representatives of local population groups, neighbouring chiefdoms and state officials.

Organizational preparations were initiated many months before the start of the ceremonies. The palace hierarchy – comprised of Nchaney title holders and elders – requested all population groups resident in the Nchaney chiefdom to contribute to the festivities in cash or kind, and to prepare delegations and cultural performances. Reactions were generally compliant. Nchaney villagers and Grassfields migrants agreed to donate food crops and money, and to rehearse their so-called traditional dances, choir presentations and masquerades.[1] Mbororo and Hausa promised to contribute meat and money for the feasting, to present dances and display their horse-riding skills.

In the course of the preparatory meetings, a disagreement arose between Nchaney notables and the representatives of the Mbororo and Hausa communities regarding the provisional rules of comportment and appearance that the palace hierarchy planned to institute for the period of the investiture ceremonies. Following these rules, men were required to remove their caps, while women should dress in a single wrap and walk barefoot and bareheaded. Hausa and Mbororo representatives pointed out that these prescriptions conflicted with Muslim ideology and practice, and thus were unacceptable to Muslims in Misaje. As the two parties could not come to an agreement, the matter was brought before the divisional officer (DO), himself a Grassfielder and familiar with royal investiture rites. He advised the Nchaney elders to exempt Mbororo and Hausa from Nchaney ritual prescriptions on account of their different religious and cultural practices. He recommended separating ritual and profane spaces by constructing a fence around the ceremonial ground on the market square, and to instruct Muslims to avoid that area when going to the mosque. The Nchaney notables agreed to build a fence, and the two parties negotiated a compromise. While Muslim elders were exempted from removing their caps, Muslim youths were required to follow the rule. Those unwilling to do so, it was decided, should stay away from the ceremonial ground. Both parties were satisfied with this arrangement, but ensuing violations of the agreement caused anger and distress on both sides.

On the opening day of the investiture ceremonies, Ganye, a respected Hausa elder in charge of the meat supply for the feasting, was attacked by *chombu ju-ju* on the grounds of wearing his cap.[2] *Chombu ju-ju* are masks of the palace that serve as messengers and local police. They are thought of as numinous beings that act through the maskers who embody them. Hausa youths were upset about the humiliation of their distinguished elder. They complained to the Nchaney palace hierarchy, who eventually instructed the *chombu ju-ju* to stop molesting Muslim elders.

The next day, which was a Friday and Muslim prayer day, *chombu ju-ju* harassed a Mbororo man who hurriedly passed the ceremonial ground as he was late for afternoon prayers. He refused to take off his cap and was encouraged by Mbororo spectators, who contended that Muslims respected only Allah and did not bend down before idols or masks.

On Saturday, the Nchaney market day, a young Mbororo man crossed a fibre rope demarcating the ceremonial ground. The *chombu ju-ju* took him to the chief's palace and intimidated Mbororo elders on their way to the mosque. The Muslim congregation decided to retaliate. Upon leaving the mosque, Mbororo men armed themselves with their herding staffs and took up positions in the market square. In the meantime, the Nchaney notables returned from the palace, bringing along their powerful *nggumba ju-ju*, a mask that should never be seen by women and comes out only at night to punish severe crimes. Muslim women heard of the event and approached the ceremonial ground in defiance of the alleged danger and wishing to witness the events. The situation turned into an open confrontation, and the two factions faced each other in a symbolic stand-off: on the one side, Nchaney notables approaching with their *nggumba ju-ju*; on the other, Mbororo and Hausa impressing their opponents with a *kariya* (staff-hurling) performance, a skill Mbororo herders are renowned and feared for (Figure 1.1).

Suddenly, Fon Richard's younger brother appeared with a rifle. A Mbororo man drew his knife, but was held back by his Mbororo neighbour. At this crucial moment, the DO – supported by the police commissioner and a few gendarmes – stepped in and took control of the situation. Under threat of army intervention, he ordered an immediate stop to the action. The crowd – frightened by previous experiences of the military – began to disperse, and the crisis was diffused. From here on, Mbororo and Hausa largely refrained from attending the investiture ceremonies, while the *chombu ju-ju* were instructed to ignore Muslim trespassers.

Some weeks after the investiture ceremony, Fon Richard invited the representatives of the Muslim community to a reconciliatory meeting. He formally apologized for the aggressive behaviour of the *chombu ju-ju* and attributed the guilt largely to his notables. Hausa and Mbororo elders accepted his apologies and confirmed their support and respect for him as the leader of the Nchaney chiefdom. Although the situation had come close to causing a disastrous breakdown of social relations in Misaje, the parties agreed to discuss the matter no further and to continue their coexistence on normal terms.

Figure 1.1: Painting of Mbororo *kariya* versus Nchaney *nggumba ju-ju* (ca. 26 cm x 40 cm). Reproduced by kind permission of the artist Marx Tawe.

To reflect the (re)constructed and imaginative character of the above narrative, I commissioned a painting from a Grassfields artist in Bamenda. The painting poignantly illustrates the encounter between the Nchaney *nggumba ju-ju* and Mbororo staff-hurlers (Figure 2.1 in Chapter 2 provides an idea of how the mask may have looked in real life). Yet as the artist's interpretation of the incident is based solely on reading the conflict narrative, it includes a few misapprehensions. Firstly, the Misaje palace is depicted as geographically set aside and with a three-pointed roof. This depiction draws on the architectural style common in the Bamiléké region, and corresponds to popular representations of chiefly structures in contemporary Grassfields art. Secondly, the Muslim staff-hurlers are shown to exit the mosque in the company of their women. This scene is unlikely, as Muslim women in Misaje generally perform their prayers at home; rather, they were supporting their men as onlookers from the square's fringes.

Critical Remarks
Before attempting an analysis of the features and causes of the conflict, I will first discuss the validity of the narrative and the representativeness of the case study.

As the above account is composed of individual and collective recollections, it is by no means an objective representation of the actual events. It is a meta-narrative or a 'master fiction' (Geertz 1985: 33) that is shaped by the partial perspectives and narrative conventions of both the informants and the anthropologist. Its underlying narratives include diverging and competing interpretations. They have a 'social energy' (Greenblatt 1994: 227) of their own, and not only reflect but also shape social reality. Finally, due to the retrospective character of their accounts, interlocutors tended to depict the events as a sequence of interdependent actions guided by intentionality and rational choice, which almost certainly was not the case. Much of the happenings may have been the result of contingency, misinformation and miscalculation. Emotions, such as fear, anger and pride, must have equally motivated individuals' actions. My informants' reassessment of their role more than three years after the event was inevitably hypothetical. Nonetheless, the above narrative provides at least a skeleton of the historical events during Fon Richard's investiture. Moreover, as I am primarily concerned with the ways in which individuals and groups have managed to overcome their differences, the account constitutes a valid basis for analysing informants' current assessments of their interethnic relations with regard to this past event.

The second point concerns the representativeness of the chosen case. Truly, the investiture conflict of 1997 was a relatively unusual case, both with regard to its origin and form. As far as I know, at no other time and in no other place in the Grassfields has a conflict emerged over the issue of wearing caps, nor have I ever heard of a symbolic stand-off, such as portrayed in the above narrative. Nonetheless, the conflict in question constitutes a valid basis for considering the circumstances under which religious and cultural differences are perceived as problematic, the strategies that are used in resolving ensuing arguments, and more generally the positive and negative impacts of conflict on social relations. As Mitchell (1983: 191) rightly argues, the value of a case study lies not in the representativeness of the events but in the validity of the analysis.

Analysis of the Investiture Conflict

In analysing the events during Fon Richard's investiture, we may first determine the main components of the story. It is a story about caps and courtyards, about staffs and masks. At the same time, it is a story about the negotiation of political and ritual authority and the intervention of state officials. We may thus interpret it as a struggle over political and cultural autonomy, played out symbolically via metonyms of cultural identity and difference.

In trying to discern different phases of conflict development, I apply Turner's (1957) model of the social drama with its four phases of breach, crisis, redress and reintegration. The conflict started with the public breach of social norms, namely Muslims' refusal to remove their caps and Nchaney notables' infringements of Muslim standards of comportment. It was followed by a phase of mounting crisis, which culminated in the symbolic stand-off of the Nchaney masquerade and Mbororo staff-hurlers. Redressive action was then taken by the DO in order to prevent the conflict's escalation. Eventually, the reintegration was achieved by a strategy best described as functional indifference.³ In order to better understand the events surrounding Fon Richard's investiture, I will embed them in their social and political background and discuss the conflict's symbolic connotations.

Modalities of Coexistence

Misaje is a small town inhabited by a variety of peoples of different ethnic and cultural backgrounds. Socio-cultural and religious differences are continuously conveyed and enacted in terms of language, clothing, demeanour, habitus, settlement pattern and many other practices that function as diacritical markers.⁴ Concurrently, gender, age and education impact upon individuals' identities and social interactions.

During the investiture conflict – as well as at the time of my research – religious and cultural differences were highlighted as the major axis of distinction, separating the Muslim community (Mbororo and Hausa) from the majority of Grassfielders. However, as this and later chapters will show, the opposition of Grassfielders versus Muslims is contentious, as ethnic and religious categories tend to overlap and many Grassfields families also include Muslim members.⁵

Occasions during which the multi-ethnic and multicultural character of the Cameroon Grassfields is accentuated include public events, such as market days, traditional celebrations and national ceremonies. During informal encounters on the road, at work, in town or at home, ethnic and cultural distinctions are also palpable.⁶ Informants perceived their living together as generally peaceful and agreeable. Most of the time, individuals have no problem in accepting others being different, be it with regard to diverging religious, economic, political or socio-cultural practices. Ethnic stereotypes are widely shared and inform people's perceptions at a more general level, while interpersonal relations are shaped by individual experiences. In popular discourse, Grassfielders are frequently characterized as superstitious and inclined to drink alcohol; Hausa may be portrayed as lazy and thieves; and Mbororo as arrogant and potentially violent. Although such stereotypes are contested by members of the respective groups, they constitute 'fields of shared meaning' (Eriksen 1998: 55).

In political terms, the coexistence of ethnic groups is guided by the principle of precedence, which informs intra-ethnic as well as interethnic relations. Local Grassfields societies claim political supremacy on the grounds of their anteriority and their relationship with their land and ancestors. Mbororo and Hausa, whose presence in the region only dates back to the early twentieth century, generally count as 'latecomers' or 'strangers' whose rights to local resources and power is mediated via their relationship with local Grassfields chiefdoms.

The analytic concept of 'the stranger' – introduced by Simmel (1908) and applied by Shack (1979) and Skinner (1963) to the African context – is helpful in understanding historical transformations in interethnic relations in the Grassfields. As the latter authors argue, before colonial rule, so-called stranger populations were both marginal and integral elements of African social and political systems. During the colonial period, however, the political status of these stranger populations changed, as the colonial powers sought to regulate their presence. The dichotomy between 'host' and 'stranger' populations became increasingly defined in legal terms. After independence, the administrative distinction was between 'citizens' and 'aliens'. Consequently, many stranger populations were either naturalized or expelled, while others willingly returned to their places of origin.

In subsequent chapters I will illustrate in more detail the degree to which group identities and relations in the Grassfields have been influenced by colonial and postcolonial policies and models of ethnicity. At this point, however, I want to stress that earlier notions of host–stranger relations are still influential in shaping interethnic relations. On the basis of living in the territory of Grassfields polities, Mbororo and Hausa are expected to pay symbolic tribute to their local Grassfields chiefs, such as Christmas gifts of cattle or money, and to participate in major festivities, such as royal investiture ceremonies. Although the concept of host–stranger relations implies a political hierarchy, it does not define the actual distribution of power. Local power relations are open to negotiation and, more often than not, are shaped by the intervention of state officials and government policies.

As I argue, the general acceptance of socio-cultural differences and of political hierarchies are two key principles guiding interethnic relations in the Grassfields. Both principles allow for differing interpretations that frequently result in disputes and ongoing negotiations. Such minor conflicts have an integrative rather than dissociative propensity, as they support communication and interaction across ethnic and cultural boundaries.

The conflict that arose during Fon Richard's investiture started off as a minor disagreement about religious and cultural differences, but developed into a near-violent conflict over local power relations. In the initial phase, all population groups, including Mbororo and Hausa, complied with the common model of contributing to the investiture ceremonies as an expression of their membership of the Nchaney chiefdom. When Hausa and Mbororo representatives made clear that they could not accept the provisional standards of comportment that the Nchaney palace hierarchy attempted to institute, the latter interpreted the Muslims' objection in political terms: as a sign of their disregard for the Nchaney chief and of their denial of Nchaney primacy.

A second, spiritual dimension of Mbororo and Hausa offences against Nchaney authority becomes evident from Argenti's description of the 1992 royal installation in Oku, a Grassfields chiefdom in the centre of the North West Region (Argenti 2001). From the perspective of Grassfielders, royal investiture ceremonies are a critical transitional period during which any breach of ritual prescriptions or social order endangers the future well-being of the polity and its population. Hence, the Muslims' refusal to remove their caps constituted a potential source of spiritual danger. Although this argument was never explicitly phrased by any of my informants, it is instructive when understanding the vigour with which the palace hierarchy tried to impose their rules of comportment.[7] Mbororo and Hausa representatives, on the other hand, sought to negotiate a compromise, with the aim of conveying their political loyalty and, at the same time, preserving their religious integrity and cultural sovereignty. The solution proposed by the DO complied with the concerns of the Muslim community and, at the same time, acknowledged Nchaney authority while limiting it to the ceremonial ground.

Up to this point, the dispute remained within locally established frameworks of negotiating cultural differences and local power relations. Subsequently, however, it developed into a serious altercation that threatened to escalate and, eventually, it was stopped forcefully. In order to understand this turn of events, it is necessary to embed the conflict in its national context and discuss the implications of the DO's intervention.

Cameroon's Economic and Political Liberalization

The 1990s were an eventful and challenging period for many Cameroonians. They experienced the introduction of democratic freedoms and, at the same time, the intensification of social insecurity and economic hardship.

By the end of the 1980s, Cameroon – like many African countries – faced a severe economic crisis resulting from fluctuations in world market prices, the mismanagement of government funds and the investment of Cameroonian capital in foreign countries (Jua 1991). In 1988, the World Bank and the IMF imposed structural adjustment programmes, including drastic cuts in the state budget and the restructuring of the administrative and banking systems. Two years later, the international donor community proclaimed political liberalization as an additional prerequisite for future aid to Africa. In response to substantial internal and external pressure, Cameroon eventually embarked on a democratization process.

The early 1990s were characterized by the rise of multiparty politics and the proliferation of the private press (Nyamnjoh 2005). Subsequent years saw the emergence of regional and ethnic elite associations as pressure groups, as well as fierce struggles over entitlement phrased in the discourse of autochthony and belonging (Geschiere and Gugler 1998; Konings and Nyamnjoh 2003; Nyamnjoh and Rowlands 1998; Socpa 2002).

During the authoritarian regime of Cameroon's first president, Ahmadou Ahidjo, emphasis was laid on nation building and the cultivation of a single national identity. Local organizations of an ethnic, regional or confessional nature were branded as potentially subversive and actively suppressed (Bayart 1979; Geschiere 2009). When Paul Biya took over the presidency in 1982, he largely maintained Ahidjo's approach. However, in the course of the country's liberalization, the government's stance on citizenship and identity drastically changed. In an attempt to weaken and diffuse the fast-growing opposition, the Biya regime urged its functionaries to return to their home areas and to win their constituency's support for the ruling party. In addition, citizenship was no longer defined in national but ethnic terms, a change reflected in the revised constitution of 1996, which gives priority to autochthonous groups and ethnic minorities regarding access to natural and state resources.[8] Conversely, migrant and stranger populations were instructed to return to their home areas to realize their political rights (Geschiere and Nyamnjoh 2000; Konings 2001). By the late 1990s, Cameroon's political transition was complete, and the country was internationally recognized as a multiparty democracy. For many Cameroonians, however, the country's political transition has been a disappointment, and initial enthusiasm was replaced by disillusionment and cynicism (e.g. Nyamnjoh 1999, 2002a).

Another characteristic of Cameroon's democratization process was a heightened degree of militancy and violence, both on the side of the population and the government. Political events frequently became unruly and were forcefully counteracted by the government, resulting in the deaths of dozens of civilians and the irregular detention of hundreds of others (Takougang and Krieger 1998). In addition, the country's economy continually degraded. Throughout the 1990s, civil servants were confronted with swingeing cuts to their salaries, as well as irregular payments. Moreover, in 1994 the CFA franc was devalued by 50 per cent, thus vitally affecting all strata of society (Konings 1996; Monga 1995).[9]

The ensuing atmosphere of political rivalry, social insecurity and aggression also had an impact at the local level and facilitated the unrest that accompanied the investiture conflict. Many Cameroonians interpreted the liberalization of political space as an opportunity to generally question established power relations. For example, prominent Grassfields chiefs who, so far, had enjoyed their subjects' full allegiance were harshly criticized by their followers for their party-political involvement; some were physically attacked, ousted or even killed (Awasom 2003b).

Party-political struggles were also deployed to redefine inter-group relations. In Misaje, political rivalry between local candidates and their counterparts in neighbouring Nkambe dominated the municipal elections of 1996 and eventually prompted army intervention, an episode whose memory shaped the investiture conflict. Elite individuals in Misaje thought it strategic to manipulate the municipal elections, with the aim of installing a council run by the ruling CPDM (Cameroon People's Democratic Movement), which would be distinct from the council of their competitors in the neighbouring town Nkambe, run by the SDF (Social Democratic Front).[10] However, the fraudulent election had unforeseen consequences, as the Misaje election was contested by SDF militants, who instructed the public to boycott council and market activities. The DO at the time was a francophone and unfamiliar with regional and local conditions, unlike his follower in office during the investiture conflict. He was out of his depth regarding the civil protest and ordered military intervention to reinstate law and order. The army came, dissolved the demonstrations, captured and abused recalcitrant militants and detained leading figures of the local SDF opposition. They made an example that would not be forgotten.

It is against this background of social insecurity and growing violence that we have to interpret the investiture conflict of the following year. The opposing parties opted for an increasingly confrontational course. Although the stand-off of the Nchaney masquerade and Mbororo staff-hurlers was essentially symbolic, these were symbols of terror and aggression. Moreover, with the appearance of a rifle and a knife, the threshold between symbolic and physical violence was crossed.

The moment of conflict escalation was also the moment when the DO intervened. Here one must keep in mind the population's prior experience of military intervention, and the implication that this would cause more violence and harm than the issue at hand was worth. Eventually, the opposing parties dispersed without the DO having to act on his threat of army intervention.[11]

Cultural Politics in 1990s Cameroon

A crucial feature of national politics that contributed to the investiture conflict was the government's emphasis on ethnic and cultural identities and minority representation. In the early 1990s, the UN and its partner organizations declared cultural authenticity as an indispensable component of individual and collective identity, and a human right that governments should preserve and encourage. In compliance with these guidelines, the Cameroonian government adopted the cultural policy of 'unity through diversity'.

Cameroon is popularly portrayed as a multicultural and bilingual nation,[12] a country characterized by ecological and ethnic diversity, and glossed as *Afrique en miniature*, or 'the microcosm of Africa's cultures' (MdlC 2002). This rhetoric is deployed both in the national and international arena. It reflects the government's efforts to comply with international demands and the tourist market, and concurrently its attempts to shift political opposition into the field of cultural expression or folklore.[13] Local cultural performances have increasingly been objectified in national celebrations and the media. Examples that illustrate this trend include a weekly television series depicting Cameroon's cultural heritage, the biennial Festival National des Arts et de la Culture, instituted in 1992, annual 'cultural fairs' organized by provincial administrations and the encouragement of local population groups to participate in national celebrations (such as National Day, Women's Day and Youth Day) with cultural performances, such as dance and choir presentations, masquerades and horse-riding displays. From the perspective of local actors, however, their groups' participation in national celebrations is primarily a political statement that confirms both their ethnic identities and national citizenship.[14]

Government policies promoting ethnic and cultural difference and minority representation also had an impact on individual and collective strategies in the investiture conflict. In his support for the Muslim community, the DO complied with the government's policy of safeguarding cultural and minority rights. At the same time, his actions may have been motivated by self-interest and personal rivalry as much as by administrative guidelines. Mbororo and Hausa interpreted the DO's backing during the initial negotiations as encouragement to defy political and cultural domination and to oppose the Nchaney palace hierarchy. The latter's obduracy, on the other hand, was hardened by the DO's apparent partiality. These views are endorsed by the allocation of guilt among my interlocutors, which will be discussed below.

The Symbolic Performance of Cultural Difference and Political Rivalry
In my analysis of the performative sequence of the investiture conflict, I have drawn on Turner's concept of the multivocality of symbols (Turner 1967: 50–52) and on Schnepel's analysis of the significance of ritual contest as compared to physical combat (Schnepel 1998). My focus in this section is on the phase of mounting crisis and on the polysemy of the deployed metonyms, namely Muslim caps, Grassfields masks and Mbororo herding staffs.

We must question how the act of wearing headgear became a symbol of Muslim resistance. Throughout the Grassfields, caps for men and headscarves for women are a common piece of clothing and indicate the wearers' social status. For Mbororo and Hausa, headgear is an integral part of their public outfit.[15] Among Grassfielders, the wearing of a cap or headscarf is less obligatory, yet the headgear is often used to convey its wearer's wealth or socio-political status.[16]

The palace hierarchy's provisional instruction that all residents of the Nchaney chiefdom should move around bareheaded was an attempt to bring about the public expression of respect and adherence to the new chief according to Nchaney standards. Among Mbororo and Hausa, however, wearing caps had mainly social and religious implications, and only in the context of the royal investiture did it assume the political connotation claimed by the Nchaney palace hierarchy. After negotiations, the two parties agreed on a provisional arrangement in which political subordination was still expressed via moving around bareheaded, but which delimited the ritual and symbolic space to the ceremonial ground.

The crucial factor that elicited and endorsed Mbororo and Hausa resistance was not the issue of removing their caps, but their numerous confrontations with Nchaney masks, namely the *chombu ju-ju*. Disagreements between Grassfielders and Muslims about the numinous nature and functions of masks go far beyond the investiture conflict. Masquerades are an integral element of the socio-political organization of Grassfields societies, and have religious and socio-political connotations (e.g. Argenti 2007; Engard 1989; Koloss 1977). Masks are understood as powerful numinous beings that can cause illness and death, and whose function is to supervise religious and social comportment. Most belong to family associations or secret societies whose members guard the knowledge of their spiritual power. As this knowledge can be transmitted and acquired, the same mask can be found in many different localities (Röschenthaler 2011). Across the Grassfields there is a wide range of popularly known masks, among them the *chombu ju-ju* and the *nggumba ju-ju* encountered in Misaje. The *chombu ju-ju* belong to the palace. As Nchaney and Muslim informants explained, they are the 'traditional police' and messengers of the *fon*. Their appearance normally indicates a spiritual danger, such as the passing of a witch or a more powerful mask. Furthermore, the chief sends them to reinforce his commands; for example, to escort culprits to the palace or to compel individuals to fulfil their obligations to the community. The power of the *chombu ju-ju* is both spiritual and physical, and they occasionally use their whips to beat offenders or frighten spectators. Their action is thought to be inspired by a numinous power, while the identity of the masker – the individual who embodies the mask – should remain unknown.

While the majority of Grassfielders believe in the efficacy and veracity of masks, Mbororo and Hausa largely refute the authority of the *ju-ju* with recourse to their Muslim faith. They deny them their numinous power and treat them as disguised human beings. Among Grassfielders, it is mandatory that spectators remove their headgear and bow down when confronted with a passing *ju-ju*. Most Muslims, however, refuse to pay the demanded respect, arguing that their religion does not permit them to bow down before idols but only before Allah. Furthermore, many Hausa and Mbororo informants complained that the *chombu ju-ju* in Misaje are pointlessly violent.[17] As one Hausa woman formulated it:

> The *ju-ju* here are more like enemies. They are used to beating women and even children, especially Hausa children. The mothers also get angry because they cannot accept that their children get beaten up like that. No, the tradition is not followed well. A man can just enter the cloth of a *ju-ju* and start beating children and women! They don't respect the function of the *ju-ju*.[18]

In order to avoid unnecessary confrontation, the head of the Hausa community instructed his people to stay indoors when maskers pass for the duration of the investiture ceremonies, which is probably the simplest and most effective strategy for dealing with irreconcilable cultural and religious differences.

During the investiture, the Muslims' initial reluctance to remove their caps was substantiated and reinforced by the repugnance they felt towards the *chombu ju-ju*. Although Mbororo and Hausa had been instructed by the DO and their community leaders to avoid the ceremonial ground, accidental confrontations could not be entirely circumvented. By attributing intentionality to accident and misadventure, the conflicting parties interpreted these encounters as the result of mutual disrespect.

In the end, the conflict culminated in the confrontation of the *nggumba ju-ju* and Mbororo staff-hurlers. The *nggumba ju-ju* is the mask of the regulatory society in Misaje.[19] It is considered much more powerful and dangerous than the *chombu ju-ju* and generally appears at night. Women are not supposed to see it, as it is believed that sight of the mask will turn them barren. When the Nchaney notables threatened to bring out their *nggumba ju-ju* during the daytime, they had in mind the mask's spiritual power, which would have lasting effect on their opponents, rendering their women barren and causing illness and death. Mbororo and Hausa were equally aware of the *nggumba ju-ju*'s alleged danger, and of the Nchaney notables' intention. But rather than shying away, their women made a point in defying the mask and challenging its efficacy.

Concurrently, Mbororo and Hausa men readied themselves to confront the Nchaney with their own particular device, namely a Mbororo staff-hurling or *kariya* performance. *Kariya* is a Hausa term and means 'protection' (Awde 1996: 82).[20] It is usually not a performative but a practical skill, which Mbororo youths acquire while herding their family's cattle. The herding staff, or *sawru* in Fulfulde, is the main tool used in guiding cattle and defending the herd against wild animals or thieves. Its metonymic character refers to cattle which, in turn, stand for Mbororo identity. Both men and women are familiar with using a *sawru*, be it as a walking stick, a herding tool or a weapon of defence. As a Mbororo friend recounted, his cousin's wife successfully defended her family against three robbers with her herding staff. And when the thieves ran off, one of them commented, 'A Mbororo man or woman with a staff is no small fight!'

Against this background it is understandable that the Mbororo *kariya* performance in the investiture conflict impressed and frightened their Nchaney opponents. Furthermore, it was generally assumed that they had fortified themselves by taking protective medicine to increase their courage and shield them against injury. Thus the Mbororo *kariya* performance, similar to the Nchaney *nggumba ju-ju*, included connotations of physical and spiritual power.

By considering the symbols of Muslim caps, Grassfields masks and Mbororo herding staffs in their social contexts, we have been able to determine at least part of the multivocality they assumed during the investiture conflict. The most vital metonym was Nchaney masks, which – while having contentious meanings for the opposing groups – primarily signified ritual authority.

A second feature of the politics of cultural performance concerns the relationship between symbolic confrontation and physical combat. I herein draw on Schnepel's (1998) explorations of ritual performances of power and authority in Orissa, India. Schnepel describes a variety of ritual performances, taking place in different historical periods, in which assertions to royal authority are based on the claimants' proximity to a deity. In his interpretation, ritual performance and royal authority in India are closely interrelated and cannot be separated into distinct domains of religion and politics. Ritual performances constitute a vital locus for the (re)negotiation of power relations; ritual contests are thus not only symbolic but 'real'. They may even be more consequential than purely physical combat as they refer to meanings and values of a higher authority.

In applying Schnepel's analysis to the investiture conflict, a number of similarities are discernable. In the Cameroon Grassfields, as in Orissa, ritual performance and royal authority are closely interlinked, hence Nchaney insistence on the observance of ritual prescriptions during royal investiture ceremonies. Secondly, the confrontation between Nchaney masquerade and Mbororo staff-hurlers was not only symbolic but 'real', where local power relations were renegotiated in the face of spiritual and physical danger. Following Schnepel (1998: 479), I suggest that their symbolic stand off was charged with greater meaning than a purely physical combat for material ends, as it ventured into the spheres of cultural ideology and social values, which are at the basis of group identities and inter-group relations.

Individual Assessments and the Allocation of Guilt

So far, I have based my analysis on a compounded version of informants' retrospective accounts. In the following I will present their individual assessments of responsibility and go beyond the simplistic dichotomy of Grassfielders versus Muslims. That is, while interlocutors generally framed the conflict in religious and ethnic terms, their individual accounts reveal that Grassfielders and Muslims did not constitute two homogeneous units, but each side included a panoply of opinions, diverging interests and cross-cutting allegiances.

The question of responsibility was prominent in informants' assessments of the conflict. Individual accounts often took the character of pre-emptive narratives that were aimed at falsifying particular explanations and allocations of guilt. As I am primarily interested in the factors that account for the conflict's ethnic framing, I will group informants' assessments according to their authors' ethnic backgrounds. However, I do not intend to create ethnicized master fictions; rather, their juxtaposition will show that informants' assessments differ as much along lines of status, gender and age as along lines of ethnicity and religion.

Nchaney Perspectives

In our conversations, Fon Richard acknowledged the investiture conflict, but emphasized that his current relationship with the Muslim community was good. In his view, the conflict arose from two sources: firstly, a misunderstanding between Nchaney notables and Muslim elders regarding mutually acceptable rules of comportment and appearance; and secondly, the partiality of the DO, who encouraged Muslim opposition against Nchaney authority in order to consolidate his own power vis-à-vis the Nchaney chief. As Fon Richard argued, royal investiture ceremonies are normally convened by the palace hierarchy, while the prospective chief is excluded from decision making. Thus, the decision that all residents in Nchaney territory should go bareheaded was not taken by him but by Nchaney notables, who did not fully understand Muslim rules of comportment. Of more consequence than this misunderstanding, however, was the involvement of the DO. In Fon Richard's view, the DO was supposed to keep a neutral position and stay away from the conflict, as this matter was to be resolved at the level of the polity rather than the administration. He identified three motives for the DO's involvement, namely personal gain (such as gifts of cattle or money for his partiality), greed for power and, not least, his ethnic background as a native of Nso. Nso is a neighbouring Grassfields polity that the Nchaney had successfully faced in a bloody and well-remembered inter-chiefdom war in the nineteenth century. In Fon Richard's view, the grievances of that century-old conflict were a crucial factor motivating the DO's stance against the Nchaney palace hierarchy.

Martin, a Nchaney sub-chief, evaluated the situation quite differently from Fon Richard. For him, blame primarily lay with the Muslims who violated the rules of 'the owners of the land'. Instead of acknowledging the legitimate supremacy of the Nchaney, they turned to the DO for assistance and even demonstrated their readiness to fight. They provoked the appearance of the dangerous *nggumba ju-ju* and, consequently, were affected by illness and death. Until they sought expiation and ritual cleansing through sacrifices performed by Nchaney village elders, the problem between the two communities would remain unresolved. By attributing guilt fully to the Muslims, Martin's view is exceptionally one-sided. His statement that inter-group relations could only normalize after the Muslim offenders had sought ritual cleansing is rather rhetorical. It reflects a procedure of social reintegration which, from a Muslim perspective, is inconceivable.

The views of Fon Richard and Martin reflect these two individuals' socio-political roles. While the *fon* is concerned with sharing political power with the DO, sub-chiefs are preoccupied with securing respect and support from their followers. Conversely, commoners' assessments of the conflict tended to be less coloured by political considerations and more informed by personal experiences and allegiances.

Hausa Perspectives

Ganye is a well-respected Hausa elder, and was one of the key representatives of the Muslim community. When he was attacked by the *chombu ju-ju* for wearing his cap while distributing meat for the festivities, it came as a surprise. However, as Ganye said, not all Nchaney were in support of the *ju-ju* attacks. Some notables took sides with the Muslim community and advised the maskers to respect Hausa and Mboror elders. Above all, Ganye stressed the involvement of the DO, whom he considered the spokesperson and protector of the Muslim community. Ganye saw the victory as one for the Muslim side, arguing that the Nchaney were intimidated by the Muslims' force of opposition and by the DO's intervention, and eventually sought reconciliation. In his assessment, the political power of the Hausa community was strengthened, and they were increasingly involved in decision-making processes in the palace.

Amina is the wife of the Hausa chief, and has a Grassfields background. She was strongly implicated in the conflict, because the Hausa chief's compound is located beside the *fon*'s palace; during the investiture ceremonies it was a central meeting point for members of the Muslim community. She mainly blamed the Nchaney, but also criticized the Mboror for their uncompromising attitude. The Nchaney wanted the Mboror to contribute cattle and, in addition, expected their presence as an expression of their adherence to the new chief. As Amina argued, the Nchaney notables should have anticipated Mboror opposition, as the latter would not accept 'traditional' laws that conflicted with Islamic ideology. The Hausa, on the other hand, tried to compromise as much as possible and to evade problems by staying at home or avoiding the ceremonial ground. Furthermore, Amina explained that she was personally confronted by Nchaney individuals who accused her of endorsing Muslim aggression.

Local Grassfielders appealed to her background as a woman of the neighbouring Mbembe (Grassfields) polity, and expected her to take their side. However, being the wife of the Hausa chief, she was bound to side with the Muslim community, and was thus treated by some Nchaney as a traitor.

The perspectives of Ganye and Amina reflect the views of two Hausa individuals who, due to their status and background, had allegiances with both sides. While Ganye highlighted differing attitudes among Nchaney, Amina pointed out divergent interests and strategies of Mbororo and Hausa.

Mbororo Perspectives

Adamu is the son and follower of the late ArDo Affang, who was at the time leader of the Mbororo community resident in Nchaney territory. He pointed out that the Mbororo community willingly supported the investiture ceremonies by contributing six zebu. But Nchaney notables did not take this into consideration when imposing their rules of comportment. In Adamu's view, the anger of the Nchaney was primarily directed against the Mbororo, although the conflict concerned the entire Muslim community.

Manu and Usman, two Mbororo brothers and regulars in Misaje, made it clear that not all Mbororo or Nchaney supported the idea of an open confrontation. They themselves did not want to get involved and were warned by their Nchaney friends to avoid the market square. Furthermore, they explained that, although the Muslims were alerted to potential problems and went to the mosque armed with staffs and knives, the elders advised their youths to concentrate on an impressive *kariya* performance and to refrain from violence in order to avoid a rupture in social and economic relations.

Hajara is a middle-aged Mbororo woman, who lives in the vicinity of Misaje. She attended the festivities on four days while making errands in town. Her account of the events was strikingly detailed and neutral. She pointed to differing approaches of Hausa and Mbororo in dealing with the impositions of the Nchaney notables. As Hausa and Nchaney are neighbours in Misaje, the Hausa elders were interested in maintaining good relations with their Nchaney neighbours. They felt uncomfortable with the offensive approach of Mbororo herders, and involved themselves in mediation. In the end, their religious affiliation was the decisive factor in rallying with the Mbororo, since the Muslim ideology of unity was seen to supersede local allegiances.

The perspectives of Mbororo men and women corroborated the views of Nchaney and Hausa informants, indicating divergent strategies and interests on all sides. Moreover, in their assessments, Mbororo informants also highlighted their own people's contribution to the conflict. While many Mbororo elders kept away from the ceremonial ground to avoid confrontations with Nchaney masks and instructed their youths to stay peaceful, the latter were less concerned and actively contributed to the acceleration of the conflict. The unruliness of Mbororo youths is a feature generally criticized by their elders, as well as by Nchaney and Hausa neighbours.

The Divisional Officer's View

When interviewed about the investiture, the DO argued that responsibility for the conflict lay with the Nchaney notables, as they tried to exert cultural hegemony over the Muslim population. He asserted that this kind of conflict was a unique incident, and that in other Grassfields chiefdoms Muslims were generally given the opportunity to circumvent 'traditional' rules that conflicted with their religious ideology. He noted that it was not only the Muslim population of Misaje town but also visiting market women who were forcefully subjected to those rules and sought his protection. The DO expressed his irritation with the Nchaney chief and his notables, who obstructed his initial efforts at mediation and who, eventually, sent the *nggumba ju-ju* to his house in revenge for the support he lent the Muslim community. While they thought the face-to-face encounter with the mask would harm the DO, he did not take the issue seriously. As he argued, his father was an *nggumba* owner in the neighbouring Nso chiefdom, and thus 'he could not be poisoned by his own food'. Similar to the *fon,* the DO interpreted the investiture conflict against the background of the long-standing rivalry between the Nchaney and Nso chiefdoms. At the same time, he justified his intervention with recourse to administrative guidelines in support of cultural autonomy and minority rights.

Two Sub-plots

In bringing together the various perspectives on the investiture conflict, we can outline at least two sub-plots to the master narrative of Grassfielders versus Muslims. On the one hand, there is the antagonism between the Nchaney palace hierarchy and the DO, who is seen not only as a representative of the state but also of the rivalling Nso chiefdom, and which reportedly influenced the actions of the Nchaney elders. On the other hand, there are the divergent approaches and interests of Hausa and Mbororo with regard to their Nchaney neighbours. While most Hausa pleaded for compromise, Mbororo youths tended to take a more aggressive approach. Both stances reflect the respective group's position in the local power hierarchy and their different ideas regarding integration into the Misaje community. While Hausa are more willing to take up a subordinate position, Mbororo wish to be integrated on an equal footing with their Nchaney neighbours. However, in the context of the investiture conflict, these different approaches were superseded by the identification of Hausa as a Muslim minority, and Mbororo and Hausa pursued a joint strategy.

When the conflict reached its peak, individuals and groups were polarized in two clear-cut factions, namely local Grassfielders versus Muslims. Once the crisis diffused, underlying schisms, internal rivalries and cross-cutting allegiances between individuals and groups resurfaced and facilitated the process of reintegration.

Reintegration and Dealing with the Past

In Turner's model of the social drama, '[t]he final phase [...] consists either of the reintegration of the disturbed social group or of the social recognition and legitimization of irreparable schism between the contesting parties' (Turner 1974: 41). This provides the researcher with the opportunity to assess socio-political changes by comparing political relations before and after the conflict. Furthermore, the phase of reintegration has its own rhetoric, non-verbal language and symbolism, and these disclose general rules of conflict resolution.

In applying Turner's analysis to the final stage of the investiture conflict, we may first note that the conflict ended in a phase of reintegration rather than schism: Nchaney, Mbororo and Hausa managed to achieve reconciliation and re-establish social and economic relations. Nevertheless, socio-political relations between the conflicting parties were altered, as were their relations with the state and its representatives. As I did not witness the situation before the investiture conflict, it is difficult for me to assess actual changes in local political relations. Nonetheless, I will outline major alterations on the basis of informants' individual assessments.

The phase of reintegration was initiated by the Nchaney chief, who invited Mbororo and Hausa representatives to a reconciliatory meeting and apologized for the maskers' excesses. He deemed it strategic to compromise and to invest in good relations with the Muslim community in order to strengthen his position vis-à-vis the DO, whom he came to consider his primary opponent in the administration of the Nchaney chiefdom. Mbororo and Hausa elders accepted the *fon*'s apologies. They saw their political authority significantly strengthened, and were confident that they would be able henceforth to assert the limits of their tolerance, if need be with the assistance of officials. The DO had proved to his superiors and the local population that he was capable of managing a critical situation, and thus reasserted his superordinate position in local power politics.

Despite the parties' eventual reconciliation and reintegration, they never succeeded in negotiating a final solution to the specific problem of cultural and religious differences regarding royal investiture rites. They ultimately deployed a strategy which I term functional indifference. By leaving the issue unresolved and accepting or ignoring the existence of inherent contradictions, they achieved a temporary compromise that kept interethnic relations flexible, while maintaining the possibility of reviving the controversy when required or seemed opportune. Lentz (2002, 2013) reports similar conflict-management strategies employed in land disputes between Dagara and Nuni farmers in the border region of Ghana and Côte d'Ivoire. Both parties considered it strategic to publicly confirm their claims, while leaving the dispute unresolved until a future incident might require its revival.

The notion of functional indifference is closely related to the concepts of compromise and avoidance. Strategies of compromise and making concessions have been described by Eriksen (1998: 14–18) for Mauritius and by Mutie (2013) regarding the coexistence of Kamba and Maasai peoples in Kenya. Mutie defines compromise as 'a negotiation process through which diverse and clashing interests coalesce in a give-and-take relationship' (2013: 332). Both authors state that compromise and concession is a pertinent strategy in overcoming ethnic and cultural differences in their respective field sites.

In the case of the investiture conflict, the process of conflict resolution involved a compromise insofar as the rivalling parties agreed to ignore the incident. Their compromise, however, did not go as far as determining a binding solution to the specific problem of wearing caps during royal investiture rites. This omission is interpreted here as a strategy of avoidance.

Elwert (2001, 2004, 2005) proposes avoidance as one of four poles in his model of conflict. These poles include destruction, warring, procedure and avoidance, and are characterized by more or less violence and stronger or weaker embedding. In his model it is the degree of embedding in social action rather than violence that determines the integrative or dissociative propensity of conflict. Avoidance strategies – as with destruction – are characterized by relatively weak embedding. They do not draw on institutions of conflict resolution, nor do they contribute to their generation, and thus they are prone to relapse to destruction (Elwert 2001: 2544; see also Eckert 2004: 15). Alber (2005: 177) defines avoidance strategies as tactics of deliberately evading or ignoring conflict by abstaining from action. She provides examples from encounters of the Baatombu with the French colonial authorities in Benin. In contrast to Elwert's assumption of the probable relapse of avoidance to destruction, Eriksen (1998: 47–48) argues that avoidance, in addition to compromise, is a relevant and successful strategy in securing peaceful coexistence in Mauritius, and a strategy supported by government policies.

As argued above, the initial, more aggressive character of the investiture conflict was bolstered by the national political developments of the 1990s and the atmosphere of social insecurity and violence. However, in the final phase of the conflict, actors switched back to established strategies of functional indifference, avoidance and compromise – strategies widespread in the Grassfields, both in preventing and resolving conflict.

In concluding this section I will discuss some of the symbols and rhetoric that informants deployed in assessing the effects of the investiture conflict, namely the symbol of blood and the idiom of forgetting. Many informants argued that 'since no blood was shed, no grudge should be kept'. From a Nchaney perspective, the spilling of blood would have implied long-term consequences, because it would have angered the ancestors and required spiritual sanctions. Similar historical incidents, such as the inter-chiefdom war between the Nchaney and Nso, are vividly remembered, and socio-political relations between these groups have remained strained. From a Mbororo and Hausa perspective, the upshot of violence would have threatened their social and economic continuity in the Nchaney chiefdom. In the investiture conflict, however, no blood was shed and its effect on inter-group relations has remained limited.

In looking back at the investiture conflict, informants expressed discomfort and confusion regarding the escalation of a minor disagreement over religious and cultural differences into an imminently violent conflict. In their view, the incident was best wiped from collective memory and should no longer enter public discourse.[21] Thus informants' conclusive statements that the incident had passed and should be forgotten reflect their strongly ambivalent feelings towards that particular period in Cameroon's political history, as well as the incident itself. On the other hand, it illustrates that all parties have a strong interest in peaceful coexistence, and that dissent and conflict are considered part and parcel of everyday life.

General Principles of Conflict Resolution

In his renowned study of the Ndembu of Zambia, Turner (1957) argued that the contradiction between the principles of matrilineal descent and virilocal residence was a major factor supporting the cyclical emergence of social dramas in Ndembu society, and that this contradiction was further complicated by larger historical changes effected through colonial rule. If we draw an analogy and apply Turner's analysis to the investiture conflict, we may assume that the givens of cultural and religious heterogeneity and the flexibility of local power relations in the Grassfields are a major source of recurrent conflict. This, however, is not the case. As I will explore in detail in subsequent chapters, interethnic coexistence is facilitated via a system of economic complementarity and a multiplicity of cross-cutting ties. The Cameroon Grassfields, alongside many other West African locales, may be cited as an example of 'integration through difference' (Schlee 2001). Nonetheless, the coexistence of groups is not entirely conflict-free, as quarrels frequently emerge over access to natural and state resources.

If the causes of the investiture conflict were not underlying contradictions rooted in the religious and cultural heterogeneity of the research area, they may be located in external factors, in particular in the national political developments of the 1990s and the intervention of state officials. In my reading, the general atmosphere of political instability and social insecurity, coupled with state policies promoting ethnic and cultural identities and minority representation, facilitated the upsurge of more aggressive strategies, as pursued by both parties in the conflict. One cannot determine with any certainty whether the investiture conflict could have emerged in a different time period, nor is it possible to fully establish the conscious strategies of all participants. I believe, however, that actors on both sides were stimulated by general socio-political developments and, quite possibly, by personal motives to 'try it on' in situations where they previously may have adopted strategies of avoidance or compromise.

I conclude this chapter with a reconsideration of the effects of the investiture conflict on social coexistence in Misaje. I take up Gluckman's (1955) argument of the socially cohesive propensity of conflict, and relate the investiture conflict to Elwert's conflict model. Following Gluckman's study of political conflict within Zulu and Barotse society in Southern Africa (Gluckman 1963), we may draw the distinction between rebellion and revolution. While revolution leads to radical and constitutional change, rebellion contributes to the reproduction of an existing political system. In addition, Gluckman elaborates on rituals of rebellion, which he sees as bounded forms that occur primarily within stationary or repetitive social systems. Such rituals are characterized by the open criticism of particular distributions of power, yet without questioning the structure of the system itself. In Gluckman's reading, rituals of rebellion demonstrate the potential for civil rebellion, but are untenable in systems open to revolution.

Applying Gluckman's analysis to the investiture conflict provides us with a model of how rituals of rebellion may lead to civil rebellion or ultimately to revolution. We may read the symbolic stand-off of Grassfielders and Muslims as a ritual of rebellion on the verge of actual civil rebellion. Whereas the transitional unrest of the 1990s had the potential for revolutionary upheaval, the investiture conflict itself was finally diffused by the intervention of government authority, and ended in the reintegration of the groups involved. While setting out as a socially cohesive conflict, it evolved into a disruptive conflict. Ultimately, its impact on the coexistence of Grassfielders, Mbororo and Hausa remained limited, as the opposing parties agreed to forego its consequences.

The more elaborate conflict model of Elwert (2001, 2004, 2005) provides two axes to assess the integrative or dissociative propensity of conflict, namely the degree of violence and of social embedding. The investiture conflict exhibited a generally low degree of social embedding, as no acknowledged guidelines or procedures existed for dealing with cultural and religious difference in the context of royal investiture rites. Initial attempts at achieving a compromise largely failed. The strategy most common among Mbororo and Hausa would have been avoidance, meaning that individuals of both groups would have stayed at home or systematically circumvented the ceremonial ground. Corresponding to Elwert's assumption that actors tend to switch from avoidance to destruction rather than procedure, both parties in the conflict opted for a relatively aggressive approach. Yet unanticipated by Elwert, they eventually switched back to avoidance – or functional indifference – in order to re-establish peaceful coexistence.

I have opened my analysis with the case study of a conflict that ignited over minor issues of religious and cultural difference, and which was fuelled by the ramifications of Cameroon's political liberalization. In Chapter 7 I will turn to the case study of a second, major conflict that erupted after a homicide in 2001, and which exhibited quite different forms of conflict management. In the chapters between these two case studies, I will provide the historical background to the coexistence of Grassfields societies, Mbororo and Hausa, and describe some of the many minor and less dramatic events that are equally significant in understanding interethnic relations and identity politics in the Grassfields.

Notes

1 In popular usage in anglophone Cameroon, the term 'traditional' (both in English and Pidgin English) is generally used to refer to cultural practices and socio-political institutions that are perceived as having a long history within the respective community. In this study, the terms 'traditional dances' and 'traditional authorities' are used occasionally when reflecting popular parlance.
2 *Ju-ju* is a Pidgin English term which stands for the complex of medicine and is also used to designate an individual mask. On the panoply of Grassfields masks, see e.g. Koloss (2000).
3 I thank Billy MacKinnon for suggesting this term. 'Indifference' is also used by Bailey (1996) to describe the moderate and pragmatic approach to ethnic difference and conflict exhibited by the inhabitants of Bisipara, a village in eastern India, in the 1950s. However, in his analysis he applied a variant of the economists' expected-utility framework (Bailey 1996: 162), a theoretical approach I do not use in this study.
4 Schlee (1994) distinguishes identity markers, ethnicity emblems and diacritical features. While the first two refer to an emic perspective, the latter implies an etic assessment. All three are indicators of ethnic and, more generally, social identities.
5 The overlapping of Grassfields and Muslim identities is most pronounced in Grassfields chiefdoms with a large Muslim congregation, such as neighbouring Nso, and the Bamoun sultanate in the francophone West Region, whose ruler converted to Islam in the early twentieth century and turned his chiefdom into a Muslim state (see e.g. Tardits 1980; Wazaki 1992).

6   For an audio-visual representation of the everyday performance of ethnic and cultural identity in Misaje see the video documentary by M. Pelican and J. Orland. 2002. *Getting Along in the Grassfields: Aspects of Village Life in Misaje* (North West Cameroon), 37 mins, with English subtitles. File name: Misaje_Documentary.mpeg, as well as the accompanying documents by M. Pelican. 2002. *Commentary on Misaje Documentary*. File name: Misaje_Commentary.pdf, and *Treatment of Misaje Documentary*. File name: Misaje_Treatment.pdf. These items are accessible via the virtual archive of the Max Planck Institute for Social Anthropology in Halle/Saale (http://corpora.eth.mpg.de/).

7   Warnier's comprehensive analysis of the technologies of power of the Mankon chiefdom sheds light on the elaborate material and symbolic practices used to secure the chiefdom's integrity, including the relevance of strict ritual prescriptions and bodily control during succession rites (Warnier 2007: 209–32).

8   See 'La Constitution de la Republique du Cameroun: Loi No 96-06 du 18 Janvier 1996'; English version 'Constitution of the Republic of Cameroon, Law No. 96–06 of 18 January 1996 to amend the Constitution of 2 June 1972'.

9   The CFA franc is pegged to the Euro and used in fourteen African countries, with different bills being used in the two zones of West and Central Africa.

10 It is important to note that the vast majority of councils in the North West Region went to candidates of the SDF (the main opposition party); only four were won by CPDM politicians, including Misaje (Geschiere and Nyamnjoh 1998: 80).

11 As further incidents of civil disobedience continued to occur in Misaje, the DO actually did call in the army at a later stage, when local villagers publicly attacked the commandant of the gendarmerie. The offenders were apprehended and taken to the divisional capital for trial and imprisonment.

12 French and English are Cameroon's two official languages.

13 In this interpretation I build on an argument put forward by a number of Cameroonian scholars, most pronouncedly by Nyamnjoh (1999). He argues that, with its politics of ethnic and cultural difference, the Cameroonian government encourages ethnic discord at local and regional levels in order to diffuse popular opposition at a national level. Nyamnjoh's interpretation ties in well with Kourouma's (2001) literary description of African despots who keep the masses singing and dancing in praise of their rule while exploiting and abusing their subjects.

14 In Mbembe's (1992) reading, national ceremonies have been used by the Cameroonian government to express and exert its power. He interprets participation by individuals and groups in these events as a strategy to partake of the government's riches.

15 Mbororo and Hausa women generally cover their heads with a head-tie and scarf, while men wear embroidered caps. Some Muslim rulers wear a turban as a symbol of their rank, while accomplished *alhaji*s bring along a specific headgear to indicate their having undertaken the pilgrimage to Mecca.

16 At the time of my fieldwork, it was fashionable among wealthy Grassfields women to wear large, gold-embroidered headdresses in the so-called Yoruba style. For men, a black crocheted cap decorated with a porcupine quill or a red feather designates its wearer's position as a sub-chief.

17 Engard (1989: 149) reports that the risk of minor injuries during masquerades is real, as maskers are not held publicly responsible for their actions. Some degree of accountability on the part of the palace hierarchy or the cult association to which the mask belongs may exist outside the context of performance.

18 B.S., Misaje, 14 November 2001.
19 *Nggumba* is originally the name of the regulatory society in the chiefdom of Bali. The same term is used in Pidgin English and is common in Misaje. Alternative terms used among other Grassfields societies are *kwifon* (Kom) and *ngwerong* (Nso). For a succinct portrayal of the Lela ceremony in Bali, in which the regulatory society plays a significant role, see Fardon (2006).
20 In Chapter 3 we will learn that the Mbororo in the Grassfields belong to two sub-groups, namely Jaafun and Aku. Informants pointed out that *kariya* is considered a speciality of the Aku. Jaafun, on the other hand, have been renowned for their stick-beating contest (*soro*), which is aimed at the public performance of self-restraint and courage, but has been banned in Cameroon.
21 A similar approach was shared by Pandey's informants towards the recollection of Hindu–Muslim riots in Bhagalpur (India), who preferred to let 'bygones be bygones' in order to ensure the reputation of their town and the future coexistence of Hindus and Muslims (Pandey 1991: 563).

2
The Power of the *Fon*
Nchaney Political History

In Kopytoff's classic essay on 'the internal African frontier' (Kopytoff 1987), Grassfields societies serve as a key example in a critique of earlier functionalist views of African tribes as homogeneous and bounded units. They are used to illustrate the recurrent formation of new polities as a result of processes of fission and fusion. Similarly, in his extensive oeuvre on Grassfields societies, Warnier (1985, 1993, 2007) has drawn attention to the composite and flexible nature of Grassfields societies as a result of exchange networks, migration and frequent intermarriage. Concurrently, he has outlined the techniques of power and subjection employed by Grassfields chiefdoms to produce territoriality and a sense of belonging within their heterogeneous populations (Warnier 2007). While these two authors largely end their analysis with the beginning of the twentieth century, I will extend the timeline to the contemporary period and consider the accommodation of ethnic and cultural 'others', such as Hausa and Mbororo in the Misaje area. Furthermore, I will examine current Grassfields institutions and their political strategies to look at the interests of Grassfields societies vis-à-vis the state and international organizations.

Carrying on from the investiture conflict and its protagonists on the Nchaney side (see Chapter 1), this chapter will engage with the chiefdom's political history and notions of Nchaney identity from the perspective of the palace hierarchy. While in colonial reports the Nchaney were known by the ethnonym Nchanti, three alternative terms are currently used in popular speech and administrative reports. Nchaney stands for the chiefdom and its people; their language is called Ncane; and Nkanchi is the head village of the Nchaney chiefdom.

Critical Remarks on Studying History and Ethnicity in the Grassfields

Anthropologists have identified colonialism as a major driving force for the emergence and transformation of ethnicities in Africa. The proponents of a most radical interpretation are Hobsbawm and Ranger (1983) and Amselle (1998), who claim that current ethnic groups are primarily the product of colonial invention. As my elaboration of Nchaney history will show, contemporary modalities of 'history telling' and ethnic self-categorization largely correspond to the colonial model. However, the contents of interlocutors' historical accounts indicate processes of inclusion and exclusion, and changes in collective self-understanding that preceded the colonial period. Moreover, processes of constructing local history and identity extend to the present and are elicited in the activities of ethnic elite associations.

According to Hobsbawm and Ranger (1983), many aspects of so-called traditional organization, history and legal arrangements in contemporary Africa are not based on locally developed customs, but were the outcome of colonial intervention and the projection of Western concepts onto colonial subjects. Ranger critically distinguishes 'tradition' from 'custom', taking 'custom' as a loosely defined and flexible body of inherited practices, while 'tradition' refers to a 'closed corporate consensual system which came to be accepted as characteristic of 'traditional' Africa' (Ranger 1983: 248).[1]

Among Cameroonians, the terms 'custom' and 'tradition' are frequently mentioned but carry connotations different from Ranger's use. 'Tradition' and its Pidgin English equivalent 'country-fashion' denote practices inherited from previous generations and still relevant in everyday life, and therefore variable and adaptable to contemporary situations. The term 'custom', on the other hand, is mainly used when referring to practices and procedures introduced or fixed by the colonial authorities. For example, the customary court is a judicial institution introduced by the British, while the traditional council is the local judiciary body of the palace that deals with village affairs. Also relevant is the notion of 'traditional authorities', which refers to local political institutions, such as Grassfields chiefs and their associates. It is important to keep in mind the local meanings of these terms when reading accounts and statements quoted in this study.

Hobsbawm and Ranger's argument about the codification of tradition, history and identity through colonial intervention remains highly relevant to a critical analysis of the Cameroonian case.[2] However, I would plead for a less radical and more subtle approach, one which admits agency as well as reflexivity on the part of both colonial authorities and colonial subjects. I will take as an example the colonial classification of Grassfields societies into 'tribes' and 'clans'. Colonial administrators and government anthropologists were well aware of the problems implied in applying these concepts to local groups. In the Grassfields, 'clan' was introduced as an administrative term to denote political and residential units. As Assistant District Officer Newton indicated in his report on the Mbembe and Nchanti Areas, the administrative definition of 'clan' differed from the anthropological one as an exogamous, unilateral group of persons, which applied to only two of the twenty-seven residential units in his survey area (Newton 1935: 39). Similarly, the colonial anthropologists and historians Chilver and Kaberry (1967; 1970: 249) stated that the concept of 'clan territory' was a misnomer. Moreover, they argued that the classification of Grassfields societies into 'tribes' or ethnic supra-units (Aghem, Bali, Mbembe, Tikar and Widekum) on the basis of cultural commonalities and shared migration histories was of doubtful validity and significance. Nonetheless, the terms 'clan', 'clan territory' and 'tribe' were commonly used in administrative English, and have also entered colloquial Pidgin English. As we will see, many interlocutors use these terms when referring to ethnic units.

In line with organizing the Grassfields into administrative units (so called 'native authority areas'), the British distinguished between 'native' and 'stranger' populations, and therewith consolidated existing power differences. In this context, the term 'native' is not derived from the idea of autochthony, which denotes a people that emerged from the very area and has no migration experience. Rather, it is a political term that refers to local population groups whose claims to pre-eminence were endorsed by the colonial administration. The term 'natives' has entered colloquial English and Pidgin English, and is commonly used to denote Grassfielders in general or local Grassfields societies, contrasting them to Mbororo, Hausa and Grassfields migrants who count as 'strangers' in a respective region. The distinction between 'natives' and 'strangers' regained significance in the 1990s in the context of legislative changes that define citizenship in terms of ethnic and regional belonging.

Taking colonial subjects not only as objects of colonial manipulation but attributing them agency and responsibility also implies ascribing them the capability and power to select, manipulate or invent information for their own purposes. Local historical accounts, at any given time, are therefore not neutral but influenced by the ideological, political and economic goals of their narrators and advocates. They may respond in form and content to structures imposed by a superior authority, and often aim at adopting strategies that promise most success.

Modalities of Nchaney Historiography

When discussing Nchaney history and identity with local informants, it became clear that historiography among Grassfields peoples entails clear hierarchies and formats. Firstly, narrating the collective history of the Nchaney is considered the monopoly of the palace hierarchy – elders and notables – while women and youths are generally excluded. Secondly, history is not imagined as a single, homogeneous body of knowledge, but as a patchwork of details known to different members of the palace hierarchy. Thirdly, even if confined to the palace, writing Nchaney history is a matter of continuous discussion, negotiation and modification, and is overshadowed by its contributors' interests and agendas. This experience, however, is not particular to the Grassfields, but has been reported for other areas of Cameroon and, contentiously, is a common feature of historiography everywhere (e.g. Kaberry and Chilver 1961; Schilder 1994).

The subsequent account draws on a variety of sources. First-hand information was contributed by Fon Richard, head of the Nchaney chiefdom at the time of my research, as well as by a group of nine Nchaney notables and elders who discussed many aspects of Nchaney history with and for me. At a later stage, a preliminary version of this chapter was sent to Misaje to be discussed with informants. This produced a number of interesting remarks, some of which have been integrated into the chapter.[3] A second source of information is visual material (photographs and maps) introduced by Fon Richard to endorse his narrative. In terms of written accounts, I have been able to draw on colonial reports (Newton 1935; Jeffreys 1951) as well as contemporary contributions. In recent times, the histories of Grassfields peoples have become the object of more or less professional academic research, and have increasingly been appropriated by members of the educated elite. For the Misaje area, no in-depth study has been carried out or published so far, although attempts have been made. For example, as the headmaster of the Misaje government school reported, he had compiled a booklet on the history of the Bessa based on oral traditions and interviews with notables and elders; but unfortunately the manuscript was lost. Although local history is not included in the curricula of primary and secondary schools, it is tacitly practised by many teachers using their own initiative. Moreover, university students of geography, environmental management, anthropology and other subjects are increasingly encouraged to carry out small-scale studies in their home villages, resulting in dissertations for Bachelors and Masters degrees (e.g. Ntoban n.d.). However, in all these academic and partly pseudo-academic endeavours, it is still the history of the palace rather than of the common man – not to speak of women – that is written down for future generations.

Against the background of these diverse sources of information, I will aim at presenting a multifaceted reconstruction of Nchaney political history that incorporates the myriad character and socio-political embeddedness of individual accounts. Moreover, the distinct character of Grassfields historiography and its preoccupation with chiefly structures will become evident when compared to the historical accounts of Mbororo and Hausa presented in later chapters.

Nchaney History and Identity: A View from the Palace

The following narrative of Nchaney political history consists of four sections that illustrate consecutive historical phases: the migration and early settlement period (probably seventeenth century), the consolidation of the Nchaney chiefdom (seventeenth and eighteenth centuries), its expansion and relationships with neighbouring chiefdoms (nineteenth century), and the accommodation of non-Grassfields groups (twentieth century). Drawing on Barth's (1969) interactionist approach, I argue that Nchaney encounters with political and cultural 'others' as well as with colonial and postcolonial governments set off processes of inclusion and exclusion. Moreover, shifting group boundaries and changing political frameworks elicited transformations in Nchaney self-understandings, as well as the adoption of new strategies of political representation.

The Nchaney Myth of Origin

At the roots of the Nchaney polity and its identity is the mythical migration of its ancestors, which culminated in their settlement at Nkanchi, probably in the seventeenth century. Fon Richard and the group of elders and notables presented early Nchaney history as follows:

> We migrated from Kimi in the Banyo area in Adamaoua; we are Tikar. This happened as a result of a serious war caused by the Muslims in the sixteenth or seventeenth century. We were called the *nchan* and were under the leadership of Ngungu, whose name means 'the carpenter bee'. He was afraid that his children might be killed. He transformed into a bee and swallowed his family. He flew to this place here [Nkanchi], which by then was a virgin place, a free land. When he got here, he vomited his children. He was no longer called Ngungu but Mbene and the place was called *fembene*, meaning 'home or palace of Mbene'. His children were called *bami babi soshung* in our language, which means 'the people of those who are seven'. These were the seven kingmakers from the seven families that make up the Nchaney. When Mbene died, he transformed into a rock. The same happened to the seven kingmakers. The place with the rocks of the *fon* and the kingmakers became a shrine, and is called *fewong*, meaning 'head of the village' or 'our country'. It is the village's sacrificial site. In case of any problem, the kingmakers go there and call the names of their gods of the land.[4]

Claims to Tikar descent, as reflected in this account, are common among Grassfields societies, and have also been remarked upon by colonial administrators (e.g. Newton 1935: 40). While most of these claims may be factually false, they have primarily political and symbolic significance, aimed at constructing a shared history and identity and at asserting political status.[5] Furthermore, Fon Richard placed the Nchaney's departure at the time of the FulBe *jihad*, which he dated to the sixteenth or seventeenth century. Actually, the FulBe *jihad* was initiated in Sokoto in 1804. But, while Fon Richard may have simply misremembered his history lessons at school, there could as well have been previous other, minor *jihads* or slave raids that affected the area.

In interpreting the Nchaney myth of origin, we may consider the precolonial history of slave raiding in the Grassfields.[6] Taking into account that 'eating' serves as an idiom for the appropriation of power (Bayart 1993), Fon Ngungu's 'swallowing' of his people could be read as an act of attaining power through sacrificing or cannibalizing his followers, that is, by selling them into slavery. As has been historically reconstructed, many Grassfields chiefs collaborated with FulBe and Chamba raiders, supplying them with slaves from their own chiefdoms, and thereby legitimizing their power (Argenti 2006, 2007; Geary 1976: 91 et passim; Nkwi and Warnier 1982: 83–88; Warnier 1995, 2007). Similarly, Fon Ngungu's 'vomiting' of his children can be read as an act of procreation, namely the creation of a new chiefdom.

A crucial component of Nchaney identity is vested in the group's relationship with the land they occupy. This connection is expressed in the ritual responsibilities of the *fon* and the seven kingmakers. They are in charge of fostering the relationship with their ancestors, who are represented in the eight stones of the village's sacrificial site. Nchaney identification with the land and the ancestors replicates a distinctive feature of many Grassfields societies. The land is generally thought to 'punish those who transgress against the moral code, and can be called upon to make judgment in disputes' (Goheen 1996: 24). Moreover, land is considered the primary means of production, and is at the root of Grassfielders' self-understanding as farmers. As Warnier (2007: 154–58) argues, the *fon*'s control over ancestral substances and over the chiefdom's boundaries is crucial to the production of locality and territorialization, which are at the heart of engendering unity and belonging among the chiefdom's heterogeneous population.

The contemporary population of Nkanchi is conceived of as descendents of the seven founding families who are represented by the seven kingmakers. Each family has its own initial settlement area, which includes a sacred site where its members can hide in case of war.[7] In addition, there is an eighth family in Nkanchi, the Che, who claim to be the original inhabitants that the seven founding families met upon their arrival, and who have retained their ritual autonomy. This is a common plot in the founding histories of Grassfields chiefdoms and is indicative of the composite nature of Grassfields societies (Kopytoff 1987; Warnier 2007: 156).

Table 2.1: Name-list of Nchaney *fons*

	Name	Approximate reign	Characterization
1	Fon Mbene (Ngungu)	seventeenth century	mythical ancestor
2	Fon Mbene II		
3	Fon Kabo		
4	Fon Krine		
5	Fon Kimenchung		
6	Fon Chimbung		
7	Fon Bamine		
8	Fon Fimban		
9	Fon Massa		
10	Fon Nchenghe	ca. 1850–1880	bad ruler, dethroned
11	Fon Fuma	ca. 1880–1933	successful ruler during a period of pre-colonial inter-chiefdom wars and colonial threats
12	Fon Ngong	1934–1950	bad ruler, dethroned
13	Fon Sale	1950–1968	successful ruler in a period of affluence
14	Fon Michael	1968–1997	local chief and government administrator
15	Fon Richard	1997–2013	

The Establishment of the Nchaney Chiefdom

After their migration and settlement at Nkanchi, the next step in Nchaney history is the establishment and consolidation of the Nchaney chiefdom. This phase is best described by presenting the name-list of Nchaney *fon*s and complementing it with anecdotes on the subsequent chiefs' reigns. Royal name-lists have been collected since the colonial period and have become an integral element of Grassfields peoples' own oral histories (Chilver and Kaberry 1967: 13). Anecdotes on the reigns of various *fon*s inform us of internal political struggles, and also illustrate the Nchaney's embeddedness in the wider historical and political framework.

The name-list of Nchaney *fon*s (Table 2.1) is based on interviews with Fon Richard and a group of palace elders conducted in 2002. It does not include the current ruler, Fon Thomas, who was enthroned in 2013. The list provides the names of fifteen chiefs, starting with the mythical ancestor Mbene (Ngungu), who allegedly moved to Nkanchi in the seventeenth century, and ending with Richard, who was enthroned in 1997. While Fon Richard and his advisors were able to recall the names of all fifteen chiefs, the group of elders and notables only remembered seven *fon*s. The following is a compilation of the information contributed by both parties. All dates indicated in the table and in the subsequent text are based on Fon Richard's historical reconstruction.

The mythical ancestor and founder of the Nchaney was Ngungu, who became known as Fon Mbene after settling at Nkanchi. He was followed by eight successive *fons*, of whom only their names are remembered. The subsequent ruler was Fon Nchenghe, who reigned for approximately thirty years. Eventually, he was dethroned, and the chieftaincy handed over to Fon Fuma. He is remembered as a good ruler who defended his chiefdom against attacks by the neighbouring polities Bum and Nso, and dealt successfully with early colonial challenges.[8] Moreover, during his reign, Hausa traders began to settle at Nkanchi, from where they later transferred to Misaje. Shortly after his death, Fon Ngong took up office. He ruled for sixteen years, but was deposed because of his harsh rule. As the Nchaney elders and notables reported, 'he beat people in the palace and did not respect human rights. He was a wicked man and even speared people'.[9]

Following Ngong's dethronement in 1950, Fon Sale was ordained to act as interim ruler until Ngong's designated successor, Michael, was old enough to take over in 1968 (Figure 2.1). Fon Sale enjoyed the reputation of a competent ruler. His reign coincided with the construction of the Ring Road (the main infrastructural axis of the North West Region) and the road to Dumbo. The British employed local workers, and also brought in skilled labour migrants from other areas of the Grassfields. Around the same time, Mbororo pastoralists began to enter the region, boosting the local economy with their demand for food crops. All in all, it was a prosperous era and a period of economic development which must have coloured people's perception of Fon Sale's rule. Concurrently, it was characterized by the accommodation of new populations, thus reflecting the chiefdom's growth and prosperity in terms of voluntarily subordinated peoples.

Fon Michael was a successful and well educated ruler. His reign lasted from 1968 to his death in 1997. Not only was he a chief but also an administrator. He was the chairman of the Ako Rural Council, which nowadays comes close to the post of mayor of Misaje. Moreover, he was married to seven wives and had more than forty children. Fon Michael was also renowned for his mystical powers, which associated him with Ngungu, the mythical ancestor of the Nchaney. Fon Michael was perceived as a skilful administrator and politician, both at the level of the local polity and the Cameroonian state. The early days of his rule coincided with Cameroon's independence. He was one of the young and dynamic rulers who succeeded in combining their traditional role with national politics, and struggled for the development of their area.[10] It was also Fon Michael who, due to his administrative responsibilities, transferred the palace from Nkanchi to Misaje, and thereby consolidated Nchaney territorial claims to Misaje town.

Fon Michael's reputation as a cunning politician is dominant in Fon Richard's portrayal of his father's rule. For example, he narrated, how Fon Michael 'snatched' development projects and deviated them to the Misaje area. The relevant point here is not the verification of such claims, but Fon Richard's

Figure 2.1: Shey Sale and Fon Michael, 1968. Reproduced by kind permission of Fon Richard.

All photographs in this chapter have been contributed by Fon Richard and are part of the Nchaney palace album. This picture was taken on 5 March 1968, on the day that Fon Sale handed over the chieftaincy to Fon Michael, and henceforth no longer bore the title of *fon* but *shey*. Shey Sale, sitting on the left, is dressed in a fine gown, tailored in the Hausa style. He is adorned with insignia of eminence, namely a long stick and a fly whip. Fon Michael, sitting on the right, is dressed in a so-called kings' cloth, a hand-woven fabric dyed in blue and white, owned by Grassfields palaces and worn only by chiefs during important rituals. Fon Michael wears a necklace made of leopard teeth, and at his feet is a calabash that symbolically contains ancestral substances transmitted from *fon* to *fon* (cf. Warnier 2007). Also noteworthy is his watch which, by then, was a symbol of modernity. Behind the two stands *kilah*, a mask in charge of protection that belongs to the Yahdo family.

framing of his father's role as a chief. Since Cameroon's independence and reunification, and increasingly with the political liberalization of the 1990s, chiefs have aspired to combine their local political roles with administrative functions. They have aimed at becoming leading figures in the struggle for government resources and rural development, and to be recognized as being on the same level as government administrators.[11]

Fon Richard was enthroned in 1997. At the time of my research, he was a young man in his early thirties with a basic educational and professional training background. At the early stage of his rule, he was preoccupied with enforcing respect and allegiance from his subjects, negotiating power relations with neighbouring Grassfields chiefdoms, and consolidating his authority over land and people vis-à-vis government and community officials (Figure 2.2). In 2013 Fon Richard passed away and was succeeded by his brother Thomas who is the current *fon*.

When comparing information about the earlier chiefs' reigns supplied by Fon Richard and the Nchaney elders and notables, a number of points are

Figure 2.2: Administrative induction of Fon Richard, 1998. Reproduced by kind permission of Fon Richard.

The photograph was taken at Fon Richard's administrative induction on 7 May 1998. It shows Fon Richard (third from the right, in 'traditional' Grassfields attire) in the company of the brigade commander of Misaje, the commissioner of the Frontier Police in Dumbo, the mayor of Misaje, the senior divisional officer, the divisional officer and the commissioner of public security of Donga-Mantung (left to right).

remarkable. In general, the material is complementary and overlaps in most respects. Differences occur with regard to the type of information, its character and orientation. While the elders and notables relied on oral tradition exclusively, Fon Richard had access to alternative sources, such as photographs and documents, mainly stored in the palace. He also referred to administrative documents, such as maps kept at the divisional archives in Nkambe, to validate his land claims against neighbouring chiefdoms. As Nyamnjoh (2003: 130) confirms, inquiries into colonial archives have become a popular strategy in which *fon*s are often assisted by their educated and external elite, that is out-migrated subjects based in urban centres. A second difference concerns the character of the information supplied. Many of the stories recounted by the Nchaney elders and notables included mythical elements that illustrate their chiefs' supernatural powers. Fon Richard, on the other hand, stressed the rulers' practical skills in negotiating power relations. A third difference concerns the political orientation of historical narratives. The knowledge of elders and notables is confined to socio-political relations within the village. Their accounts focused on the relationships between the *fon* and his subjects, the ruler and his councillors or sub-chiefs, or between families. Conversely, Fon Richard's knowledge and interest centred on inter-village, inter-chiefdom and interethnic relations, and the relationship between the *fon* and the colonial and postcolonial administration.

The Expansion of the Nchaney Chiefdom and Inter-Chiefdom Relations

Along with the consolidation of the Nchaney chiefdom in the seventeenth and eighteenth centuries, there also arose the desire to expand, occupy new areas and incorporate new populations. Accordingly, the *fon* of Nkanchi succeeded in asserting his primacy over the four villages of Kibbo, Bem, Chunghe and Nfume, which – while retaining their ritual authority – became part of the Nchaney chiefdom. Today, their inhabitants count as Nchaney on the grounds of residing in Nchaney territory, speaking Ncane, adhering to Nchaney cultural practices and respecting the Nchaney *fon*'s pre-eminence.

When Newton visited the Misaje area in the mid 1930s, he found a Nchaney chiefdom comprised of five villages, which he identified as the Nchaney 'clan territory'. However, the disruption of the local power balance through colonial intervention was only too obvious to him. As he explained, all five villages were placed under the *fon* of Nkanchi by the German administration for taxation purposes. He warned against treating them as equal, knowing that the chiefs utilized the colonial endeavour of ordering and encoding power relations for their own ends. Both Newton (1935: 40–41) and Chilver and Kaberry (1967: 29) reported that Bem and Chunghe claimed nearby origins, the people of

Kibbo recounted having moved together with those of Dumbo, and those of Nfume claimed to have come from Kano in Nigeria.

The case of the Nfume is particularly interesting, as even today their historical narratives contain the claim that they came from northern Nigeria and describe the processes of linguistic, religious and ethnic change that were part of their integration into the Nchaney polity. Moreover, as a Nfume interlocutor explained, part of his people originally settled in neighbouring Bessa territory, and thus consider themselves Bessa, while others moved to Nfume and eventually adopted Nchaney identity.

> Our old fathers who came first used to speak Hausa and also bent down for prayers [i.e. were Muslims]. When they died, and the next generation lived together with other population groups who had stayed here already, our people began to follow their fashion. We took over their language and also the Christian faith. Those of us who remained at Mbissa and became members of the Bessa clan adopted Nsari as their language. Those who came to Nfume adopted the Ncane language [...] If it is to identify ourselves, we conceive [of ourselves] as members of the Nchaney clan in the first instance. Since we have come to stay [here], we are Nchaney and we are together with them. For our brothers who are at Mbissa, they are members of the Bessa clan, and they first of all are with the Bessa. But when it comes to 'country-fashion' [local cultural practices], for example in case of installing a new chief, marriage arrangements or war alliances, the family relationship with our brothers at Mbissa becomes important.[12]

As this narrative vividly illustrates, Grassfields ethnicities are all but fixed, bounded or homogeneous, but allow for flexible, overlapping and changing identifications. Moreover, it attests to the mobility of Grassfields peoples within and across polities; a feature that in the nineteenth century put many Grassfields chiefdoms under stress and resulted in violent struggles over people, land and power (Nkwi 1987). Those conflicts contributed to the consolidation of the political and territorial authority of Grassfields chiefdoms, as well as their distinct identities. Even today, the memory of these battles remains vivid and is occasionally used to frame contemporary inter-chiefdom relations in historical terms. This also applies to the Nchaney chiefdom, which shares boundaries with the chiefdoms of Bessa, Bum, Kemezung/Bebe, Noni and Wimbum (Figure 2.3). These neighbouring Grassfields societies speak different and for the most part mutually unintelligible languages. Yet thanks to a high degree of multilingualism, communication is relatively unproblematic (Brye and Brye 2001).

Informants characterized the relationship of the Nchaney with the Kemezung and Bebe to the north and the Wimbum to the east as amicable. The relationship perceived as the closest is that with the Noni, situated to the south of Nchaney territory, with whom they share linguistic similarities, cultural institutions and frequent intermarriage. The Noni actually fall under

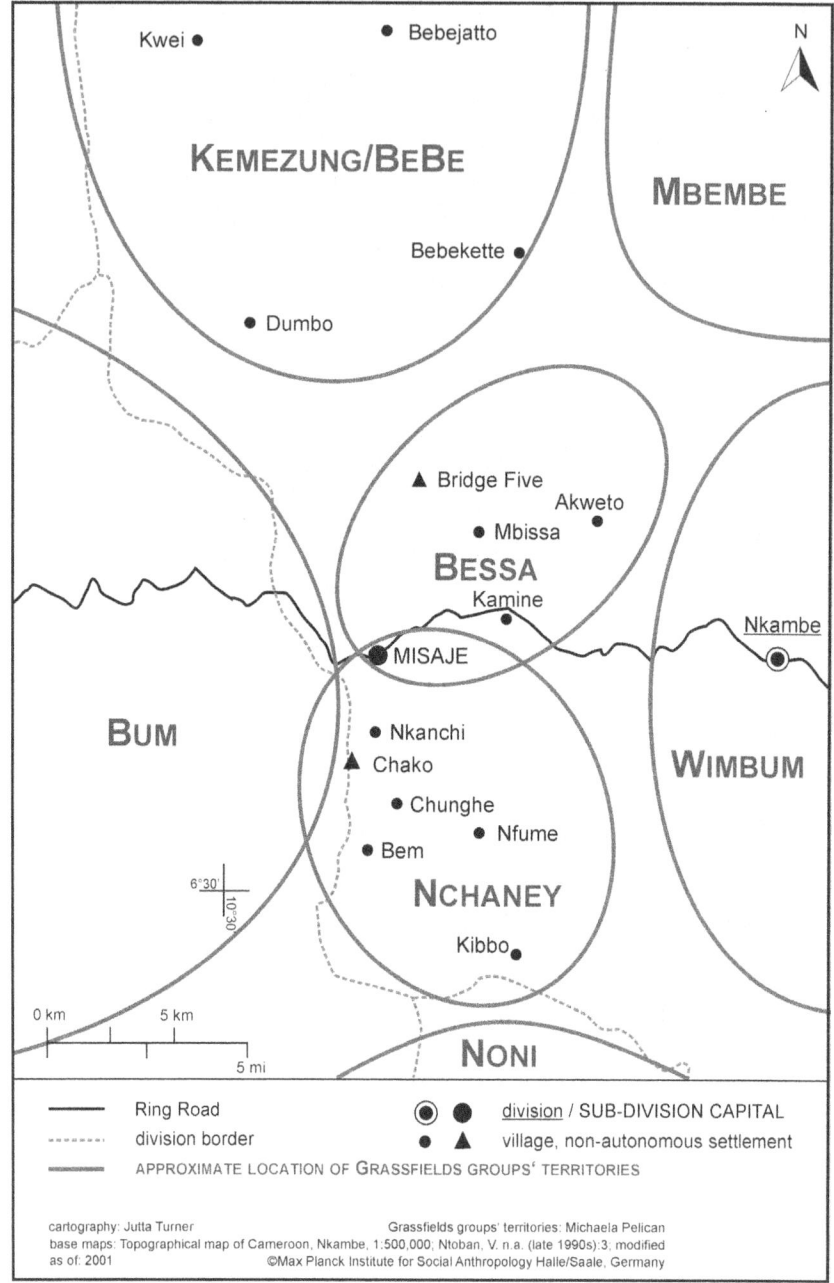

Figure 2.3: The Nchaney polity and neighbouring chiefdoms. Reproduced by kind permission of the Max Planck Institute for Social Anthropology, Halle.

the political hegemony of Nso, one of the most powerful and prominent Grassfields chiefdoms. Inter-chiefdom relations that Nchaney interlocutors described as overshadowed by historical struggles include their relationship with Nso, Bum and Bessa.

The Nchaney and the Banso (people of Nso) share an ambivalent relationship that goes back to the Nchaney–Banso war in pre-colonial times. Its memory still influences the perception of inter-chiefdom relations, and occasionally even interpersonal rivalry is perceived in historical terms. For example, as we saw in the previous chapter, Fon Richard and the then divisional officer explained their political divergences as rooted in the Nchaney–Banso war. The second ambivalent inter-chiefdom relationship is with Bum, a relatively large and influential chiefdom situated to the west of Nchaney territory. Mention of Bum aggression against the Nchaney is found in several colonial documents (Bridges 1933; Chilver and Kaberry 1967: 32; Newton 1935: 41). Yet despite conflict and competition between the two chiefdoms, interpersonal relationships have hardly been affected. This observation is supported by Nkwi in his study of inter-chiefdom relations in the Cameroon Grassfields, who interprets the coexistence of trade friendships at the individual level and of hostile relations at the institutional level as 'a marked characteristic of traditional [Grassfields] diplomacy' (Nkwi 1987: 96).

Somewhat convoluted is the relationship between the Nchaney and the Bessa, the second local Grassfields group inhabiting the Misaje area and relevant to this study. From a Nchaney perspective, their relationship with the Bessa is characterized by numerous cross-cutting ties. They share kinship relations based on frequent intermarriage and common descent with at least part of the Bessa population. In political terms, however, their relationship has been strained by competing claims over both the territory of Misaje town and the post of mayor of Misaje.

In contemporary usage, the ethnonym Bessa refers to the inhabitants of three villages: Mbissa, Kamine and Akweto. In colonial reports, however, they were treated as independent chiefdoms, although Newton (1935: 40) noted that Akweto and Kamine shared common ancestry and jointly constituted a 'clan' as defined in anthropology. The postcolonial administration later elevated the *fon* of Akweto over those of Kamine and Mbissa. Conversely, shared ethnic identification as Bessa (or members of the Bessa 'clan') has gained traction only in recent years in the context of Cameroon's politics of belonging and the widespread formation of ethnic elite associations. As members of the Bessa Cultural and Development Association (BECUDA) explained, they worked hard to reconcile their chief and foster a sense of collective identity on the basis of common origins and language. Consequently, the Bessa chiefs and elite members were less interested in stressing cross-cutting ties with their Nchaney neighbours but in opposing Bessa and Nchaney ethnicity. This development was also recognized by Fon Richard, who mainly blamed the Bessa elite for the contemporary friction in Nchaney–Bessa relations. However, tensions between Nchaney and Bessa are not just a contemporary feature, and anecdotes of how the Nchaney tricked the Bessa in the past are numerous.

While Grassfields chiefdoms in the nineteenth century were preoccupied with consolidating their borders and with producing territoriality and unity within their heterogeneous populations (Warnier 2007), in the twentieth century they were confronted with the arrival of new population groups as well as the intervention of the colonial and postcolonial administrations. The following section narrates the Nchaney's encounter with Hausa, Mbororo and Grassfields migrants from the viewpoint of the palace hierarchy (alternative perspectives will be explored in subsequent chapters). Differing from settlers from earlier periods such as the Nfume, who also originated from northern Nigeria, these groups were integrated into the Nchaney polity while retaining their cultural differences. Conversely, their accommodation has impacted on Grassfields identity and self-understanding. Moreover, as we will see below and in later chapters, it has engendered a range of popular misconceptions and ethnic stereotypes that have persisted up to today.

Nchaney Accommodation of Cultural 'Others'

Hausa, Mbororo and Grassfields migrants count as 'latecomers' to the region. Despite long-term settlement in Grassfields territory, they have generally maintained (and cultivated) their cultural difference. At the same time, their integration into the overarching regional society has not been on equal terms, but has hinged on their recognition of the political and territorial authority of Grassfields chiefs. The arrival of Hausa and Mbororo occurred during the colonial period, during which delineated notions of ethnicity, such as 'tribe', 'clan' and 'clan territory', were introduced. These idioms have been incorporated into local understandings of ethnicity. Thus the Nchaney palace hierarchy perceives and claims all population groups living in its territory as 'clan' members irrespective of ethnic or cultural differences.

> Mbororo, Hausa and [Grassfields] migrants are members of the Nchaney clan. The Fulani [Mbororo] and the Hausa staying on Nchaney land are considered members of the Nchaney clan. They are looked upon as children but they can move anytime. The same applies to Pinyin and Bamenda people staying on Nchaney land; that is, membership of a clan is tied to residence on its land. The Pinyin and Bamenda people are under the Nchaney; that is, they are members of the Nchaney clan because they cannot carry their problems to their home village. They have to be judged by the *fon* and therefore it is necessary that they are members of the traditional council.[13]

'Clan' membership is primarily defined in terms of territorial identity and the acknowledgement of the political and judicial supremacy of the *fon* of Nkanchi, as illustrated in the investiture conflict analysed in the previous chapter. Shared cultural features play no role here; nor is there any need for reference to a shared history.

Among the first people to settle on Nchaney territory and preserve their distinct ethnic identity were early Hausa traders and their followers. As we learn from Fon Richard, the arrival of Hausa traders coincided with the rule of Fon Fuma, who welcomed them because of their business activities.

> The first Hausa chief, Mallam Awudu, was brought in from Nkor by Fon Fuma around 1900. We had no Hausa people this way and Fon Fuma was interested in having them staying with us because of their engagement in trade. The Hausa usually bought kola nuts in Nso and passed through Nkanchi on their way to Bissaula in Nigeria. The Nchaney were interested in kola nuts, Hausa caps and salt, because there was no salt by that time; instead they used the ashes of burnt plantain peelings. They were also interested in lime stone, *kanwa* [potash]. The Nchaney had palm oil, traditional caps and wives to offer in exchange. At first, the Nchaney dressed in bark clothes. The Hausa traders and the Germans brought clothes, mainly shirts and shorts as trade goods.[14]

In 1935, Newton was already describing the presence of Hausa traders as having a significant impact on the population of the Mbembe and Nchanti areas in terms of clothing, manners and religion (Newton 1935: 21). While Nchaney informants generally endorsed the spatial and political integration of Hausa settlers, many viewed them as culturally different and somehow dubious. In particular, their initial activities as Islamic scholars knowledgeable in the Muslim faith and in healing (*mallam* in Hausa and Fulfulde) caused suspicion and rumours among local Grassfielders, some of which have persisted up to today. This is well illustrated in the following quotes from two interviews with Nchaney informants, who accentuate the perceived cultural and moral gap between themselves and Hausa.

> The Hausa people are truly poor. From the beginning their wives never went out of the fenced compound. They were not used to farming. They were actually depending on the Fulani [Mbororo]. The Hausa man from the word go is an idle sitting man, just relying on the Koran to beg from the Fulani. It is a matter discussed on and agreed upon.[15]

> The Hausa, at first, only came working as *mallams*, that is, sitting in front of their houses doing some unidentifiable work. At night they would go out to steal, both from Aku [a Mbororo sub-group] and from 'country-people' [local Grassfielders]. Only later on, they got involved in the cattle business when the Pinyin people were already buying and selling.[16]

As later chapters will show, the distinction between Hausa and Grassfielders is not as obvious as these stereotypical assumptions suggest. Many members of today's Hausa community in Misaje have at least partial Grassfields parentage (remember Fon Richard's statement that the Nchaney had 'wives to offer in exchange' for Hausa trade goods) or are Grassfielders who have converted to Islam and retain allegiances with both groups.

Moreover, this view of the Hausa as idlers and thieves enraged Hausa informants who read a preliminary version of this chapter. They argued that Nchaney interlocutors misinterpreted the relationship between Hausa and Mbororo as one of dependency. Since giving alms to the poor is a commandment prescribed in the Koran, receiving support is not shameful. Furthermore, a young Hausa man pointed out that it was Hausa traders who 'brought civilization to them [the Nchaney] long before the white man came. Hausa people even took them to Nigeria; they worked for Hausa as porters'.[17] Finally, Hausa informants refuted the accusation of theft, incriminating Mbororo youths instead, and insisted that Hausa merchants partook in cattle trade long before the Pinyin.

A second distinct category of individuals to be welcomed in Nchaney territory were migrants from neighbouring and distant Grassfields areas. These essentially moved to Misaje in connection with the construction of the Ring Road in the 1950s, and in relation to the cattle trade which has been flourishing since the 1940s. Nchaney informants hardly mentioned Grassfields migrants in their historical accounts. However, Fon Richard and his councillors were able to recall the names of a few early migrants, like Pa Ngwa, a Meta man who came in 1922. Fon Richard grouped the migrant population in three major categories: the people from Bamenda and Pinyin who came for business (the cattle trade in particular) or farming; migrants from Nso who were mainly involved in road construction; and individuals from the neighbouring Wimbum area who engaged in business or were alleged societal outcasts, exiled or driven away by threats of witchcraft.[18]

More detailed than Nchaney accounts of the establishment of Hausa and Grassfields migrants in Misaje were narratives regarding the recent history of a third group of settlers, Mbororo pastoralists. This probably has to be viewed against the fact that the Nchaney derive greater economic benefits from Mbororo herders and their cattle than from Hausa or Grassfields migrants. As I will outline in more detail in Chapter 3, the Mbororo in the Misaje area belong to two sub-groups that settled at different periods. The Jaafun, who arrived in the first half of the twentieth century, established themselves in the highlands near Nkambe and descended with their herds to the lowlands of Misaje and Dumbo for seasonal transhumance. The second group, the Aku, entered the region in the second half of the twentieth century and settled permanently in the lowlands around Misaje town. According to Fon Richard, his father

Michael was actively involved in the establishment of Aku herders and their leadership in the Misaje area.

> ArDo Affang originally came here in 1952. But before him, the first *arDo* [Mbororo group leader] was ArDo Maguwa from whom ArDo Burti took over ... When ArDo Burti became *arDo*, my father was working with the council. Burti was stubborn and destructive, and also ate tax money. My father Fon Michael, in his position as municipal administrator, that is, chairman of the local council, sacked him. After that, Affang became *arDo* in 1973, on July twentieth. That was the same day I, Fon Richard, was born, which also gave me the name Affang. It was the native authorities who chose the *arDo*. By the time ArDo Affang was made *arDo*, it was my father who imposed it on him since, by then, he only had twenty to thirty cattle. Actually, it was Fon Michael who brought ArDo Affang here, because they had been friends in Nigeria at Boko, where my father schooled and completed standard six. The time ArDo Affang came here, he had only two children and twenty to thirty animals. The rest of the family were all born here.[19]

This account only reaches back to the 1950s, when the first Aku pastoralists settled in the Misaje area. In its structure and content it resembles the description of the reigns of Nchaney *fon*s discussed in the royal name-list above; that is, it is largely concerned with offices and institutions. As we will see in Chapter 3, Mbororo history told from an Aku or Jaafun perspective is different, and we will hardly come across the kind of information supplied here.

Thanks to the relatively recent arrival of Mbororo pastoralists in the region, many Nchaney still remember the changes initiated by their influx and settlement. The distinction between Jaafun and Aku plays a significant role in the Nchaney perception of Mbororo. The following extract from an interview with a Nchaney elder illustrates Grassfielders' perception of Jaafun and Aku as ethnically and culturally distinct, not only from the Nchaney but also from each other. The term Mbororo is commonly used among Grassfielders when talking of Jaafun, while Aku are simply referred to as Aku.

> In Misaje Sub-Division, we used to have Mbororo people [Jaafun] only during the dry season; that is, from December till mid March. Then, they went back to Ndu, Nkambe and Nso where they stayed in grass houses. There were no permanent graziers. They only lived in grass huts; that is, they were identified as nomads. It is only in 1952 that the other race,[20] the Aku graziers, came to Misaje Sub-Division from Nigeria. They actually are two different people with two languages.[21] The Aku people farmed the same like us and generally took care of their animals so as to avoid farm damage. They may now get involved in stealing and misbehaving because of the effects of social integration. But the first race, the Mbororo [Jaafun] were more careless and wild, causing a lot of farm damage. The knifing system was very common with the Mbororo [Jaafun].[22] They attacked their own people as well as 'country-people' [local Grassfielders], and sometimes even respected us

more than themselves. In case of farm damage, they escaped overnight back to the uplands. They did not care about the farmers.[23]

Most Nchaney informants agreed that rampant farmer–herder conflicts are a feature of the past and were mainly associated with the Jaafun. Conversely, they assessed their socio-economic relations with the Aku as generally good, despite issues over cattle theft, lamented by both Nchaney and Aku elders.

The above accounts on Nchaney political history illustrate an ever widening radius of the Nchaney polity and ethnicity, starting with the mythical ancestors' establishment at Nkanchi and ending with the accommodation of Hausa, Mbororo and Grassfields migrants as members of the Nchaney 'clan'. Moreover, these narratives show the extent to which local conceptions of ethnicity have been modified in response to colonial and postcolonial intervention, and the ways in which idioms like 'natives', 'tribe', 'clan', 'clan territory' and 'first arrivals' and 'latecomers' have been used to bolster political claims.

Local Political Representation and the State

Since Cameroon gained independence, the postcolonial state has been a vital party to be addressed when seeking political representation and access to resources. With the country's democratization and the advent of ethnic elite associations, its relevance has further increased. In this section, I will focus on the deployment of ethnicity and history in local politics and in strategies of representation vis-à-vis the state and international organizations. In order to capture the variety of political actors in the Misaje area, I will include representatives of other Grassfields societies (Bessa and Kemezung) in my analysis. As we will see, political representation is no longer limited to local chiefs; ethnic and regional elite associations have also become influential agents in claiming political offices and economic assistance from the state and international organizations.

Changing Avenues of Political Representation

During the colonial period, political representation of Grassfields societies vis-à-vis the administration was vested in the *fon*. After Cameroon's independence and reunification, Grassfields *fon*s continued acting as representatives of their peoples, but their political and administrative powers were considerably curtailed. After abolishing the House of Chiefs in 1972, President Ahidjo issued a decree in 1977 in which he confined the role of chiefs to auxiliaries of the administration. Chiefs were supposed to mediate between the administration and the local population, and to assist in executing government directives and tax-collection. Moreover, chiefdoms were classified as first, second and third class chiefdoms on the basis of their relative power, with leaders correspondingly remunerated for administrative tasks.[24]

With their chiefs largely excluded from national politics, Grassfielders and others had to look for alternative ways of representing their interests with regards to the state. Educated individuals, including some Grassfields *fon*s, entered the ruling party and achieved positions of pre-eminence as parliamentarians, court presidents, ministers, mayors, municipal councillors and party leaders. In the Misaje area, the late Fon Michael was successful in occupying an administrative function as chairman of the Ako Rural Council and in attracting government projects to the area. Yet, until recently, he was the only Nchaney to acquire a prominent political position, while other groups, like the neighbouring Wimbum, have produced a number of influential officials.[25]

Legislative changes and the introduction of a multiparty system in 1990 opened up new avenues of political representation. A number of Grassfields chiefs engaged in party politics, much to the dislike of their subjects, who preferred their chiefs to remain neutral mediators in the democratic struggle between civil society and the state.[26] With the introduction of democratic voting, debates about ethnic belonging and local citizenship gained in significance and facilitated the emergence of ethnic elite associations. As a result, nearly every chiefdom in the Grassfields has its own elite association, which acts as the group's representative in relations with the state and international organizations.[27]

Local Grassfields Chiefs as Political Actors
Fon Richard saw himself as the legitimate representative of the Nchaney 'clan'. He claimed to know Nchaney history best, as he based his version on accounts of palace notables and official documents. References to colonial maps and assertion of good relations with their erstwhile colonial masters were part and parcel of his vocabulary, not only in interviews with the anthropologist, but generally in dealing with neighbouring chiefdoms and the Cameroonian government.

Officially, Fon Richard was non-partisan; but in order to further his interests as the head of the Nchaney 'clan', he joined the North West Fons' Conference (NOWEFCO), founded in 1995 to unite local chiefs in support of the ruling party. Besides NOWEFCO, there existed NOWEFA, the North West Fons' Association, which was founded in 1993 and affirmed its political neutrality. Fon Richard Chefon's preference for NOWEFCO was not motivated by party-political considerations but by the fact that NOWEFA was dominated by first-class *fon*s, while NOWEFCO declared all chiefdoms to be equal, irrespective of their administrative classification. In 1998, the two associations held a joint meeting and decided to fuse as the North West Fons' Union (NOWEFU).

As Fon Richard explained, the *fons*' associations put forward a number of requests to the government. They demanded that government officials respect Grassfields tradition and political protocol, called for the reinstatement of the House of Chiefs and stipulated the need for government support to develop their respective 'clan areas'. Fon Richard had little success in attracting development aid to Misaje or the Nchaney area. Instead, he was pre-occupied with securing his own interests, with bolstering his authority over his subjects and with furthering his influence over neighbouring groups and government officials.

Ethnic Elite Associations as Political Representatives

Elite associations are not a new phenomenon in Cameroon, but date back to the 1950s, when the first high-school graduates ascended to government positions. Many of them developed from college associations or church groups, and their members' prime objectives were to assist each other socially and economically.[28] Many members of the educated elite also aimed at supporting their home areas. But during the regime of President Ahmadou Ahidjo, Cameroon's first head of state, their regional and ethnic loyalties were restrained, as these were considered inimical to the aspired ideal of national identity (Geschiere 2009; Nyamnjoh and Rowlands 1998). With political liberalization in the 1990s, elite associations experienced a renaissance. Many associations founded in the 1980s and 1990s are registered as 'socio-cultural and development associations'. They represent particular ethnic groups or specific regions and aim at providing the necessary contacts and assistance to access resources for local development. Most associations assert their political neutrality, but as their members tend to exploit personal party-political connections to the benefit of their ethnic or regional group, they are often politically predisposed.

Over the past few decades, not only has the character and function of elite associations changed, but so too has the meaning of the term elite. In the writings of Bayart (1993) and Geschiere (1997), elite – and its French equivalent *évolués* – refers primarily to early generations of educated and qualified individuals who left their home villages, adopted an urban lifestyle and occupied a position in the public service. In contemporary understanding, and in colloquial Pidgin English and English in Cameroon, the meaning of the term 'elite' has shifted. Everyone with a basic education who has spent time in an urban environment and enjoys a slightly improved quality of life claims the rank of an elite person. Thus contemporary elite associations often comprise educated individuals as well as labour migrants, businessmen and local politicians.

In Misaje Sub-Division there are four elite associations. The three local Grassfields groups (Nchaney, Bessa and Kemezung) each have their own cultural and development association, while there is also the Misaje Area Elite Association (MELA) that represents all inhabitants of Misaje irrespective of their ethnicity. All three ethnic elite associations were founded in the 1990s by labour migrants from the respective areas who consider themselves members of the Nchaney, Bessa or Kemezung external elite. Since the 1940s, many Bessa villagers have left for the economically prosperous South West Region to work on the rubber, banana and palm oil plantations.[29] By now they are well established; many have jobs in local industries or run small businesses. Nchaney labour migrants cluster mainly in the Douala region, where they migrated to work on coffee and palm oil plantations. The three ethnic elite associations are also part of the regional association MELA. During the period of my research, MELA representatives actively participated in public events, such as national ceremonies, the investiture of the new DO and the burial of Misaje elite association members. Besides its representative and advisory function, however, MELA has not been successful in generating economic support for the development of the Misaje area.

The association most effective at the time of my fieldwork with regard to local politics and representation was the Bessa Cultural and Development Association (BECUDA). The following elaborations are based on interviews with BECUDA officials, the analysis of internal reports on the association's activities as well as first-hand participation in BECUDA meetings in the Bessa area.

BECUDA was founded in the mid 1990s, with branches in the southwest of the country, in the cities of Douala and Yaoundé and in the Bessa home area. It claims to represent the Bessa 'clan', which it defines as the collective of nine settlements under the rule of the *fon*s of Akweto, Kamine and Mbissa.[30] Historically, the Bessa have been less centralized and unified than the Nchaney. But BECUDA effectively promoted a strong notion of belonging among Bessa individuals, emphasizing cultural criteria such as their common language, Nsari, as well as the need for collective action and representation. They united the population of the three politically independent chiefdoms under one ethnic category, the Bessa 'clan'. The three Bessa *fon*s are automatically honorary members and patrons of the association.

Besides local group activities, BECUDA runs an elite circle whose members meet when required to give advice on current issues troubling Bessa abroad and at home. So far, BECUDA activities have focused on the conservation of Bessa culture, the encouragement of child education, the containment of witchcraft, the resolution of land disputes and farmer–herder conflicts, and the improvement of rural infrastructure in the home area. Moreover, BECUDA members have been encouraged to contribute personal funds for self-help and development projects, and to lobby the government for support. In 2000, for example, they collected more than 180,000 CFA (€ 275) to sponsor ten Bessa children at secondary school. In 2002 they donated a computer and printer to the Misaje council to welcome the newly inducted mayor, a Bessa man from Kamine.

This last gesture illustrates BECUDA's intention of channelling development aid via ethnic representation and good relations with the administration. As the previous mayor was a Nchaney, the Bessa felt it was their turn to hold the position of mayor. BECUDA encouraged Bessa candidates from the ruling party (CPDM) and the opposition (SDF) to stand for the municipal elections in 2001. Finally, the Bessa SDF candidate won, and despite a strong pro-CPDM faction within the association, BECUDA unanimously congratulated the new mayor. Thus, despite political differences, common ethnic identification was given priority.

Closely linked to the struggle for the position of mayor is a surreptitious debate about the ownership of Misaje town. During the colonial period, Bessa and Nchaney competed for the seat of the customary court, based on the assumption that the group on whose territory the court was to be established would benefit most from administrative facilities, social infrastructure and the anticipated economic boom. The same scenario was repeated in 1996 when the Misaje Sub-Division was created with Misaje town as its headquarters. Subsequently, rumours emerged that the Bessa wanted to challenge Nchaney assertions of their ownership of Misaje town. Although never stated publicly, BECUDA officials in interviews claimed the Kimbeng River as the natural border between Bessa and Nchaney territory, implying that only a fraction of Misaje town was situated on Nchaney land, while the largest part was on Bessa territory. If the Bessa asserted their territorial claim, the Nchaney *fon*'s political and physical presence in Misaje town would be critically challenged. The concealed dispute about the ownership of Misaje town and its resources surfaced in 2003 in a conflict between the Bessa mayor and Fon Richard about the administration of vacant plots in Misaje. Eventually, the DO stepped in and urged the two parties to reconcile so as to stifle the growing rumours of an ominous boundary dispute between the two neighbouring chiefdoms.

As these examples illustrate, popular actors in contemporary politics are not only local Grassfields chiefs, but also party-political activists and ethnic elite associations. However, as the case of Misaje also demonstrates, not all ethnic groups are necessarily represented in the same way. While Nchaney interests are currently represented primarily by their *fon*, the Bessa rely on their elite association and their Bessa mayor for political representation vis-à-vis the state. In the most favourable case, the different agents of representation collaborate and effectively nullify party-political differences. Yet in attaining assistance from the government or international organizations, personal relations with influential individuals are a crucial prerequisite.

Although traditional authorities, external elites and local politicians have been relatively ineffective in attracting external aid to the Misaje area, they have significantly contributed to the strengthening of ethnic identities and boundaries by portraying themselves as representatives of specific ethnic groups.

A Nchaney Model of Identity

The aim of this chapter has been to shed light on the composite nature of Grassfields societies, and to outline the historical processes that have engendered changing notions of Nchaney political and ethnic identity. In concluding, I will discuss historical and current conceptions of Nchaney ethnicity, integrating them in a single model.

The narratives of Nchaney history reveal an ever widening radius of Nchaney political influence and self-understanding. In this process, three phases can be discerned: from the formation of the Nkanchi village, to the consolidation of the Nchaney chiefdom, to the recognition of its 'clan territory' by neighbouring polities as well as the colonial and postcolonial administration. These three phases in the polity's historical development are reflected in contemporary understandings of Nchaney identity. This can be represented in a three-layered model, which, while an abstraction, serves as a heuristic device (Figure 2.4). With the widening of group boundaries, the contents and meanings of Nchaney self-understanding have changed. Contemporary conceptions of Nchaney identity include three layers (Nkanchi village, Nchaney chiefdom, Nchaney 'clan territory') and allow for single as well as multiple ethnic identifications.

The most confined understanding of Nchaney identity refers to members of the seven founding families and the Che, the original inhabitants of Nkanchi. Here Nchaney identity is based on shared migration history and religious responsibilities (with the exception of the Che), shared language and a common body of socio-cultural practices. The next layer of identification refers more broadly to the Nchaney chiefdom, made up of five villages. In this case, Nchaney identity is defined by residing on Nchaney territory, speaking the Nchaney language, adhering to Nchaney socio-cultural practices and respecting the primacy of the *fon* of Nkanchi. Yet, each of the five villages is ritually independent. The third and loosest conception of Nchaney identity refers to all

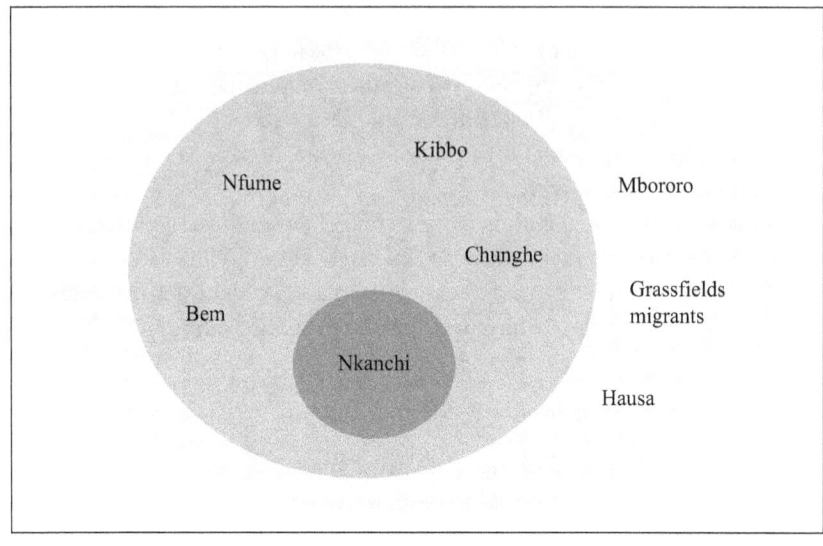

layers of identity	members	migration history	common first language	socio-cultural practices	territory	submission to the *fon*'s political authority
Nchaney village	descendants of the eight families of Nkanchi	shared by seven of the eight families	x	x	x	x
Nchaney chiefdom	five villages: Nkanchi, Bem, Nfume, Kibbo, Chunghe		x	x	x	x
Nchaney 'clan territory'	members of the Nchaney chiefdom, Mbororo, Hausa, Grassfields migrants				x	x

Figure 2.4: Layers of Nchaney identity. Source: Author's fieldwork.

permanent residents on Nchaney 'clan territory', a concept introduced by the colonial administration. In this case, Nchaney identity is defined in terms of territoriality and entails at least symbolic homage to the political authority of the *fon* of Nkanchi as head of the Nchaney 'clan'.

Due to its inclusive and multilayered character, Nchaney identity provides a suitable framework for the accommodation of a heterogeneous population. Moreover, with the incorporation of colonial and postcolonial models of group classification, it serves as an effective tool of self-representation vis-à-vis the state. Yet, while this model accounts for the capacity of Grassfields societies to accommodate ethnic and cultural 'others', we ought to keep in mind that it primarily reflects the perspective of the palace hierarchy. From the viewpoint of ordinary Grassfielders, the territorial belonging of recent immigrants and cultural 'others' may well be contestable. Concurrently, Mbororo and Hausa have developed distinct interpretations of their integration into Grassfields societies, as reflected in the investiture conflict as well as in subsequent chapters.

Notes

1 In a later article, Ranger (1993) critically discusses his use of the terms 'custom' and 'tradition' and admits that his argument was too polarized.
2 As this study is confined to northwest Cameroon, I mainly engage with the British colonial era, but similar processes occurred in French-administered Cameroon (see e.g. Geschiere 1993; Tardits 1980).
3 Most local readers were appreciative, but also very critical. In particular, they approved of the use of colonial sources and visual materials which, in their view, verified the account presented of Nchaney history. They criticized my limited choice of interview partners, and recommended that I question not only the *fon* of Nkanchi but also members of neighbouring groups to cross-check his claims. Another criticism pointed to the fact that my analysis of Nchaney history and identity did not take into account age or gender differences.
4 Fon Richard, Misaje, 9 January 2002; Nchaney notables and elders, Nkanchi, 6 January 2002.
5 The so-called Tikar question – that is, the widespread claim to Tikar origins among Grassfields groups and its political implications – has been widely discussed among Cameroonist historians and anthropologists (e.g. Chilver and Kaberry 1967, 1971; Fowler and Zeitlyn 1996; Jeffreys 1964; Kopytoff 1981; Price 1979; Yenshu and Ngwa 2001).
6 I thank Nicolas Argenti for suggesting this line of interpretation.
7 The names of the founding families are Basse, Bame, Sanda, Gwala, Ngonje, Ndomo and Yahdo.
8 According to Fon Richard, the Germans set up a military camp in what is the current market square in Nkanchi, which is called *kibalaki*, meaning 'the (German) barracks'. Fon Fuma supplied them with provisions and instructed his subjects to cultivate crops next to the German encampment. The Germans also needed carriers for their patrols. While officers travelled on horseback, local carriers accompanied them on foot from Nkanchi to Tulawa, a second military camp on the road to Bissaula. As Newton (1935: 9) confirms, the villages situated close to the road to Nigeria, including Nkanchi, frequently came in contact with the German colonial administration. They were required to provide men for the chain of mail-runners from Bamenda to Kentu.
9 Both Newton and Jeffreys must have toured the Nchaney area while Fon Ngong ruled. Indeed, Jeffreys's notes on Misaje include a letter of complaint by the council clerk, H.N. Laban, written in 1941 and addressed to the Misaje native court. Laban reported the uncooperativeness of the Nkanchi village head in building a rest house for the resident's visit to the area, and described the instigation of a fight by the village head (Jeffreys 1951: 116–17).

10 Another example was Fon John Yai, the late chief of Bum, whose political engagement has been described by Geschiere and Nyamnjoh (1998).
11 Similarly, Warnier (2007: 266) argues with regard to the Mankon chiefdom that the authority of Grassfields chiefs no longer rests on their exclusive control over ancestral substances, but on having access to state resources as well as influence over their elite associations.
12 B.K., Nfume, 11 January 2002.
13 Nchaney elders and notables, Nkanchi, 6 January 2002.
14 Fon Richard, Misaje, 13 January 2002.
15 M.C., Misaje, 18 December 2001.
16 B.J., Misaje, 24 September 2001.
17 J.M., Misaje, 23 July 2003.
18 While I do not subscribe to Fon Richard's portrait of Wimbum migrants as alleged and ousted witches, this is a common representation among Grassfields societies, particularly with regard to migrants from neighbouring polities (see Argenti 2007; Warnier 2007).
19 Fon Richard, Misaje, 13 January 2002.
20 'Race' and 'tribe' are colonial notions that entered local parlance in anglophone Cameroon and are still in use today. In this particular case, the interlocutor probably used 'race' to underline his argument of Aku and Jaafun being distinct ethnic groups.
21 Jaafun and Aku are both Mbororo sub-groups and speak the same language, Fulfulde, albeit with slight dialect variations. Yet, Grassfielders perceive them as two distinct ethnic groups, just as Nchaney and Bessa are viewed as distinct linguistic and ethnic groups.
22 The knife is an integral part of a Mbororo man's herding equipment. Mbororo youths are thought to be quick in using their knives in brawls.
23 M.C., Misaje, 18 December 2001.
24 This classification system was introduced by the British colonial administration; for a critical discussion of its impact on inter-chiefdom relations, see Yenshu and Ngwa (2001). The five first-class chiefdoms are Bafut, Bali, Kom, Mankon and Nso; they have been influential since the colonial period. The classification of second- and third-class chiefdoms is an ongoing process, and is related to demographic, political and administrative developments. The *fon* of Bum, for example, was promoted to the status of second-class chief during my research in 2001; the *fon* of Nkanchi was made a second-class chief in the 1970s.
25 In 2007, Dr Fuh Calestus Gentry (originally from Nfume) was appointed secretary of state in charge of mines and power. So far, his success in attracting development projects to the Misaje area has been limited.
26 The political dealings of Fon Angwafo III of Mankon have been the subject of a number of publications (Angwafo 2009; Awasom 2003b; Nyamnjoh 2002b, 2003; Rowlands 2002). On the party-political involvement of Fon Ganyonga III of Bali, see Fokwang (2009).
27 It seems there are regional variations regarding the prominence of ethnic or regional elite associations. While in the South West Region, associations are formed more on the basis of regional units, in the North West Region they are mostly organized on an ethnic basis (see also Mercer et al. 2008).

28 For an example, see Njeuma's description of the Record Club, a branch of the *alma mater* association of the Sasse College in Soppo, southwest Cameroon (Njeuma 1987).
29 On the topic of labour migration to the southwest and coastal areas, see also Ardener et al. (1960: 211–29) and Geschiere and Nyamnjoh (1998: 77), who provide accounts for the neighbouring Bum as well as the Esu in Menchum Division.
30 In BECUDA documents, the ethnonym Bessa appears in a variety of spellings: Bessa, Besaah, Bessah, Bessaah. The most common spelling is Bessa, also used in linguistic publications (e.g. Brye and Brye 2001).

3

From Pastoral Society to Indigenous People

Mbororo Identity Politics

While the Mbororo presence in the Grassfields dates back to the early twentieth century, since the 1990s Mbororo activists have come to play a crucial role in local and national identity politics. As I will show in this chapter, what it means to be Mbororo has changed drastically over time – from identifying with specific lineage and migration groups to stressing Muslim identity, to renouncing *pulaaku* (FulBe code of conduct) and, most recently, to making claims of being an 'indigenous people'. Moreover, current Mbororo strategies of political representation clearly show the imprints of their prolonged cohabitation with Grassfields societies. At the same time, they reflect divergent visions within Mbororo society of Mbororo identity and future and their national integration.

The historical migration and settlement of Mbororo pastoralists in northwest Cameroon has attracted the attention of earlier researchers. Some have studied their establishment in the colonial and postcolonial period (Awasom 1984; Boutrais 1996), and others have focused on the conflictual relationship between Grassfields farmers and Mbororo herders (e.g. Chilver 1989; Harshbarger 1995). While their findings will be integrated in this and the next chapter, my analysis will go beyond the focus of these studies by extending its time frame to the current period and by considering the relevance of both intra-ethnic and interethnic relations for Mbororo self-understandings.

The Mbororo belong to the FulBe ethnic category and are classically associated with cattle pastoralism.[1] Their language is Fulfulde, which they share with other FulBe sub-groups, although there are regional and dialect variations. Most Mbororo who settled in the Cameroon Grassfields are agro-pastoralists and combine cattle husbandry with subsistence agriculture. They belong to two sub-groups, Jaafun and Aku, who arrived at different periods and settled in distinct areas.

After local Grassfields societies, the Mbororo constitute the second largest population group in the research area. While within the North West Region they make up 5 to 15 per cent of the total population, the Mbororo in Misaje Sub-Division comprise more than 400 (registered) graziers and their families, and account for approximately 25 per cent of the sub-division's population.[2]

In the context of migration, settlement, political accommodation and social change, emic conceptions of Mbororo identity have undergone a number of transformations, which are the subject of this chapter. As with my previous elaborations on Nchaney history and identity, I am primarily interested here in the ways in which history is used in constructing Mbororo identity and in validating political claims. Concurrently, my focus is on processes of inclusion and exclusion, and on the ways in which Mbororo perceive themselves in relation to internal and external 'others'.

FulBe Categories of Identification

The FulBe constitute a complex ethnic category whose members are represented in at least eighteen countries across the Sudanic belt (Boutrais 1994). Their extended dispersal accounts for considerable variation, reflected in different forms of socio-political organization and economic specialization (Diallo and Schlee 2000). Nonetheless, they share a common identity based on the Fulfulde language and a shared complex of moral values and social practices known as *pulaaku*.

Pulaaku is a topic widely discussed in FulBe studies, though there is no general agreement on its exact meaning or content.[3] Despite informants' essentializing attitudes, it is a relative, contextual and dynamic concept. In its most general application it denotes FulBe ideals of social and moral comportment. As Virtanen points out, '*pulaaku* is essentially public – and conditional – behaviour as it is expected in the presence of defined social others' (Virtanen 2003: 27). To date, most studies of *pulaaku* have focused on internal categories of social others. Little attention has been paid to the degree to which *pulaaku* is performed towards a non-FulBe audience,[4] a subject addressed in the final section of this chapter.

The antonym of FulBe is *haaBe* (sing. *kaaDo*), meaning non-FulBe. It has an inherent pejorative connotation, as it conveys FulBe superiority vis-à-vis all black African non-FulBe who are characterized by the absence of specific FulBe qualities (Boesen 1989, 1994; Ogawa 1993). Within the FulBe ethnic category, there are various sub-ethnic categories that individuals identify with. It is thus important to determine the categories that have emerged as most relevant in the historical and regional context of the Cameroon Grassfields.

The Mbororo in northwest Cameroon are agro-pastoralists and distinguish themselves from other FulBe groups, such as the sedentary Town FulBe (also called Huya) in northern Cameroon, by stressing their pastoral identity. Mbororo and Huya are complementary terms applied by each group to denote the respective other; both terms have a somewhat derogatory connotation, particularly in their usage in northern Cameroon (Dognin 1981; Walker 1980). As a particularity of the Grassfields, migrants from northern Cameroon and Nigeria – including Town FulBe – are subsumed under the ethnic category of Hausa. Being numerically few, they are socially, economically and spatially integrated into Hausa communities. In northern Cameroon, on the other hand, they are a dominant majority and the primary object of Mbororo self-distinction (Burnham 1996).

Individuals in the Grassfields rarely use the generic term Mbororo in their self-identification. They tend to introduce themselves as Jaafun or Aku, thus referring to distinct sub-ethnic categories that developed as a result of different migration trajectories. Moreover, the appellation Mbororo is often used interchangeably with Jaafun. In order to avoid terminological confusion, I will use the sub-ethnic distinctions of Jaafun and Aku, and adhere to Mbororo as a generic term for pastoral FulBe.

Beyond the distinction of Jaafun and Aku, Mbororo classify themselves into lineages (Fulfulde: *lenyol*, sing.; *lenyi*, pl.) which serve as primary categories of identification and sociality. The lineages represented in northwest Cameroon are numerous. Most are clearly identified as Jaafun or Aku; some allegedly have switched categories, and a few include both Jaafun and Aku factions. Lineage identification is mostly transmitted patrilineally, and is based on the idea of distant relation rather than descent from common ancestors known by name. Large lineages are generally sub-divided into 'houses' (Fulfulde: *suudu*, sing.; *suudi*, pl.). This is a rare phenomenon in the Grassfields, because the lineages here are relatively small.

Lineage organization plays an important role in Mbororo social life (Dupire 1970). Historically, members of the same lineage tended to congregate spatially and follow the same migration route. Lineage solidarity is still emphasized, mostly in terms of preferential marriage arrangements and mutual assistance. Lineages are ranked according to a variety of criteria, including historical depth, anteriority in terms of arrival and establishment, numerical importance and wealth in cattle. As the French geographer Jean Boutrais (1996: 557–629) argues, lineage hierarchy is particularly pronounced in northwest Cameroon and is mirrored in their altitudinal dispersal. While the more prestigious lineages have appropriated the highland pastures, latecomer and numerically minor lineages are found at the fringes of the Bamenda Highlands.

Among Mbororo in the Grassfields, sub-ethnic and lineage ascriptions constitute the two major categories of identification. Jaafun and Aku as well as many lineages represented in the research area are also found in other parts of Cameroon or neighbouring countries, yet their modes of identification are not necessarily the same. As Virtanen (2003: 77) points out, pastoral FulBe in the Adamaoua Region do not refer to themselves as Jaafun or Aku but by their lineage names. Moreover, they emphasize their otherness from nomadic WoDaaBe and sedentary Town FulBe, two FulBe categories largely absent in the Cameroon Grassfields. As these differences in self-ascription between Mbororo in the Grassfields and Adamaoua illustrate, the respective categories of identification depend on the presence or absence of specific 'FulBe others'.

(Re)Constructing Mbororo History

Mbororo historical consciousness differs significantly from Grassfielders' modes of history making. While the latter aim at a collective history of a polity, the Mbororo focus on social rather than political units. Being a pastoral people and highly mobile, the Mbororo essentially produce migration histories that are confined to particular migration groups, such as lineages and family units. Furthermore, Mbororo historical memory is relatively shallow and generally limited to two or three generations. Similarly, Mbororo individuals hardly keep track of events that have no immediate effect on pastoral society, which renders dating their movements difficult. These characteristics of Mbororo oral history and the resulting methodological predicaments have been pointed out by Boutrais (1996) in his seminal work on the Mbororo in northwest Cameroon, based on research carried out in the 1970s. He came to the conclusion that the Mbororo have no collective historical consciousness; being a pastoral society, they are generally oriented to an 'immobile' or continuously reproduced present (Boutrais 1996: 43, 65). Undertaking my fieldwork thirty years after Boutrais's research, I had similar experiences. Yet certain Mbororo factions, such as the Mbororo of Sabga whose case will be discussed later, have developed a distinct consciousness regarding their history and identity, mainly in response to changing political conditions in the 1990s.

The Mbororo population of Misaje Sub-Division is diverse, including members of more than twenty lineages with complex interrelationships. Since presenting the migration history of each lineage would exceed the focus and limits of this study, I will focus on the Daneeji, one of the two major lineages residing in Nchaney territory. To illustrate changing understandings of Mbororo history and identity, I will later shift my regional focus to Sabga and the provincial capital Bamenda, where educated and politically active Mbororo have come up with new strategies of identification and representation.

In reconstructing Mbororo history I rely on two types of sources. An initial, more general overview of Mbororo migration and their establishment in the Grassfields draws on secondary sources, in particular the in-depth studies of Boutrais (1996) and of the Cameroonian historian Nicodemus Awasom (1984). Conversely, Mbororo histories in Misaje and Sabga are based on firsthand information, namely interviews with elderly Mbororo men and women. Unlike Grassfielders, who deem group histories the monopoly of the palace, there are no socio-political restrictions on history telling among Mbororo. However, individuals considered most conversant with Mbororo history and customs are elders of both sexes, while Mbororo youths are generally thought of as less interested and informed. A preliminary version of this chapter was discussed with Mbororo informants in Misaje and Sabga. Their critical comments confirmed the segmentary character of Mbororo self-identification and the growing recognition of historiography as a political strategy.[5]

Mbororo Migration and Intra-group Relations

As a first step, I will provide a historical sketch of Mbororo pastoral mobility and the establishment of Mbororo in the Cameroon Grassfields. In this context, I will focus on the emergence of Jaafun and Aku as distinct sub-ethnic categories.

The starting point of this historical reconstruction is the early nineteenth century, when the Mbororo who later became known as Jaafun dwelled in northern Nigeria. As is common among Mbororo, their lineage name is derived from the toponym Jafun, also spelled Jahun, a small settlement situated between Kano and Hadejia (Figure 3.1). When, in the first decade of the nineteenth century, the FulBe *jihad* was declared, it had far-reaching consequences for Muslim and non-Muslim peoples in northern Nigeria and Adamaoua. The Jaafun, like most pastoral FulBe, did not actively participate in the *jihad*, but the combined effects of political destabilization, famine and bovine disease provoked their departure from the Kano area. They left for the Bornu region of Nigeria where they were badly received and continued to Bauchi. The majority moved on to Yola, attracted by the prospects of fertile pastures and political security under FulBe hegemony. As most families had lost large parts of their herds on the long and hazardous journey, they engaged in agricultural and trading activities in order to reconstitute their stock (Brackenbury 1923a). Many started to acquire red zebu (Fulfulde: *boDeeji*) from their WoDaaBe neighbours, which replaced the white zebu (Fulfulde: *daneeji*) they had previously herded.[6] While this shift was motivated by pragmatic reasons, it also had symbolic implications. Red zebu soon became an icon of Jaafun identity (Boutrais 1996; Pelican 2012a).

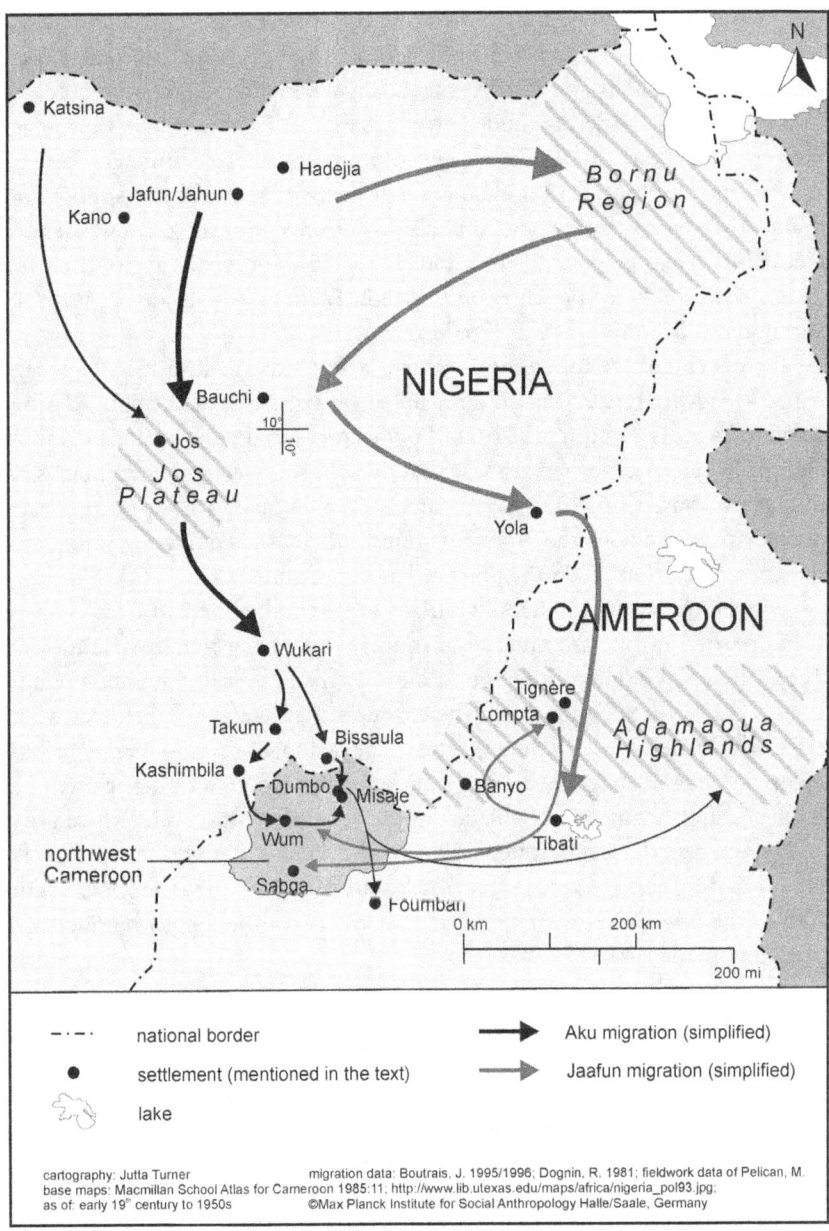

Figure 3.1: Aku and Jaafun migration to northwest Cameroon. Reproduced by kind permission of the Max Planck Institute for Social Anthropology, Halle.

In reaction to an outbreak of rinderpest in northern Nigeria and across Africa at the end of the nineteenth century, many Jaafun continued their journey from Bauchi and Yola to the Adamawa Highlands in contemporary Cameroon. They settled around Banyo, Tibati and Tignère, where they benefited from fertile pastures. Concurrently, however, they encountered the hostility of the local population, who denied them access to the salt springs and frequently attacked people and animals. It was only with the establishment of German colonial power and their forceful pacification of the region that the Jaafun were able to settle with confidence in Lompta, which was set up as an autonomous Mbororo district (Pfeffer 1936).

By the end of the nineteenth century, Jaafun – originally a specific lineage name – had become a generic term for all lineages that had migrated from Kano to Yola. As Dognin (1981: 142) points out, besides their joint migration and their preference for red zebu, Jaafun lineages were recognized as practising the *soro*, a contest in which groups of young men take turns at beating each other with sticks with the aim of demonstrating their courage, stamina and self-control. In Cameroon the practice has been banned.[7]

Similar to the Jaafun, the Aku initially settled in the Kano area, from where they departed in the late nineteenth century due to the rinderpest outbreak. They followed a different migration trajectory than the Jaafun, taking them to the Jos Plateau (see Figure 3.1). There, they settled with their herds of white zebu, which later – as with the red zebu of the Jaafun – became a marker of Aku identity. Aku as a category emerged only when the two groups met again in the Bamenda and Adamaoua Highlands in the first half of the twentieth century, and it became clear that despite their common Kano origin, they had culturally grown apart. It was in this context that Jaafun herders applied the generic term Aku to the newcomers with white zebu, deriving it from a greeting popularly used among the latter.

The Mbororo in the Cameroon Grassfields

While the nineteenth century saw Mbororo southward migration and the subsequent emergence of Jaafun and Aku as distinct sub-ethnic identities, the twentieth century witnessed the establishment of Mbororo graziers of both categories in the Cameroon Grassfields.

The Establishment of Jaafun in the Bamenda Highlands
The first Mbororo to enter the Grassfields were an offshoot of the Jaafun at Lompta. They comprised about thirty families under the leadership of ArDo Sabga (also spelled Sawga), who left Lompta due to internal rivalries. They arrived in the Bamenda Highlands in the late 1910s and established themselves

in the Grassfields chiefdom of Babanki Tungo, where they located four salt springs. Their settlement was named Sabga after its initiator, and later became the headquarters of the Mbororo population in the Grassfields. ArDo Sabga's authority was endorsed by the colonial administration, who recognized him as a Mbororo representative.

Subsequently, more Mbororo were attracted to the Bamenda region. The 1920s witnessed the influx of Jaafun of various lineages, who dispersed to different areas congregating under their respective leaders. Those Jaafun residing in the northern parts of the Bamenda Highlands had no access to salt springs but relied on Hausa and Grassfields merchants supplying them with salt from the Benue region.

The 1930s and 1940s were characterized by ecological changes which affected pastoralists' strategies. The 1940s were also the period when individual Mbororo began to settle permanently. The main motive for this was to secure their pastures, since vacating an area – if only for seasonal displacement – gave way to the possibility of occupation by other pastoralists. Also in the 1940s, a last influx of Jaafun reached the Bamenda Highlands. At the same time, the first Aku entered the Grassfields, most of them being in transit to the Adamaoua Highlands.

Besides ecological conditions, political factors have been equally relevant. As Boutrais (1996: 84) points out, the establishment of Mbororo in northwest Cameroon would probably not have been successful without being facilitated by the British colonial administration. The British supported the influx of Mbororo pastoralists as a means of diversifying the regional economy and augmenting their tax revenue. Concurrently, local Grassfields chiefs welcomed the establishment of pastoralists in their chiefdom's territory, as long as they paid tribute and acknowledged their hosts' territorial and political primacy. Even though population densities were relatively low, and farmland and pasture were abundant, crop damage was a recurrent problem, as the Mbororo practice of extensive grazing and seasonal transhumance collided with the Grassfielders' system of shifting cultivation. As a consequence, Grassfields farmers began to look on the settlement of pastoralists with reservation, and occasionally responded with public protest and violence. The British colonial administration was faced with the predicament of implementing its policy of indirect rule and, at the same time, protecting the Mbororo against the hostility of Grassfields farmers and exactions by local chiefs. This dilemma resulted in frequently changing policies regarding the pastoral sector and the management of farmer–herder relations (Njeuma and Awasom 1989, 1990).

By the late 1920s, the Mbororo were subordinated to Native Authorities – that is, local Grassfields chiefs and their palace hierarchy. The position of *arDo* (a Mbororo group leader), initially a socio-political role, was transformed into an administrative function with tax collecting responsibilities.[8] In the 1940s, the Mbororo made an attempt to evade political subordination by appealing to the British administration for autonomous representation; they largely failed. The British headquarters in Nigeria denied them a politically independent minority status, and classified them as 'strangers' rather than 'natives'. In response, Mbororo leaders formed the Fulani Council which, although its existence was never officially acknowledged, effectively acted as an intermediary between the Mbororo population and the British administration.

During the same decade, grazing rules were introduced to restrict and control pastoral activities. Pastoralists were required to obtain a grazing permit, a document that the Mbororo perceived as validating their claims to pasture land vis-à-vis the administration, neighbouring farmers and rival lineages. With the imposition of grazing rules, the British also encouraged sedentarization. Many Mbororo successively changed their strategy from seasonal migration to transhumance, with part of the family remaining in a permanent rainy-season camp. They subsequently invested in consumer goods and also adopted a distinct identity in reference to more mobile Mbororo groups.

The Fate of Aku Pastoralists in the Grassfields

By the mid twentieth century, the Jaafun in the Grassfields were spatially and politically established. A second wave of pastoral immigration started in the late 1940s. These were Mbororo who had left their initial settlements in northern Nigeria in the early twentieth century and had sojourned for a considerable period on the Jos Plateau. They were attracted to the Grassfields by the prospect of new pastures, as their previous settlement areas had started to exhibit signs of overpopulation and overgrazing. They were grouped under the sub-ethnic category Aku on account of speaking a Hausa-ized Fulfulde and rearing white zebu.

The influx of Aku pastoralists was facilitated by changes in colonial administrative policies. While in the 1940s the British aimed at reducing the pastoral population through grazing rules, they subsequently altered their assessment criteria and reconsidered the northern lowlands of the Bamenda region – namely Misaje, Fungom, Wum and We – as suitable grazing zones. The Jaafun avoided those areas due to tsetse infestation, which their cattle could not endure. Conversely, they attracted incoming Aku graziers whose white zebu were largely tsetse resistant and better adapted to lowland pastures. Moreover, the Aku were welcomed by the local Grassfields authorities and the administration on account of their envisaged cattle-tax contributions, which significantly augmented the revenue of the Native Council (Awasom 1984: 124–27; Kaberry 1960).

A few years later, the pastoralists were confronted with a situation of political insecurity to which many responded with flight. In 1961, the population of British Cameroon was given a chance to vote either for reunification with formerly French-administered Cameroon, or for incorporation into independent Nigeria. The Mboro were excluded from voting, because they were legally considered 'strangers'. Even among them, opinions differed. While most Jaafun were in support of reunification with the hope of attaining full citizenship, many Aku favoured the alternative of joining Nigeria, as they were already familiar with political and ecological conditions there. With the pendulum swinging towards reunification, Mbororo and Hausa became the targets of local Grassfielders' animosity against perceived foreigners from Nigeria. A violent rebellion in the Bamiléké area (involving those known by the French appellation *maquisards*) eventually provoked the displacement of pastoralists, and many Aku decided to take refuge in neighbouring Nigeria.

In the second half of the 1960s and the 1970s, Aku influx into the Grassfields was again considerable. Pastoralists were displaced by political instability in southern Nigeria, culminating in the Tiv revolts and Biafra war. Moreover, as a consequence of drought in the Sahel from 1969 to 1973, southward chain migrations were set in motion. In entering the Cameroon Grassfields, migrant pastoralists caused the displacement of already established Mbororo.

Cameroon's transition to independence and reunification in the early 1960s was accompanied by administrative changes that impacted on Mbororo economic strategies and altered their legal status. With the introduction of the French administrative and legal system, the Mbororo were released from their subordination to Native Authorities in collecting taxes. However, since Cameroon's entry into the French Central African Currency Union in 1963 and the adoption of the CFA franc, cattle taxes rose continuously. Because cattle could no longer be traded across the Nigerian border, the supply to southern Cameroonian markets increased, with the effect that cattle prices fell. Gradually, the fiscal burden on the Mbororo became onerous. Concurrently, administrative control over the pastoral sector increased, and pastoral movement was constrained. Government representatives encouraged Mbororo to settle and to diversify their economic activities. Eventually, in the context of constitutional changes in 1972, Mbororo graziers were granted Cameroonian citizenship.

For most Mbororo in the Grassfields, their migration trajectories ended in the 1970s. Many had settled permanently even before then, and by now their children and grandchildren consider themselves 'locals' of the region (Awasom 2003a; Mimche 2014). Before looking at the ways in which Mbororo interlocutors in the Misaje area portray their settlement and integration into the local community, I will elaborate on intra-ethnic relations, namely the relationship between Jaafun and Aku, as both sub-groups are represented in Misaje Sub-Division (Figure 3.2).

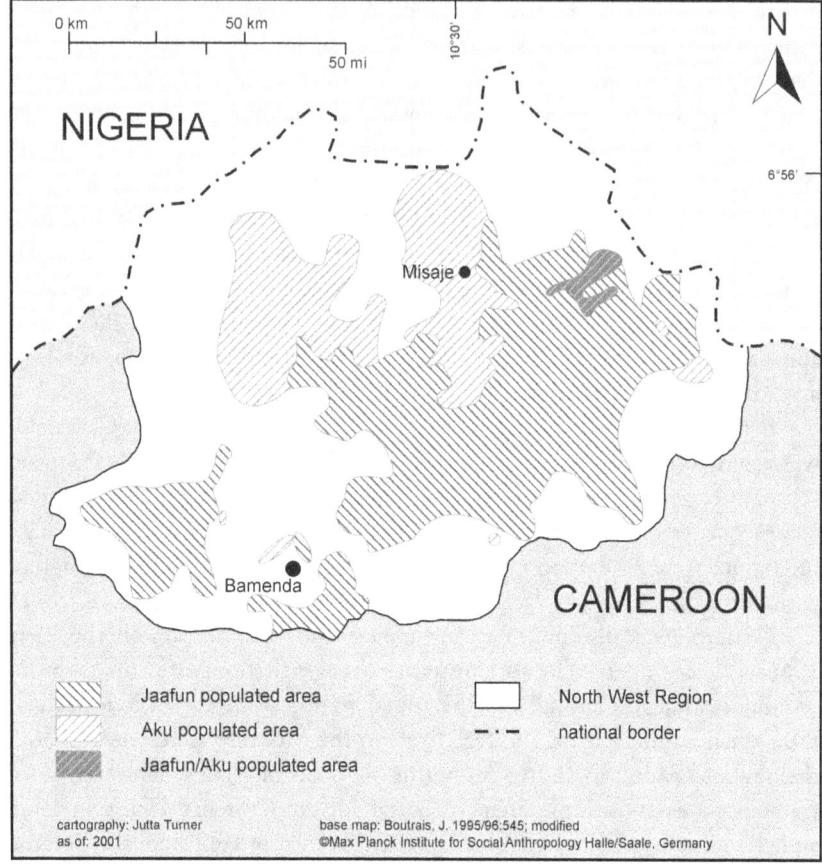

Figure 3.2: Spatial distribution of Jaafun and Aku in the North West Region. Reproduced by kind permission of the Max Planck Institute for Social Anthropology, Halle.

Jaafun–Aku Relations

The historical pattern of Mbororo migration and settlement in the Grassfields gives an idea of the complex relationship between Jaafun and Aku. As firstcomers, Jaafun herders were in a politically advantageous position vis-à-vis the Aku, whose establishment was limited to areas neglected by the Jaafun. The spatial divide between Jaafun in the highlands and Aku in the lowlands has become characteristic of their asymmetrical relationship. Similarly, their different preference for cattle breeds is based on asymmetrical ecological prerogatives. Red zebu (*boDeeji*) are generally deemed finer than white zebu (*daneeji*) and admired for their intelligence and beauty. Given that the highland areas facilitate the raising of all cattle breeds, Jaafun preference for *boDeeji* can be read as an expression of claiming cultural supremacy and of disassociating themselves from the Aku. The Aku choice of *daneeji*, on the other hand, is informed by white zebu's better adaptation to the harsh conditions of the lowlands (Boutrais 1996: 378–95).

Despite these ecological restrictions, the connection between Jaafun and red zebu, and Aku and white zebu, is primarily ideological. White zebu are also called *akuji*, meaning 'Aku cattle', while red zebu are called *mbororoji*, 'cattle of the Mbororo' (with Mbororo standing for Jaafun). Yet as early photographs of Mbororo immigrants in the Grassfields illustrate, diversification and experimentation with cattle breeds has been common since the early settlement period (Figure 3.3). Nowadays, pure-bred flocks are exceptional, and it is only wealthy Jaafun graziers who can afford keeping a separate *boDeeji* group in addition to their main herd of cross-breeds.

Jaafun and Aku tend to keep territorially and socially apart, and their relationship is coloured by unspoken grievance and rivalry. Due to socio-cultural

Figure 3.3: Early Mbororo grazier in the Cameroon Grassfields, 1930s.
Source: Basel Mission Archives / Basel Mission Holdings, E–30.85.003.
Reproduced by kind permission of Basel Mission / Basel Mission Holdings.

The photograph was taken by Wilhelm Zürcher between 1932 and 1937, and the original caption reads, 'A Mbororo man with his herd'. The cattle in this photograph illustrate the degree of heterogeneity of Mbororo herds by the 1930s. The four animals on the left look like they have been cross-bred with *gudaali*,[9] whereas the cattle on the right are of the red zebu breed (*boDeeji*). In the background can be seen a Mbororo camp consisting of two beehive grass huts. Unfortunately, no further information is available on the identity of the herdsman or the compound's location.

conventions of restraint and modesty (*pulaaku*) informing FulBe comportment, conflicts of interest are rarely expressed openly. Instead, feelings of discord are generally concealed, and conflicts are resolved by acquiescence.

In the constrained relationship between Jaafun and Aku, Jaafun generally perceive and pride themselves as culturally and morally superior. They characterize the Aku as conservative, illiterate, poor and ill-mannered. In contrast, they depict themselves as sophisticated, knowledgeable in Islamic practices and teaching, and open to economic innovation (Pelican 1999: 28–32). The Jaafun stress on cultural and economic superiority can be read as a strategy to maintain their privileged position as first-comers. Concurrently, it indicates their resentment about the Aku establishing themselves in the lowlands, as a consequence of which they were deprived of grazing land. In accordance with *pulaaku*, most Jaafun withdrew from their former dry-season pastures, but express their grievance indirectly by belittling the Aku.

Aku, on the other hand, are well aware of the Jaafun resentment. They see themselves as closer to the pastoral ideal and less spoilt by the socio-cultural influence of Grassfielders, the market economy and Western education. Against the background of their marginalized status within Mbororo society in the Grassfields, they tend to be less concerned with their reputation than the Jaafun. Many Aku have expanded their settlement areas; some have even ventured into the privileged highland pastures monopolized by the Jaafun. Nowadays, individual Aku families are found dispersed all over the Grassfields.

History and Self-understanding of Mbororo in the Misaje Area

The contemporary Mbororo population of Misaje Sub-Division is composed of a total of twenty-one lineages, fourteen of them Aku and seven of them Jaafun, some of which comprise only a couple of families.[10] The Misaje Sub-Division is divided into six *ardorates*.[11] These are administrative units, each headed by an *arDo* who operates as a political representative vis-à-vis the administration and neighbouring groups.

The Aku who settled in the lowlands around Misaje and Dumbo dominate four of the six *ardorates*; they constitute approximately 65 per cent of the overall Mbororo population of Misaje Sub-Division. Jaafun graziers are concentrated in the more elevated terrain towards Nkambe and are in control of two *ardorates*. In comparing Aku and Jaafun in terms of herd size, the Aku own approximately 60 per cent of the cattle in Mbororo possession in Misaje Sub-Division. In the areas where the Jaafun constitute a majority, they generally have larger herds than their Aku neighbours. In those *ardorates* where they are represented only sparsely, they tend to be impoverished individuals.[12]

In my research I focused on the two southern *ardorates* of Misaje Sub-Division, which largely overlap with Nchaney territory. They comprise approximately 140 Mbororo graziers who belong to thirteen lineages, ten of them Aku and three of them Jaafun. At the time of my fieldwork, the two *ardorates* were headed by ArDo Bala of the Daneeji and ArDo Adamu who had just taken over from his father, the late ArDo Affang of the Gamanko'en, both dominant Aku lineages in their respective areas. ArDo Bala passed away in 2010 and the *arDo*ship was handed over to his son Musa.

My elaborations are based on conversations with middle-aged and elderly Mbororo men and women. Vital information was also contributed by non-Mbororo, namely Nchaney, Pinyin and Hausa informants, for whom fragments of Mbororo history were part of their personal life or group history. Rather than presenting a wide array of settlement histories, I will concentrate on the life histories of ArDo Bala, the head of the Daneeji lineage and *ardorate*, and his former wife Hajja Maimouna of the same lineage.[13]

Local Accounts of Aku History

In recounting the history of the Mbororo in the Cameroon Grassfields, informants occasionally started by telling a version of the FulBe myth of origin, which is shared in slightly different versions by most FulBe groups across Africa (Jeffreys 1946, 1966; Virtanen 2003: 85–96). In short, it tells how the FulBe ancestors received a gift of cattle from a water spirit who instructed them to lead a pastoral life.

Pastoral identity is an important aspect of FulBe identity in general, and Mbororo identity in particular. Similar to Grassfielders, who define themselves through their relationship with the land and their ancestors, Mbororo identity is rooted in their relationship with cattle. The image of a cow is emblematic of Mbororo identity, and is pictured widely on handmade artefacts, furnishings and Mbororo association banners. Besides the pastoral connotation of Mbororo ethnicity, Muslim identity is a second essential component. Myths about Mbororo descent from Arab scholars, common among pastoral FulBe in other regions (e.g. Virtanen 2003: 86–99), are less popular in the Misaje area. Yet with the Mbororo and Hausa constituting a Muslim minority vis-à-vis Grassfielders, who are predominantly Christians or adherents of African local religions, their Muslim identity is stressed as a vital marker of ethnic and cultural difference. While these tales are familiar to Mbororo as well as members of neighbouring communities, lineage histories are less formalized and mostly known to their own members.

In 2000, the Daneeji comprised a total of thirty-two (registered) graziers with approximately 750 animals. They were split into three clusters. The majority resided near Nfume, in the area administered by ArDo Bala. A second group stayed near Chako, in the *ardorate* of the late ArDo Affang. Another group settled close to Bridge Five, under the direction of a third *arDo*.[14] The Daneeji are one of the few lineages in the Grassfields that differentiates its component 'houses' (Fulfulde: *suudi*). In Nigeria, they allegedly comprise sixty-two 'houses', but only a handful are represented in the Misaje area.

At the time of my fieldwork, ArDo Bala and Alhaji Yaroko were the two most respected and influential elders among the Daneeji in the Misaje area. They were both in their seventies and had entered the Grassfields in the second half of the 1950s. ArDo Bala settled near Nfume, while Alhaji Yaroko first established himself in Bum territory and later moved to Chako. Hajja Maimouna was ArDo Bala's former wife and had accompanied him from Nigeria to Cameroon. She was a well-respected elder and knowledgeable about Aku pastoral lifestyle and custom. Hajja Maimouna and Alhaji Yaroko both accomplished the pilgrimage to Mecca, which is acknowledged in the courtesy title (in Hausa and Fulfulde) of *hajja* for women and *alhaji* for men.

ArDo Bala and Hajja Maimouna were Daneeji from Kano, where they had been neighbours with other lineages, such as the Ringimaji and Tukanko'en (Jaafun lineages). ArDo Bala fondly remembered his youth, moving back and forth between the dry season camp around Hadejia and their rainy season settlement near Kano. Towards the end of the dry season, he and his brothers used to drive the cattle and sheep to the salt springs at Basansani (in Niger), while the majority of the family returned to Kano to engage in farming. They bartered milk for food crops and entertained good relations with their farming neighbours.

By the age of twenty-five, ArDo Bala married Maimouna, who was then fourteen. Two years later, they transferred to Bauchi, leaving behind their parents. They spent six years around Bauchi and progressed to the Benue area. From Wukari they ascended the Mambila Plateau and later entered the Grassfields. While on the Mambila, they resided with members of the NaatirBe lineage. Around 1957, ArDo Maguwa, who had moved to Cameroon three years earlier, invited his relatives on the Mambila Plateau to join him at Dumbo. As Daneeji and NaatirBe entertain a joking relationship, members of both lineages followed his call.

Unlike others who sold their animals prior to their departure and reconstituted their herds by buying *gudaali* (a special cattle breed from northern Cameroon) in Cameroon, the migration group of ArDo Bala moved together with their white zebu. They followed the cattle trade route from Wukari via Takum and Kashimbila to Wum and Dumbo.

> We were so many that I can't remember. We could have been more than one hundred. You see, all this area around Kibbo was occupied by Daneeji, but now only

I alone of the Daneeji of east Kano am left in this place. Some have gone back to Kano, others moved on to the Adamaoua and the Central African Republic. I was tired of running up and down, so I settled.[15]

ArDo Bala and his elder brother established themselves at Nfume. They encountered other Daneeji families who belonged to different 'houses'. Alhaji Yaroko's family, for example, originated from Katsina and shares no relations with the Daneeji from Kano. ArDo Bala and his family have lived in the Cameroon Grassfields for forty-three years. Over that period, many things have changed. ArDo Bala and Hajja Maimouna came to Cameroon with many cattle, but soon herds began to dwindle due to disease and increasing cattle sales. Hajja Maimouna assessed the situation as follows:

> We did not know that somebody's cattle could all get finished. Only in Cameroon did we see it happen. The thing that decimated our herds was *pettoowu* [Fulfulde term for rinderpest]. We still work hard to bring them [the herds] back [to their initial size]. So for now, whenever someone's cattle get finished, he can hardly reconstitute his herd. He just stays like a *kaaDo* [non-FulBe, here farmer]. At first, when our cattle diminished, we women helped our husbands. We sold milk and made cotton thread. But here the women do nothing. They do not sell milk, they do not even carry water. That is what brought us poverty. Women have become queens! We see it, but they do not see it. The men sell cattle to solve all the problems of their women.[16]

Soon after he settled at Nfume, ArDo Bala engaged in farming and cattle trading to reduce the economic burden on the cattle herd. After some years the couple separated, and Hajja Maimouna remarried in northern Cameroon. She spent twenty-seven years at Ngaoundal before returning to Misaje, where she lived with one of her sons. While Hajja Maimouna proceeded to Ngaoundal, ArDo Bala remained at Nfume. When the government decided to split the territory under ArDo Affang's control, Bala applied for the post of *arDo*. As he framed it, 'This is the sixth year, since I started counting cattle'.[17]

The historical account of ArDo Bala and Hajja Maimouna contains a lot of relevant information, among which I will concentrate on three topics: migration experiences, lineage relations and social (including gender) transformations. ArDo Bala and Hajja Maimouna were of the first generation of Mbororo immigrants and could well remember their past in Nigeria and their trajectory to Cameroon. Both interlocutors precisely recalled their migration routes, the years spent at each location and the challenges they encountered. However, as Boutrais (1996: 65) points out, pastoral memory is preoccupied with trajectories rather than motives of migration.

A central topic addressed in the above historical account concerns the relationship between Daneeji 'houses', and between the Daneeji and other lineages. Throughout our conversations, ArDo Bala and Hajja Maimouna stressed their identity as Kano Daneeji, distancing themselves from Katsina Daneeji who dwelled on the Jos Plateau before coming to Cameroon. They both emphasized the shared origin of and initial proximity between Daneeji and Jaafun from Kano.[18] At the same time, they clearly distinguished Aku from Jaafun lineages, and insisted that the two groups had culturally grown apart. As Hajja Maimouna explained, in terms of dialect, clothing and socializing, Aku are closer to Hausa. Jaafun, on the other hand, are more similar to Huya (Town FulBe of northern Cameroon). Thus the cultural similarity between Jaafun and Daneeji from Kano has diminished. The latter now associate with other Daneeji 'houses' and with Aku lineages from different areas, with whom they co-reside and intermarry. It becomes clear that over the lifetimes of ArDo Bala and Hajja Maimouna, their criteria of cultural alignment shifted from shared origins to shared location. Secondly, their account demonstrates that in the Bamenda region the sub-ethnic level of identification (Jaafun versus Aku) has gained prominence over lineage identification.

Besides shifts in identification, ArDo Bala and Hajja Maimouna outlined significant socio-economic and socio-cultural changes. The subject of social change is crucial for an understanding of recent transformations in Mbororo self-understanding and political representation, which will be discussed below. Among the most crucial factors shaping pastoralists' lives is their degree of mobility. ArDo Bala described his parents practising a transhumant, agro-pastoral lifestyle while residing in northern Nigeria. Together with his brother, ArDo Bala adopted a more mobile lifestyle. They eventually decided to settle permanently upon their arrival in the Grassfields, arguing that they felt tired after many years of roaming. These shifts in mobility are typical of the strategies of many Mbororo graziers.

The adoption of a more sedentary lifestyle impacted on the pastoralists' socio-economic organization, in particular their gender roles. As ArDo Bala and Hajja Maimouna pointed out, Mbororo women usually assisted their husbands in supporting the family by selling milk. But once established in the Grassfields, they encountered a number of obstacles and eventually reduced milk sales to a minimum (Pelican 1999: 106–30; 2004b). Since Grassfielders were not accustomed to milk consumption, the demand for milk products was limited. At the same time, the productivity of Mbororo animals declined as an effect of their restricted mobility and veterinary medication. Moreover, adherence to Islamic rules became a symbol of progress, wealth and status, and was expressed, *inter alia*, in the restriction of women's mobility. Hajja Maimouna rightly emphasized the changes in Mbororo women's lives; yet, ironically, she attributed responsibility to women themselves rather than to socio-economic factors.

In order to safeguard their pastoral resources, many Mbororo started to combine their herding activities with small-scale subsistence agriculture. While Jaafun relied primarily on employing local farmers to cultivate their fields, Aku tended to perform most tasks themselves. Economic diversification was also encouraged by the British colonial administration and subsequently the Cameroonian government, both as a means of augmenting rural production and as a way of improving farmer–herder relations. ArDo Bala grew up with both cattle grazing and farming. Retrospectively, he prided himself on being the first Aku in the Misaje area to build a permanent house and cultivate crops. In addition, he ventured into the cattle trade, selling animals in Nigeria and southern Cameroon. Most of his sons have copied his attitude and have diversified their economic activities; they run small shops, work as drivers and peripatetic photographers, cultivate crops for sale and rear cattle. Somewhat misleading is Hajja Maimouna's comment that a person whose herd was depleted had to stay like a *kaaDo* (non-Mbororo), that is, make their living from farming. While this argument has frequently been made, the empirical data from Misaje shows otherwise. It is rather the more enterprising individuals, like ArDo Bala, Alhaji Yaroko and ArDo Affang, who engaged in agriculture, not as a response to poverty but thanks to their relative wealth. Impoverished Mbororo, on the other hand, tend to be conservative in their economic activities and to capitalize on their pastoral expertise, working as paid herdsmen or cattle drovers.

Changes in Mbororo mobility and economy also affected the sociocultural sphere. With growing wealth, many Mbororo aimed at improving their living conditions by investing in consumer goods and Islamic education. Mbororo youths gradually adopted practices and consumption patterns of their Grassfields peers – such as frequenting local bars, attending Grassfielders rituals and festivities, or dating Grassfields partners – which their elders considered incompatible with their Mbororo and Muslim identity (Boutrais 1996: 967–70; Frantz 1986). In the same vein, Hajja Maimouna complained that, while Mbororo women were previously ashamed of admitting to a pregnancy, 'they nowadays start buying clothes from the moment a child is in the mother's womb'.[19] She deemed this contemporary practice a breach of *pulaaku* and a sign of moral decay. Moreover, in comparing the situation in Misaje to Ngaoundal in northern Cameroon, she emphasized that Mbororo cohabitation with their Grassfields neighbours posed unforeseen challenges to their cultural practices and identity. Similarly, as Mbororo elders worried about the acculturation of their youngsters as a result of living in a non-Muslim environment, they emphasized the practice of an Islamic lifestyle and encouraged the pursuit of Islamic education as opposed to Western or Christian schooling. It is only in the past decades that Mbororo individuals have become aware of the practical advantages of Western education and have started to send their children to school.

The historical narrative of Daneeji establishment in the Misaje area has illustrated two significant points raised at the beginning of this chapter, namely the absence of a collective history shared by all Mbororo in the research area, and, secondly, shifting categories of identification contingent on the historical context and the envisaged 'other'. Both features are rooted in the economic and socio-political organization of the Mbororo as a pastoral, mobile and segmentary society. However, as the subsequent example will show, these features are not absolute. Prolonged sedentarization and Cameroon's political liberalization have promoted the emergence of new modes of historiography, self-identification and political representation.

A Different Setting: Historiography and Ethnicity in Sabga

I will now change sites and turn to Sabga, the oldest and most prestigious Mbororo settlement in northwest Cameroon. Sabga was mentioned above, in the historical overview of Mbororo establishment in the Grassfields. Here, I will focus on contemporary practices of historiography and self-representation, discuss the ways in which they diverge from local practices in Misaje, and highlight the reasons that account for their different structure and significance.

With a population of approximately 3,000 inhabitants in 2013 (census data of the Independent Electoral Commission of the Tubah Council office), Sabga is the largest Mbororo settlement in northwest Cameroon (see also Davis 1995). It is situated in the chiefdom of Babanki Tungo, some 40 kilometres northeast of Bamenda. It derives its name from ArDo Sabga, the first Mbororo leader who settled in the Grassfields in the late 1910s. The Sabga community has retained its prestige as first-comers, and counts as the headquarters of the Mbororo in the Grassfields. Its leader is administratively classified as a second-class chief and bears the title of *laamiiDo* (Fulfulde for paramount *arDo* or superior chief).[20] Thanks to its proximity to Bamenda, the provincial capital and a large city, as well as the centre of the cattle trade, the Sabga community has been exposed to urban stimuli and pastoral development programmes more than any other Mbororo group in the Grassfields. This applies to the colonial and postcolonial period, and became even more pertinent in the 1990s, an era coloured by national political liberalization and increasing NGO activities.

Over the past two decades, Sabga Mbororo have participated in a number of non-governmental development projects. Since 1992, members of the Sabga community have operated a dairy cooperative in collaboration with the American NGO Land O'Lakes. Exchange visits were organized, and individuals were trained in various techniques promoting the milk and meat productivity of their cattle. In 1996, Sabga graziers established a business relationship with Sotramilk, a commercial dairy-processing company in Bamenda, supplying fresh milk on a regular basis (Pelican 2004b). Sabga people have also been in contact with the Association pour la Promotion de l'Elevage au Sahel et en Savane (APESS), a pastoral development NGO based in Burkina Faso. APESS mainly runs educational and pasture improvement programmes, and is largely Swiss-funded (Hagberg 2004; Kremling 2004). Imam Umaru, the current religious head of the Mbororo community in Sabga, has attended several APESS meetings in Cameroon and Burkina Faso.[21] He adopted the Fulfulde script, developed by APESS on the basis of the Arabic alphabet, and in the late 1990s began to organize classes for women and children. Moreover, besides its involvement in various development programmes, the Sabga community has produced some educated Mbororo individuals as well as successful businessmen. While Sabga is arguably neither the only nor necessarily the most progressive and prolific Mbororo community in the Grassfields, its historical eminence and the popularity of some of its well-to-do individuals have contributed to its reputation.

Sabga's success story also has its negative side, which finds expression in recurrent confrontations over landownership and access to resources with neighbouring communities and influential individuals. For example, in 1999, an argument emerged between the *fon* of Babanki Tungo and the *laamiiDo* of Sabga concerning the territorial authority of the two community leaders. The *fon* of Babanki challenged the *laamiiDo*'s status as a second-class chief, arguing that Sabga was not an independent village but a quarter of Kejom Ketinguh, the capital of the Babanki chiefdom. The *laamiiDo* of Sabga responded by indicating his community's long-standing establishment, which qualified them as autonomous citizens of the area in their own right (Awasom 2003a). Similarly, members of the Sabga community have long been at odds with an influential entrepreneur of Grassfields-Mbororo background who has interfered in local politics and has made repeated claims on their grazing land (Pelican 2010, 2013).

Against this background and the community's long-standing establishment, it is not surprising that self-representation in Sabga takes a different form than among Mbororo in the Misaje area, where such challenges have started to arise only recently. Among the most striking features of Sabga self-representation is the codification of its history by Imam Umaru, written in Fulfulde in Arabic script.[22] Compared to the historical narratives of Mbororo in Misaje, it becomes evident that the codification of Sabga history is not just a case of preserving historical knowledge, but rather an example of the 'invention of tradition' (Hobsbawm and Ranger 1983), namely the production of written historical accounts. Moreover, Imam Umaru expressed his intention to rewrite the history of Sabga in the Fulfulde script introduced by APESS, which would add another dimension of invention.

Sabga historiography not only stands out regarding its codification, but also in its content and structure. It claims to provide not just a historical account of one specific lineage but to represent the history of all Jaafun in the Grassfields, starting with the initial departure of FulBe from Mali. In the following I quote selected sections of the Fulfulde text, read out to me by Imam Umaru, in English translation to illustrate its structured and authoritative character. In this respect, the Sabga history resembles much more the Nchaney one than the Aku style of history telling encountered in the Misaje area.

> After the death of ArDo Manya at Falkoumré, ArDo Vami, also called Hoba, took over the *arDo*ship. He left Falkoumré and went to Galim with his followers, to a place called Lompta. His son left Lompta and went to Banyo where he settled with his people. A disagreement arose between Hoba and Tonga, the son of ArDo Manya. ArDo Hoba lost his support and the *arDo*ship was given to Tonga. Hoba's son, Sabga, heard the news and returned to Lompta to take his father to Banyo. ArDo Hoba later retrieved the *arDo*ship. By then it was still the colonial rule of the Germans, that is, when the Germans and British fought over the control of Cameroon. The white men met them [the Jaafun] at Banyo […]

> Abdullahi Sabga ruled from 1916 to 1957. He was followed by Adamu Jaki *bi* [Fulfulde: son of] Sabga who ruled from 1957 till 1961. The third *arDo* of Sabga was ArDo Buba *bi* Sabga.[23] He ruled from 1961 to 1990 and was followed by ArDo Adamu Jooro Bure who ruled from 12 August 1990 to 12 November 1998. The present *arDo* is ArDo Ahmadou Sabga. He started his rule on 13 November 1998. He is the last ArDo of Sabga for now, that is, the fifth generation.[24]

LaamiiDo Ahmadou passed away in 2007. His succession caused unrest among the Mbororo of Sabga (see also Pelican 2010, 2013). Yet eventually, his brother Mahmouda was confirmed in office and is the current *laamiiDo* of Sabga.

In comparison to the way history is told among the Aku in the Misaje area, Imam Umaru's account stands out in many ways. The history of the Mbororo of Sabga is primarily a political history. It is structured strictly chronologically and focuses on internal power struggles and the establishment of a lineage hierarchy. Throughout the text there are references to external events, such as encounters with the British and German colonial powers, whereby Mbororo history is framed in time and space. The second part resembles the structure of the Nchaney list of chiefs. It serves the purpose of legitimizing the authority of the Sabga community over other Mbororo lineages, and of validating their rights and claims vis-à-vis neighbouring communities and the government. In the same way as Fon Richard used photographs and documents to illustrate and authenticate his own account, the Sabga Mbororo quickly produced

Figure 3.4: Historical Sabga rulers. Reproduced by kind permission of Imam Umaru, religious leader and local expert on the history of the Sabga Mbororo community.

This image is a photo collage of two pictures: on the left we see ArDo Sabga, on the right LaamiiDo Buba, his son and third in line to the Sabga leadership. The stamp on the rear of the photograph indicates the date (6 November 1979) and the studio that produced the collage (Photos J.N. Akonsah, P.O. Box 7, Mankon).

photographs of their rulers when I asked for them, a selection of which is presented here (Figures 3.4 and 3.5).

The *laamiiDo* of Sabga and his community are occasionally invited to participate in public events organized by the provincial or national administration in order to represent the Mbororo population of northwest Cameroon. Such occasions are usually intended at demonstrating the cultural and ethnic diversity of the North West Region and the Cameroonian nation. Thanks to its proximity to Bamenda, Sabga is also the Mbororo community most exposed to tourism, which admittedly is very small scale and of limited economic relevance. Nevertheless, Sabga individuals are willing and interested in welcoming visitors from abroad and familiarizing them with their cultural practices and pastoral lifestyle.

In looking at the multidimensional participation of the Sabga community in historical reconstruction and cultural representation, it becomes clear that we can observe not only the proliferation of history, culture and identity, but

Figure 3.5: Grassfields and Mbororo rulers, 1993. Reproduced by kind permission of Imam Umaru.

According to the information provided by Imam Umaru, we see on the left the *fon* of Nso with his palace stewards; on the right is the late LaamiiDo Jooro Bure, and next to him his brother Ahmadou, who subsequently succeeded him to the throne. They are joined by the *imam* (front row middle), the *kaigamma* (chief of slaves/serfs, front right) and two elders who remained unidentified. The photograph was taken in the Babanki palace in November 1993.

also their gradual objectification and folklorization. Both are significant steps in strengthening ethnic consciousness and political awareness among Mbororo, an objective adopted more pronouncedly by MBOSCUDA, a Mbororo NGO popular in the Grassfields.

Agents of Representation: The Mbororo, the State and International Organizations

Significant changes in Mbororo self-understanding and political representation occurred in the 1990s in response to Cameroon's liberalization. As we saw in the previous chapter on Nchaney history and identity, the Mbororo are not the only group who have adopted new strategies of political representation vis-à-vis state and international organizations, yet their case is one of the most striking regarding transformations in collective self-identification and representation.

Mbororo Responses to New Political and Legal Avenues
Ndudi Umaru, a Mbororo from northern Cameroon and the protagonist of Boquené's biography, portrays his people as homeless, marginalized and without consciousness of their past.

> No Mbororo can link himself either to a country or a flag that he would pass on from generation to generation. The Mbororo have no fatherland. So it isn't astonishing that everywhere they wander with their herds, the Mbororo are treated like people of no importance. They do not have the right to any consideration. The least of the farmers is not worried about saying to them, 'Why did you come here? You do not even have a country. And if you're chased from here, where will you go?' Because the Mbororo are without homeland, they are also without memories. None of them worry about knowing where their ancestors spent their lives. (Bocquené 2002: 95–96)

This self-perception of the Mbororo as an insecure and disadvantaged people was endorsed by many Mbororo interlocutors, particularly with regard to their relationship with their Grassfields neighbours and with state agents.[25] In their view, the attempts of Grassfields rulers to integrate them via patron–client or host–guest relations constituted a source of dependency and exploitation. Conversely, while the British colonial administration classified the Mbororo as 'strangers' and denied them autonomous political representation, under Ahidjo's regime they qualified as Cameroonian citizens. Yet at the same time, they were subsumed under the category of 'northerners' on account of their Muslim identity and FulBe ethnicity. Consequently, Mbororo who were born and grew up in the Grassfields still counted as 'strangers' to the area with limited rights to the region's natural and state resources.[26] It was only with Cameroon's political liberalization in the 1990s that the Mbororo eventually seized the opportunity to engage in the political arena and to express their interests and grievances directly to the state (Davies 1995; Mouiche 2011).

The North West Region, being the seat of the principal opposition party, the SDF, constituted a centre of virulent struggles between the opposition and the ruling CPDM. Unlike the majority of Grassfielders, Mbororo generally distanced themselves from party politics. During the presidential election in 1992, most Mbororo avoided taking sides and voted for the Muslim, northern Cameroonian candidate, Bello Buba of the NUDP. In the same year, a group of Mbororo youths met in the capital Yaoundé and formed MBSOCUDA, the Mbororo Social and Cultural Development Association. Alternative associations were formed at this time, yet over the years MBOSCUDA advanced to become the most vocal and effective organ of Mbororo self-representation in relations with the state, international organizations and neighbouring communities (Pelican 2008).[27]

Supplementary paths of political lobbying have subsequently been explored, often with the support of or due to the initiative of MBOSCUDA members. Analogous to the North West Fons' Union (NOWEFU), Mbororo leaders in the Grassfields formed their own political associations, such as the North West Ardos Union and the North West Lamidos Forum (Awasom 2003a). Another strategy of endorsing Mbororo interests vis-à-vis the state is by securing the support of high-ranking officials. In 2002, the Mbororo of the Grassfields counted two members of parliament as ambassadors to their cause, namely Peter Abety, minister for special duties, and Manu Jaji Gidado, attaché at the presidency. In the meantime, Abety has been discharged from office, while new sympathizers have been won among current officials.

Transformations in Mbororo Self-understanding

Two features are most noteworthy with regard to recent transformations in Mbororo self-understanding. Firstly, due to the efforts and activities of MBOSCUDA, a new consciousness of pan-Mbororo identity has emerged that transcends generational, gender, lineage, sub-ethnic and regional differences. Secondly, Mbororo identity has been redefined in political and legal terms, which is reflected in the growing self-confidence of Mbororo vis-à-vis the state and neighbouring communities.

MBOSCUDA is a national, membership-based organization with approximately 30,000 members and branches in nearly all administrative regions.[28] Its formation was an initiative of young, mostly educated Mbororo individuals who were searching for answers to their shared experience of a crisis of Mbororo identity. Initial questions addressed included: 'Who or what are we? Where do we come from? Where are we heading to? If let alone what will become of us as a people, our cattle herding culture and pastoral way of life? What can be done to improve our lives?' (Salihu 1999: 3). MBOSCUDA founding members explicitly distanced themselves from Town FulBe (Huya) in northern Cameroon and stressed their identification with (agro-)pastoral FulBe. They argued that the two groups' interests and problems differed substantially, and that the Mbororo in particular lacked efficient strategies of political representation regarding the state. To emphasize the distinction between Town FulBe and pastoral FulBe, they deliberately opted for the ethnonym Mbororo in naming their association. They decided on a number of objectives and programmes, aimed at the revitalization of Mbororo cultural practices, the improvement of Mbororo women's socio-economic situation, the promotion of Mbororo children's education and the improvement of pastoral conditions. These programmes were intended to be realized at a regional level with the support of local communities.

MBOSCUDA's most active branch is in the North West Region, whose members have been influenced by the socio-political and organizational strategies of their Grassfields neighbours. Here, transformations in Mbororo self-perception are more evident than in other parts of the country. The following elaborations focus on MBOSCUDA activities and community responses in the North West Region; they are not representative of other regions. The current influence of MBOSCUDA in northwest Cameroon was not a given from the beginning. One of its initial difficulties was to convince members of the Mbororo community of the advantages of joint action and collective political representation. As a result of their pastoral heritage, Mbororo were used to pursuing their interests via individual strategies, such as patron–client relationships. Their solidarity networks focused on the kin or lineage group. Moreover, interaction between Jaafun and Aku was limited. MBOSCUDA activists, however, encouraged collective strategies. In this context, the Fulfulde phrase *taa waDDa pulaaku* ('don't make *pulaaku*') became a popular slogan among MBOSCUDA sympathizers (Davis 1995). In their view, *pulaaku*, or the way of behaving like a *pullo* (the singular of FulBe) was an outdated strategy and no longer compatible with the requirements of their current economic and political situation. They thus called on individuals to transcend socio-cultural barriers and to express disagreement openly. Many Mbororo elders took offence and accused MBOSCUDA of eroding Mbororo morale and identity. Gradually, MBOSCUDA officials adopted a more inclusive strategy, involving Mbororo elders and Muslim scholars in the planning and execution of their programmes. Besides this, they addressed the sub-ethnic divide between Jaafun and Aku and stressed awareness of an overarching Mbororo identity.

By the second half of the 1990s, MBOSCUDA was widely established among Mbororo in the Grassfields. In order to realize their community development projects, MBOSCUDA officials secured the collaboration of international NGOs, such as the German Development Service and Village AiD, a UK funding-partner agency. Concurrently, international development discourses impacted on MBOSCUDA's programme orientation (Hickey 2002). In line with global discourses on human, minority and indigenous rights, MBOSCUDA shifted its initial focus from redefining Mbororo identity to asserting Mbororo political and legal status. Current projects include women's training in alternative income schemes, the establishment of Anglo-Arabic schools[29] and the provision of legal advice in land disputes as well as in cases of human rights abuse and illegal extortion by government officials (Duni et al. 2009). Furthermore, MBOSCUDA has been involved in the administrative process of devising a national pastoral code, and has made efforts to familiarize its constituencies with the implications for pastoral livestock production (Django et al. 2011). On account of these activities, MBOSCUDA is well-regarded among Mbororo in the Grassfields, many of whom have benefited from its ongoing projects.

One of MBOSCUDA's most relevant programmes at the time of my research was Ballotiral, a partnership programme funded by Village AiD, which involved collaboration between representatives of three regional NGOs.[30] *Ballotiral* is a Fulfulde word and means 'working together'. The programme's main objective was to support Mbororo social and political integration into the regional community. Among other activities, it ran adult literacy circles and provided legal counselling to Mbororo individuals. The programme was initiated by two founding members of MBOSCUDA from the North West Region who had been influential in the association's development over the early years, and who established the contact with Village AiD. Subsequently, both left Cameroon for the UK, where they continued to support MBOSCUDA and the Mbororo community by facilitating international contacts and promoting Mbororo interests in global networks. With their outreach activities, MBOSCUDA and Ballotiral promoted civil awareness among Mbororo in northwest Cameroon and redefined Mbororo status vis-à-vis the state.

In the course of Cameroon's political liberalization, its constitution underwent a number of changes, and Cameroonian citizenship became defined via membership of an indigenous or minority group. As stated in the preamble of the Cameroonian constitution of 1996, the state guarantees the protection of minorities and the preservation of the rights of indigenous populations.[31] Mbororo thus share the same rights as local Grassfielders if they can prove to the state that they are indigenous or a minority. When in 2000 new computerized identity cards were issued, MBOSCUDA and Ballotiral encouraged the Mbororo population to register. While in the previous system Mbororo were generally registered as being born in northern Cameroon, the new identity cards indicated their actual birthplace. Mbororo hence qualified as regional citizens with claims and rights to natural resources and political representation in their home area.

A few years later, MBOSCUDA went a step further. In line with the UN proclamation of the first decade of 'indigenous peoples' (1995 to 2004), the organization began to promote the Mbororo as an 'indigenous minority' whose cultural survival had to be protected. Consequently, MBOSCUDA officials enrolled in government programmes for the development of indigenous minorities and autochthonous peoples. At the same time, the UN and the International Labour Organization recognized the Mbororo and the so-called Pygmies as 'indigenous peoples' of Cameroon. Moreover, in 2005, MBOSCUDA was granted consultative status by the Economic and Social Council (ECOSOC) of the United Nations. However, as I have argued elsewhere in more detail (Pelican 2009a, 2010, 2013), Mbororo claims of indigeneity and demands for political and legal entitlements associated with them have not gone unchallenged. The complexities of defining indigeneity in relation to local idioms of historical primacy ('first-comers', 'natives') and in relation to national discourses of autochthony has engendered a new potential for conflict with Grassfields neighbours, as well as with the Cameroonian government. Moreover, it has prompted disagreement and friction within the Mbororo of northwest Cameroon and beyond about the meanings of Mbororo identity and about appropriate national and international representations of Mbororo culture and society.[32]

In 2005, for example, dissent emerged within MBOSCUDA's leading echelons concerning the association's envisaged collaboration with Cameroonian forest peoples, popularly known as Pygmies. The situation escalated when both groups were to be subsumed under the category of 'indigenous peoples'. As a consequence, the two Mbororo individuals living in the UK mentioned above, who had crucially facilitated MBOSCUDA's international contacts, quit the association. As one of them explained, they could no longer cope with their colleagues' 'complex of Mbororo superiority', nor tolerate the misuse of MBOSCUDA to advance the personal interests of elite Mbororo. In the same year, Mbororo leaders submitted a petition to the British high commissioner accusing Mbororo intellectuals of misappropriating international aid. Furthermore, they expressed dissatisfaction with the representation of the Mbororo as an 'indigenous people', which they felt was suggestive of Mbororo backwardness and poverty. Conversely, in 2007 a conflict emerged in Sabga over the right to determine the next ruler after the death of the late *laamiiDo* (Pelican 2010, 2013). When the regional administration intervened in the selection procedure and forcefully imposed a Mbororo ruler of their liking, elite members of the Sabga community demanded the right to political self-determination as an 'indigenous people' of Cameroon. They used their international connections to pressure the government, and MBOSCUDA filed a report with the UN Human Rights Council on their behalf. While these interventions effected an intergovernmental exchange and follow-up over the subsequent years, they finally proved inconsequential. Eventually, the Sabga community had to come to terms with its ruler as well as the internal fission provoked by the protracted conflict.

Despite the divergent outcomes of these interventions, MBOSCUDA's international connections and their recourse to global discourses on human, minority and indigenous rights have been instrumental in redefining the political and legal status of the Mbororo community. At the same time, they have given rise to internal rivalries and estrangement between Mbororo and other minority groups. However, the message that Mbororo have rights and claims has been conveyed at the local, national and international level, and has impacted on Mbororo self-understanding throughout the Cameroon Grassfields. As Mbororo informants in Misaje pointed out, they no longer see themselves as disunited and marginalized pastoralists, but as an empowered Cameroonian minority whose members can defend themselves against illicit infringements and the venality of state officials.

The consolidation of Mbororo identity and their growing self-confidence have not only affected their relationship with the state, but also interpersonal relations with members of neighbouring communities as well as between Mbororo. In Chapter 7, I will analyse a case in which a Mbororo individual's assertiveness towards his Grassfields neighbours has added to the deterioration of social relations between Mbororo and Grassfielders in the Misaje area.

Mbororo Identity and the Presence/Absence of (FulBe) 'Others'

To conclude, I will review some of my findings regarding Mbororo approaches to history, their notions of identity and the relevance of *pulaaku* in interethnic relations. Let me take up Boutrais's observation that the Mbororo preoccupation with the present and the limitedness of their collective historical consciousness is a characteristic of pastoral societies (Boutrais 1996: 65). A similar approach to history is reflected in the accounts of Mbororo informants in Misaje. However, as more recent developments among urban-exposed Mbororo communities like Sabga illustrate, long-standing sedentarization combined with the emergence of new political and legal avenues have facilitated a change in their approach to history. Sabga historiography, indeed, reflects the current strategies of a sedentary Mbororo community that legitimates its claims to political representation and economic resources in roughly the same terms as Grassfields chiefdoms.

As we saw in the previous chapter on Nchaney history and identity, Grassfielders' understanding of their ethnicity is multilayered and inclusive, and enables multiple ethnic identifications in terms of shared migration and descent, linguistic and socio-cultural commonalities, common territory and acceptance of the political authority of Grassfields rulers. Mbororo notions of ethnicity, on the other hand, are rather exclusivist and essentializing. Becoming Mbororo through intermarriage, religious conversion or by practising cattle pastoralism is virtually impossible. To be recognized as Mbororo, one should be born as Mbororo and have internalized the ideals of *pulaaku*. Transformations in Mbororo identity thus refer less to shifting boundaries than to shifts regarding the meaning and content of Mbororo ethnicity.

Their focus on the self, on ethnic and cultural integrity is an expression both of the Mbororo (provisionally) mobile lifestyle, which exposes them to continuously changing 'ethnic others' or host-communities, and of their resultant socio-political marginality as a migrant minority. However, changes in Mbororo identity as a consequence of their interaction and cohabitation with other groups are reflected, for example, in the contemporary sub-ethnic divide between Jaafun and Aku. While the Aku were influenced by their coexistence with Hausa in Nigeria, the Jaafun adopted a lifestyle similar to their Town FulBe (Huya) neighbours in northern Cameroon. The effects of residing in the Grassfields are mirrored in, among other things, the selective adoption of political institutions and organizational practices of their Grassfields neighbours, as well as in changing generational and gender dynamics.

Another crucial variable shaping Mbororo self-understanding is the presence or absence of 'FulBe others'. In northern Cameroon, Mbororo distinguish themselves from sedentary Town FulBe (Huya) by stressing their pastoral identity and their mastery of *pulaaku* (Burnham 1996; Virtanen 2003). In northwest Cameroon, the category of Town FulBe is largely absent. Here the primary criterion of ethnic distinction is not *pulaaku* but Islam. With regard to internal categories of identification, historical and situational shifts from the lineage category to the sub-ethnic to the Mbororo category have been observable. Contemporaneously, the sub-ethnic divide between Jaafun and Aku is pertinent in individuals' self-identification. At the same time, in the context of new political strategies, identification with the overarching Mbororo category has gained in popularity.

The impacts of state policies and administrative impositions on Mbororo identity have become most noticeable in the past twenty years as a result of the opening of political space for Mbororo self-representation. The recent emergence of a kind of frail Mbororo nationalism resonates with Anderson's notion of 'the imagined community' (Anderson 1983). The newly gained political and civil self-confidence of Mbororo in the Grassfields is mainly the result of the joint efforts of national and international NGOs, and has been facilitated by their use of print, audio-visual and virtual media.

Finally, let me address the question of the contemporary relevance of *pulaaku* in interethnic interaction. *Pulaaku* commonly denotes a complex of social values, such as modesty, self-control, common sense and courage that are supposed to guide public interaction between FulBe. With regard to non-FulBe (or *haaBe*), *pulaaku* serves as an indication of 'otherness' and sociocultural distance. As Boesen (1994, 1997) and Guichard (1996, 2000) show, pastoral FulBe in Benin treat their *haaBe* neighbours neither in the same way as their FulBe companions, nor do they make any effort to respect their rules of comportment. The *haaBe* generally comply, tolerating FulBe oddness as an expression of their 'otherness'.

In the contemporary Cameroon Grassfields, the responses to *pulaaku* as a strategy of aloofness and constraint are different. First of all, Grassfielders are less likely to accept Mbororo 'otherness', but urge them to participate in village life and to comply with general social rules. Secondly, the slogan 'don't make *pulaaku'*, popular among Mbororo youths in the 1990s, demonstrates that many Mbororo have come to consider *pulaaku* as obstructive with regard to their interaction with Grassfields neighbours and state representatives. Mbororo in the Grassfields no longer want to stress their 'otherness' vis-à-vis their Grassfields neighbours, but demand their integration as local and national citizens with valid rights and claims.

Most recently, however, with the rise of the indigenous rights movement, Mbororo identity politics has again taken a novel turn. This current phase is characterized by concurrent but divergent visions of a Mbororo future and integration in Cameroon society, be it as an indigenous minority with special entitlements due to its distinct culture, or as a Cameroonian people that wishes to be integrated on equal terms with other population groups. The concurrent negotiations of Mbororo identity and representation are ongoing. Moreover, with the growing extension of Mbororo youths to urban areas for reasons of employment, education or marriage, novel challenges are emerging and will engender new debates about what it could mean to be Mbororo.

Notes

1 The FulBe are known by various ethnonyms that differ regionally, including FulBe, Fulani, Peul, Foulah, Fellata, Halpulaar'en and Tukulor. In anglophone Cameroon, the terms FulBe, Fulani and Mbororo are used interchangeably.
2 The numerical data is derived from the cattle tax statistics of 2000/2001, made available by the Misaje Council. The number of Mbororo graziers is probably considerably higher if we single out close relatives (e.g. father and sons or brothers) who group under one grazier's name for the purpose of tax collection. The term 'grazier' was introduced in the colonial period to denote cattle herders. It will be used here interchangeably with pastoralist and herder.
3 See e.g. Boesen (1998, 1999a, 1999b), Breedveld and de Bruijn (1996), Diallo (2005: 475–76), Regis (2003), VerEecke (1993, 1996) and Virtanen (2003), to give only recent publications that explicitly engage with *pulaaku*. For a review of earlier literature on *pulaaku*, see Boesen (1999a: 54–62), Oppong (2002: 35–37) and Virtanen (2003: 25–46).
4 For notable exceptions to this tendency, see Boesen (1994, 1997) and Guichard (1996, 2000).
5 Compared to feedback on Nchaney history, Mbororo interlocutors' responses were fewer, which is largely due to the fact that the majority of Mbororo are not literate in English. However, two major criticisms emerged. Firstly, informants criticized our focus on selected lineages while omitting the migration histories of all other lineages represented in the Misaje area. This comment illustrates that their core category of identification is not the Mbororo sub-group but their specific lineage, which cannot be substituted or represented collectively. Secondly, Mbororo informants in the Misaje area were fascinated by the history of Sabga. This interest reflects the celebrity and social prestige of the Sabga community, rooted in their historical primacy in the Grassfields.

Moreover, it indicates that new trajectories of self-representation – promoted by educated Mbororo – are also gradually spreading to the peripheries.
6. The Fulfulde term *daneeji* literally means 'white'. It is at the same time the term for white zebu and the name of an Aku lineage. The Daneeji thus are 'the people of the white cattle'.
7. On the practice of *soro*, see Bocquené (2002: 119–32), Bovin (1974/75), Brackenbury (1923b: 274), Virtanen (2003: 113–21) and Whitting (1955).
8. Initially, the title *arDo* referred to the leadership of a migration group. It was a temporary position based on individual knowledge of migration routes, leadership skills and political influence (Kintz 1985).
9. *Gudaali* are stocky, short-legged zebu. The breed is from northern Cameroon, where it was developed to suit intensive grazing methods (Boutrais 1996: 395–400).
10. The lineages represented in Misaje Sub-Division comprise Gamanko'en, Daneeji, Danagu'en, Joranko'en, Bogoyanko'en, Galeeji, NaatirBe, Gorkanko'en, Butanko'en, Jallanko'en, Dauranko'en, Witi'en, Sisilbe, Ba'en (Aku lineages) and Ringimaji, Tukanko'en, Kesanko'en, Dabbanko'en, Bodi'en, Rahaji, Bawanko'en (Jaafun lineages).
11. *Ardorate* is a local (slightly corrupted) derivate from *arDo* (leader), equivalent to sultanate from sultan, emirate from emir, or *lamidate* from *laamiiDo*. It is commonly used by administrators as well as local informants.
12. This information was extrapolated from the cattle tax statistics of 2000/2001 provided by the Misaje Council, as well as from personal observation.
13. An overview and analysis of the history of the Gamanko'en in the Misaje area is provided in Pelican (2006: 168–73).
14. Another small group of Daneeji have settled near Sabongida, but they are outside the reach of this study.
15. ArDo Bala, Nfume, 16 January 2001.
16. Hajja Maimouna, Misaje, 1 December 2001.
17. ArDo Bala, Nfume, 16 January 2001.
18. The two informants here refer to Jaafun as a specific lineage and not as a sub-ethnic category.
19. Hajja Maimouna, Misaje, 1 December 2001.
20. In Cameroon there are only three Mbororo *lamidates*, namely, Sabga in the North West Region, Didango in the West Region and Lompta in the Adamawa Region. All other *lamidates* are Town FulBe (Huya) *lamidates*.
21. *Imam* is the title for a Muslim cleric or prayer leader. It originates from Arabic and is used in Fulfulde and Hausa.
22. The use of Arabic script for writing short notes or letters is not uncommon among Mbororo. Many have undergone a basic Islamic education and are familiar with the Arabic script, while only few have acquired a Western education.
23. The text refers to the Sabga rulers by the title *arDo* instead of *laamiiDo*.
24. Imam Umaru, Sabga, 15 November 2000 (original in Fulfulde).
25. On the collective self-depiction of pastoral FulBe as marginalized and feeble, see also Boesen (1994, 1997) and Guichard (1998) for Benin, and Dafinger (2013: 144–56) and Dafinger and Pelican (2002, 2006) for Burkina Faso.
26. Following Hickey (2007), Mbororo informants in Sabga recollected that, during a visit to the North West Region, President Ahidjo actively discouraged them from engaging in politics.

27 A rival to MBOSCUDA is SODELCO (Société de Développement d'Elevage et du Commerce). While both organizations were founded around the same period, SODELCO does not define itself as an ethnic but occupational association, and is open to cattle rearers of all ethnic backgrounds. Its main clientele, however, is wealthy Mbororo cattle rearers. The relationship between SODELCO and MBOSCUDA has been strained from the start due to ideological differences as well as personal rivalries between the associations' leaders. In terms of community development and ethnic lobbying, MBOSCUDA has outweighed SODELCO by far.
28 MBOSCUDA press release, Bamenda, 16 March 2005.
29 Anglo-Arabic schools are co-educational schools that provide primary school education in English as well as instruction in Arabic language and Muslim religion.
30 In its pilot phase from 1998 to 2003, Ballotiral operated exclusively in Donga-Mantung. After the programme was completed, the project team disintegrated and MBOSCUDA took over their activities and extended them to all seven divisions of the North West Region (Duni et al. 2009; Hickey 2002).
31 See 'La Constitution de la Republique du Cameroun. Loi No 96–06 du 18 Janvier 1996', p. 1, and English version 'Constitution of the Republic of Cameroon, Law No. 96–06 of 18 January 1996 to amend the Constitution of 2 June 1972', p. 2
32 The indigenous rights discourse has gained traction in many parts of Africa (see also Feyissa and Zeleke 2015; Hodgson 2011; Maruyama 2010; Maruyama and Pelican 2015; Pelican 2015). For the case of, Kenya, Schlee (2012) gives an example of how different actors have used and abused parts of his academic writings to claim indigeneity.

4
A Shift to Economic Competition?
Farmer–Herder Conflict and Cattle Theft in the Misaje Area

At the heart of this chapter is the question of why farmer–herder conflict, a long-standing and pertinent issue widely addressed in research and policy across West Africa, continues to be perceived in ethnic terms – despite economic diversification and alternative lines of conflict. To resolve this conundrum, I will examine transformations in the economic activities of Grassfielders and Mbororo, and the ways these transformations have impacted on the groups' socio-economic relations. Moreover, I will address two sources of public contention – farmer–herder disputes and cattle theft – and analyse them in their practical and discursive dimensions. As I argue, it is only by taking into account colonial and postcolonial economic policies as well as the role of governmental and non-governmental agents that we can understand the endurance of established discourses and ethnic stereotypes that characterize the perception of farmer–herder relations in the Cameroon Grassfields.

Farming and Herding in the Misaje Area

The two main production systems practised in the Grassfields are shifting cultivation and extensive grazing. My descriptions are limited to the Misaje area, as there are slight variations in farming and herding practices in different regions of the Grassfields.

The majority of Grassfielders in the Misaje area make their living from farming. Within Grassfields societies, the cultivation of food crops is generally considered the responsibility of women, while men concentrate on cultivating tree and cash crops, such as palm trees, fruit trees, kola nut trees and coffee. The main crops cultivated in the research area are maize, coco yam, sweet potato, beans, sugar cane and a variety of vegetables. Ecologic conditions and crop preferences vary slightly within Misaje Sub-Division. The Nchaney area is known for its small-scale coffee and palm oil plantations, which are complementary to subsistence agriculture. Bessa territory extends to the upland region of the Nkambe Plateau; it supports the cultivation of groundnuts and fruit trees, such as plantain, banana and mango. Dumbo is renowned for its red groundnuts, a particularly oily species preferred for the production of groundnut oil and snacks. Around Misaje town, cassava is cultivated, a perennial crop introduced by migrants from the Bamenda area. The climatic conditions and soil quality in the Misaje lowlands render farming quite a challenge. Most of the soil is stony and sandy, and the temperature is generally higher than in the Bamenda Highlands. Grassfields farmers prefer to cultivate along the valleys, which are cooler and moister than the hilltops. They practice shifting cultivation and enhance the soil fertility via mixed cropping. The majority of local farmers cultivate only rainy-season crops. Dry-season farming is relatively rare and limited to riversides and swampy areas.

Maize is the main food crop. It is consumed on a daily basis as maize porridge, which is the staple dish of the area. Moreover, it is processed into maize beer (Pidgin English: *shah*) which is extensively consumed during social gatherings and in drinking places (so-called *shah houses*). Frequently, Nchaney and Bessa farmers are not able to cultivate enough maize for home consumption and beer brewing to last throughout the year. During the months before the new harvest, families rely on alternative crops, such as sweet potato and coco yam. As the corresponding meals are considered of lower quality and nutritional value than maize porridge, this period is generally experienced and framed as one of scarcity and hunger.

The predicament of seasonal scarcity has also coloured the reputation of local Grassfielders among neighbouring groups. Informed by Muslim doctrine, Mbororo and Hausa tend to view their Grassfields neighbours as drunkards because of their consumption of maize beer.[1] In the eyes of migrants from the Bamenda area, local Grassfielders are lazy because they cultivate only once a year. From the perspective of Nchaney and Bessa farmers, however, it is more reasonable to complement their farming with alternative economic activities, such as working for their Mbororo neighbours, than cultivating dry-season crops that run the risk of being eaten by cattle.

Animal husbandry is practised by members of all population groups in the Misaje area. While many Grassfielders tend poultry, goats and occasionally pigs, the Mbororo constitute the majority of cattle herders in the Grassfields. They live with their families and herds 'in the bush'. Their compounds are situated in their animals' grazing area and within walking distance (between thirty minutes and three hours) of the nearest farmers' hamlet.

The majority of Mbororo in the Misaje area are Aku. They mainly rear white zebu (*daneeji*), *gudaali* (a cattle breed introduced from northern Cameroon) and cross-breeds that are well adapted to the hot and humid climate of the Misaje lowlands. The area offers good pasture and extensive grazing land, though herders have noticed signs of pasture degradation, such as the vanishing of certain grass species or the spread of shrubs and trees. During the dry season, most Mbororo in the Misaje lowlands graze their animals in swampy areas and along riverbanks. A few herders undertake short-distance, seasonal transhumance, mostly within Misaje Sub-Division.

Pastoral duties are shared among family members (Pelican 1999: 41–53). Cattle herding is the domain of youths.[2] During the day, boys and occasionally girls take the animals to alternating pasture grounds and watering points within their grazing area. In the evening, they drive them back to the compound where the cattle spend the night in a paddock, often just a fenced plot, so as to prevent them from straying onto neighbours' farms. Calves and cows are kept apart at night, and dams are milked in the morning. The processing and selling of milk is considered the women's domain. Aku women in the Misaje area are generally accustomed to selling milk, but often the yields are low and just enough for home consumption. Among Jaafun, the practice of selling milk has become stigmatized as a sign of backwardness and poverty, and as contradicting Islamic rules of modesty (Pelican 1999: 118–125; 2004b). The overall responsibility for animal health and herd management lies with the household head. He regularly checks on his animals, provides them with salt and medical treatment, and frequents the nearby cattle markets to keep himself informed about cattle prices and pastoral developments.

Mbororo generally do not produce for the market, though sporadically they are required to sell single animals to cover their living expenses (Pelican 2012a). Almost all herders are agro-pastoralists, complementing cattle husbandry with subsistence agriculture. Many Mbororo herders in the Misaje area have relatively small herds of thirty to fifty animals. However, there are also very wealthy herders with many hundred cattle who entrust their animals to hired herdsmen.

Mediating Farmer–Herder Relations

As Grassfielders are generally associated with farming and Mbororo with herding, their economic relations are commonly framed in terms of farmer–herder relations. There is a substantial body of academic literature on this subject. At the same time, many governments and international development organizations are interested in applied studies on which they may draw in devising economic policies (Hussein 1998). In the following I will give a brief overview of academic research on farmer–herder relations in western Africa. Secondly, I will outline administrative policies shaping farmer–herder relations in northwest Cameroon.

Researchers differ in their assessments of farmer–herder relations. The general frame of reference, however, is defined by the poles of economic complementarity or symbiosis on the one hand, and competition or conflict on the other. In the classical literature on FulBe in West Africa, the relationship between pastoral FulBe and their farming neighbours is often depicted as symbiotic, and characterized by economic complementarity and interdependence (e.g. Dupire 1970; Stenning 1959). This perspective is upheld by current research; according to Diallo (2001, 2008), for example, FulBe in western Burkina Faso and northern Côte d'Ivoire are integrated into local society by virtue of their economic specialization and take part in an ethnic division of labour. This interpretation ties in with Schlee's model of 'integration through difference' (Schlee 2001). However, in much of the recent literature on farmer–herder relations, an alternative assessment prevails. The relationship is no longer described as inherently symbiotic and complementary but as overshadowed by competition and conflict over natural resources.[3]

As Breusers et al. (1998) rightly pointed out, farmer–herder relations – potentially everywhere and at any time – entail competition and conflict over natural resources; concurrently, they include friendly and mutually beneficial relationships. The stress on either symbiotic or conflictual aspects of farmer–herder relations is thus partly the result of emic and academic discourses. At the same time, it is virtually impossible to provide a general assessment of farmer–herder relations, as they are embedded in their respective historical and regional contexts. I thus believe that a comparative approach, as Andreas Dafinger and I have pursued elsewhere (Dafinger and Pelican 2002, 2006), is most fruitful in producing new insights. As we have argued, some of the most significant factors in shaping farmer–herder relations – besides ecological, demographic and political conditions – are the presence or absence of historically produced interethnic alliances as well as different administrative and legal frameworks. In many parts of West Africa, FulBe presence dates back to the pre-colonial period, and disputes between farmers and herders are normally resolved at the local level; that is, between the parties to the conflict themselves or via the mediation of local institutions. In other areas, such as northwest Cameroon, FulBe pastoralists are relative newcomers. Here, from the very start, farmer–herder relations have been mediated by the colonial and later postcolonial administration with the aim of securing government interests. Consequently, state agents are a relevant third party in dispute settlement.[4] As we will see below, the involvement of state agents is generally considered to be driven by self-interest and corruption, and thought to perpetuate and aggravate farmer–herder disputes.

The coexistence of farmers and herders in northwest Cameroon coincided with the advent of the British colonial period. In the 1930s, British administrators firstly addressed the issue of recurrent confrontations between Grassfields farmers and Mbororo herders. At the same time, they faced difficulties in reconciling their interests and liabilities vis-à-vis the two population groups. On the one hand, they endorsed the presence of the Mbororo and their herds as a means of diversifying the regional economy and of augmenting their tax income. On the other, they were obliged to consider Grassfielders' concerns, since they constituted the majority population. The British subsequently experimented with varying approaches, but never succeeded in eradicating the sources of farmer–herder conflict (Boutrais 1996: 772–802; Chilver 1989; Frantz 1986; Njeuma and Awasom 1989, 1990). Most consequential among these varying policies was the idea of spatial separation. By allocating farmers and herders separate user zones, the colonial administration reduced not only the potential for conflict, but also the possibilities for social interaction and mutual integration (Dafinger and Pelican 2002, 2006). Moreover, by encouraging the coexistence of economically specialized entities that corresponded to distinct ethnic groups, the British endorsed complex ethno-occupational identities.

In the French administered zone of Cameroon, the situation was different. The French colonial administration adopted a relatively lax attitude regarding the administration of the pastoral sector and farmer–herder relations (Boutrais 1996: 176–85). By contrast, the British tended to overemphasize the potential for conflict between farmers and herders. They thus endorsed corresponding discourses and shaped farmers' and herders' perceptions of each other. Moreover, with their shifting policies that favoured graziers and farmers alternately, they influenced both groups' expectations towards the postcolonial government.

With Cameroon's independence, the French administrative system became more influential in the design of contemporary state policies; however, regional variations have endured. In the North West Region, the spatial division of farming and grazing zones has remained operative, and the administration is still charged with the mediation of farmer–herder disputes. The prescribed administrative procedure is relatively complicated, and individuals frequently explore alternative legal avenues.

In the field of economic policies, there has been a shift towards encouraging economic diversification across ethno-occupational groups (Moritz 2006). These policies are informed by the idea of economic growth via rural development and market production. At the same time, they rest on the assumption that economic diversification contributes to the improvement of farmer–herder relations. Comprehensive knowledge of both economic systems and a better understanding of each other's predicaments are thought to enhance mutual sympathy and cooperation.

Economic Diversification in Northwest Cameroon

In the Grassfields, the process of economic diversification started in the colonial period. For farmers this meant the introduction of new productive resources, primarily cash crops and cattle; for herders it entailed incentives to adopt a sedentary lifestyle. Yet legal entitlement to cultivate within grazing areas was provided only in 1962, and the size of farming plots was restricted to 0.4 hectares per family.

In the 1980s many governmental and international development organizations ran programmes to diversify and intensify farming and grazing methods. Most of them, however, failed in the long run and had no significant impact on farmer–herder relations. Another factor promoting economic diversification, however, was the nationwide economic crisis that set in during the late 1980s and fully impacted on rural and urban populations in the 1990s. In particular, impoverished Mbororo saw the exigency of taking up agriculture as an alternative to or as complementing their herding activities. Grassfielders, on the other hand, tended to concentrate on farming and to withdraw from cattle husbandry, which is a capital intensive activity. At the same time, the 1990s also witnessed an increase in criminal activity, which in the Misaje area expressed itself in a growing rate of cattle theft. Thus, while the economic crisis did not initiate a process of economic diversification, it significantly contributed to competition within and between ethnic groups.

Mbororo Agro-pastoralism

Mbororo have long been identified with cattle husbandry by their Grassfields neighbours and the colonial and postcolonial administrations. They generally stress their pastoral identity and consider alternative economic activities, such as farming or trade, subsidiary. Nowadays, most Mbororo in the Grassfields are agro-pastoralists. However, Jaafun and Aku differ in their attitudes to agriculture and in their farming practices.

Among Jaafun lineages, practising agriculture is associated with low esteem. Upon their establishment in the Grassfields, many Jaafun families benefited from the favourable ecological and climatic conditions of the highlands. Thanks to the productivity of local farming communities, they were able to supply themselves with food crops via barter and purchase. In conjunction with increasing wealth and sedentarization, many Jaafun invested in augmenting their herds and families, as well as in Islamic scholarship, while farming became stigmatized as emblematic of Grassfielders or *haaBe* (non-Mbororo). Furthermore, many Jaafun exhibit a rather resentful attitude towards physical labour, thus looking down on their Grassfields neighbours who, on the contrary, appreciate physical robustness and stamina. In return, Grassfielders tend to view the Mbororo – in particular their women – as lazy, weak and conceited.

Aku herders, on the other hand, entered the Grassfields only in the second half of the twentieth century and missed the era of pastoral success. They have a different attitude to farming. The familiarity of many Aku lineages with agriculture dates back far into the past. A number of individuals pride themselves on their farming expertise and successfully bolster their pastoral activities with agriculture. A significant difference between the farming practices of Aku and Grassfielders lies in their respective systems of the division of labour. While women are the primary farmers among Grassfielders, Aku women are exempted from heavy tasks and only participate in planting and harvesting. The majority of farm work is done by men and children and by hired farm labourers.

Due to increasing economic hardship over the past twenty to thirty years, farming has generally become more popular among Mbororo in the Grassfields. Consequently, many Mbororo families cultivate larger plots than the officially acknowledged 0.4 hectares. The practice of employing local farmers to cultivate their farms or refurbish their compounds is common among pastoral FulBe in various parts of West Africa, and contributes to their socio-economic integration into local communities (e.g. Waters-Bayer and Bayer 1994; Vabi 1991). Aku interlocutors explained that they often hire the same men and women over consecutive years. Over time, some of the work relationships have developed into friendships (Pelican 2004a, 2012b).

Local farming women frequently work for Mbororo when they need cash for specific occasions (such as church contributions, group meetings, celebrations) or when they lack maize for home consumption or the production of maize beer. Since they are busy cultivating their own farms, they only take on work on small plots which require a few days' work. Conversely, men are more reluctant to work on Mbororo farms, as many consider it beneath their dignity to cultivate other people's land. A few younger men, however, engage in farm work as a form of seasonal labour. They arrange for a number of larger consecutive contracts, working different people's farms and make a considerable amount of money.[5]

Most farm labourers I talked to were quite happy and satisfied with their current work arrangements. Some recalled negative experiences with Mbororo who paid low salaries or treated them badly. Others claimed that they would rather give someone a helping hand than work for 'a slave's salary', an argument that was primarily rhetorical and politically motivated. The practice of local Grassfielders working for Mbororo has occasionally been politicized by Grassfields chiefs or members of the local Grassfields elite who see it as a source of inequality and potential conflict. Fon Richard, for example, claimed that herders did not initially cultivate farms but bought food crops from Grassfields farmers, and herewith supported the local economy. Conversely, by exploiting Grassfields women's labour, they contributed to the creation of poverty and hunger. As he argued, women were seduced to spend money on luxury items instead of cultivating food for their families. While these may be genuine concerns, his disapproval was also informed by the critical impact of salaried work on the occasional free labour provided by his subjects on his farms, a chiefly prerogative. Similarly, as we will see in Chapter 7, Grassfields elite associations consider the collective refusal to collaborate with graziers – that is, neither working on their farms nor selling crops to them – an effective strategy for expressing their discontent with their Mbororo neighbours.

The Emergence of Native Graziers in the Misaje Area

In the same way that Mbororo became agro-pastoralists, Grassfields farmers ventured into cattle husbandry. Initially, Grassfielders only knew semi-feral dwarf cattle that were kept at chiefs' palaces for ritual consumption (Boutrais 1998; Chilver and Kaberry 1967). With the arrival of the Mbororo, zebu cattle entered northwest Cameroon, and beef gradually became accessible to the wider population.

In the early twentieth century, cattle husbandry was the exclusive domain of the Mbororo. Yet, as Grassfielders and Mbororo got accustomed to each other, and as Grassfields individuals successfully accumulated capital through trade or cash-crop production, they developed an interest in cattle husbandry. A new category of cattle herders emerged, known as 'native graziers'.[6] Grassfields chiefs were among the first to build up their own cattle herds on the basis of gifts and tributes demanded from Mbororo immigrants. They were followed by well-to-do Grassfielders who invested in cattle husbandry as a means of augmenting their wealth, as well as by Grassfields individuals who worked as herdsmen for Mbororo and were paid in calves (Njeuma and Awasom 1990).

Among all Grassfields societies, the Pinyin earned the reputation of being skilled graziers and cattle traders.[7] Their affinity for cattle husbandry may be rooted in their pre-colonial specialization in rearing small livestock (Warnier 1985: 36–47). Many are farmers as well as cattle graziers, and entertain close economic and social relations with their Mbororo neighbours. Pinyin migrants are well represented among native graziers in Misaje. Before the introduction of public education, Pinyin boys frequently stayed with Mbororo families for an apprenticeship in cattle rearing.[8] The Pidgin English-Fulfulde derivation *boy na'i* or *boyjo*, meaning 'cattle boy', is generally used in referring to a Grassfields

Table 4.1: Cattle herding statistics for the Misaje area, 2000/2001. Sources: Misaje Council, 2000/2001; author's fieldwork.

Misaje Sub-Division	Mbororo		Local Grassfielders		Grassfields migrants		Hausa		Totals	
registered graziers	407	87%	29	6%	23	5%	10	2%	469	100%
cattle owned	17,734	87.5%	902	4.5%	1,279	6%	385	2%	20,300	100%
average herd size	44 animals		31 animals		56 animals		38.5 animals		43 animals	

(often Pinyin) herdsman, while a Mbororo herdsman is called by the Fulfulde term *gaynaako* (pl. *waynaaBe*). Over time, individuals across all ethnic groups engaged in cattle husbandry, which has generally become an accepted economic activity.

Table 4.1 details the ratio of cattle ownership among different categories of graziers in Misaje Sub-Division. The calculation is based on the *jangali* (cattle tax) statistics of 2000/2001 made available by the Misaje Council. The distinction by ethnic background, however, has been made on the basis of additional information collected by my research team, as ethnicity is not a valid parameter in cattle tax statistics.

Local Grassfielders in the Misaje area developed an interest in cattle rearing as a result of the permanent establishment of Aku herders. With the emergence of neighbourhood and friendship relations between the two groups, a few adventurous individuals began to rear their own cattle.

Cattle rearing is generally considered a male enterprise. Compared to farming, it is a relatively new and supplementary activity for Grassfielders, and hence occupies a subordinate position in their scale of values. As Fon Richard explained, it is considered 'a borrowed culture; that is, to have cattle is just a means of investing money'. The decision to engage in cattle husbandry is taken individually, and there is generally no correlation of economic activities between related households.

Native graziers differ to some extent from Mbororo herders in their aims and practices of cattle rearing. Cattle are not kept for milk or meat but with the aim of reproduction and marketing. Furthermore, native graziers tend to practise less extensive grazing than Mbororo, keeping their animals close to their compounds or within a limited grazing range. While Mbororo herders fence their farms, native graziers prefer to enclose their grazing area so as to prevent cattle from straying into their own and other people's farms.

Native graziers learned the handling of cattle from their Mbororo neighbours. A Nchaney interlocutor, whose father was among the first native graziers, described some of the tasks: taking the animals to drinking points, occasionally feeding them salt and locking them in the night paddock. He stressed his familiarity with most technical aspects of cattle herding. Furthermore, he prided himself on communicating with his father's cattle in Fulfulde, which he learned from his Mbororo friends.

Local Grassfielders' engagement with cattle rearing impacted positively on interethnic relations; pre-existent friendships were intensified and new relationships emerged. The integrative property of Grassfielders' economic diversification was most effective in the initial phase, when native graziers depended on their Mbororo neighbours for professional instruction and assistance. At a later stage, however, Nchaney graziers decided to detach themselves from Mbororo herders for administrative purposes. While farmers were required to pay poll tax, graziers were taxed according to the number of their animals. Native graziers were asked to pay *jangali* (cattle tax) to the Mbororo *arDo* charged with its collection. This arrangement continued until the late 1970s, when Nchaney graziers felt that Mbororo *arDo'en* (pl. of *arDo*) treated them unfairly and suspected them of misusing their tax receipts. Consequently, they asked the administration to appoint a Nchaney *arDo*. In the administrative understanding, an *arDo* is not a political leader but a person representing cattle herders and their liabilities and interests to the state. Thus an *arDo* functions as a tax collector, supervises inoculations and is involved in the administration of grazing land. The separation of native and Mbororo graziers occurred in such a pronounced way only in the Nchaney area because of the sheer number of graziers and cattle. Conversely, in other areas, the group of native graziers was too small or ethnically diverse to gain enough strength and stand on its own.

The 1980s were the heyday of native cattle grazing in the Misaje area. Subsequently, herds gradually began to diminish, and individuals became disheartened and gave up. For example, the number of Nchaney graziers reduced from twenty-eight in 1983 to eleven in 2000. Informants mentioned cattle theft as the primary source of their losses. Besides that, a couple of internal factors contributed to the decline of native cattle grazing. In the beginning, native graziers were interested in learning all details of cattle rearing; after some time, however, they realized that successful cattle husbandry required the herders' familiarity with animal needs and a profound knowledge of cattle diseases. With rising cattle numbers, many native graziers turned to employing Mbororo herdsmen to take care of their animals. Around the same period, the reputation of school education as a road to government jobs reached the countryside. As several interlocutors outlined, parents preferred to send their own children to school than to do an apprenticeship in cattle grazing.

This shift from cooperating with Mbororo neighbours – in order to learn the practicalities of cattle rearing – to employing Mbororo herdsmen includes not only a change in the assessment of cattle grazing, but also in the perception of interethnic relations. While native grazing became an expression of individual affluence, Mbororo graziers have increasingly been associated with paid herdsmanship and life 'in the bush'. Furthermore, by employing professional herdsmen, the responsibility for the herd has shifted from the cattle owner to the *gaynaako* (herdsman), who most often is a young man and receives only a small salary. The *gaynaako*, on the other hand, considers himself just a workman, and has little interest in the well-being of the herd other than getting his payment. This predicament is not particular to native graziers but to all graziers employing herdsmen (Moritz et al. 2011).

Other factors limiting the success of native graziers emerged from within Grassfields communities. Envy is generally considered a crucial negative social factor and is thought to be at the roots of witchcraft assaults and related attempts at thwarting individual success. Among Grassfielders, the family and close social environment count as the prime source of occult aggression. Native grazing, commonly perceived as an expression of individual affluence, is thus liable to attract the envy of relatives, friends and neighbours. Furthermore, jealousy is also thought to colour the relationship between farmers and native graziers, particularly in the face of crop damage. Thus, native graziers see themselves confronted with the envy of their relatives and friends as well as their Mbororo neighbours, whom they hold responsible for frequent incidents of cattle theft. Against the background of these multiple adversities, for many Grassfielders, cattle husbandry has become an economic and social burden rather than a source of status and wealth.

Transformations in Interethnic Relations

The process of economic diversification has impacted significantly on socio-economic and political relations between Grassfielders and Mbororo in the Misaje area. Informants recognized both positive and negative effects regarding their own situation and the coexistence of the two population groups.

The majority of Grassfielders approve of Mbororo cultivating their own farms. It is considered fair and normal that every individual should have the opportunity to produce enough food to support their family. However, queries arise when Mbororo farming activities exceed the subsistence level, and individuals begin to sell their food produce in the market. As interlocutors occasionally remarked, Mbororo not only sell animals and animal products, such as cattle, sheep, horses and milk, but also goats, fowl, guinea fowl and eggs – goods initially provided by Grassfields farmers. Moreover, their farms seem to produce so well that some Mbororo are able to sell maize, coco yam, sweet potato and cassava, as well as vegetables and spices, which are also the main products of Grassfields farmers. Over and above Mbororo competition in the market, Grassfields farmers are concerned that the government privileges graziers' claims to land over farmers' needs.

Conversely, from the perspective of many Mbororo, the positive effects of graziers' and farmers' economic diversification prevail. In contrast to the widespread conviction of administrators and Grassfields individuals that Mbororo herders dislike native graziers, Mbororo interlocutors acknowledged their presence, and some entertained friendly relations with them. Many herdsmen, however, considered work arrangements with native graziers more of a nuisance than a benefit. Taking into account the generally low rate of remuneration and the risk of animal disease and cattle theft, they expressed their reluctance to assume the responsibility for native graziers' animals.

By cultivating their own food, Mbororo have not only modified economic but also political relations with their farming neighbours. In the initial phase of their establishment in the Grassfields, Mbororo herders were dependent on Grassfields farmers for their food supply and access to grazing land. Grassfielders, on the other hand, relied on the Mbororo for providing meat which, before their arrival, was available only through hunting and rearing small livestock. With growing self-sustainability, Mbororo dependency has not only decreased but also changed in character. Mbororo no longer rely on local Grassfielders for farm produce but labour; that is, they have switched from being customers to employers, while Grassfields farmers have become clients and – as their chiefs and elite associations see it – have submitted themselves to a situation of economic 'enslavement'.

In assessing the impact of economic diversification on intergroup relations, a shift from economic complementarity to competition is observable, namely in the field of commerce and over limited natural resources such as land. At the same time, economic relations between Grassfielders and Mbororo continue to entail various forms of interdependency, though no longer at the production level but that of services. In consequence, socio-political relations have changed as well. While Grassfielders expressed their concern that the power balance between themselves and Mbororo has shifted to their detriment, Mbororo are increasingly confident of their integral economic position within local and regional society, a development that also contributed to bolstering their political self-confidence, as illustrated in Chapter 3.

Farmer–Herder Disputes and Cattle Theft: Economic Conflicts and Discourses

Farmer–herder disputes and cattle theft are both current issues of public contention in the Grassfields. Farmer–herder disputes date back to the early twentieth century, and have been a persistent concern of the colonial and postcolonial governments. Similarly, incidents of cattle theft have occurred ever since the introduction of cattle into the region. The current extent of cattle theft, however, is a feature of the 1990s.[9]

While the subject of farmer–herder conflict has been central to my research, it turned out to be challenging in methodological terms. First-hand observation of actual incidents was hardly feasible, and it was only in 2009 that I had the opportunity to personally witness a case, albeit in a different region of the Grassfields. I base my analysis on administrative documents as well as conversations with individuals and parties involved in farmer–herder disputes. Moreover, I draw on a staged performance by the local NGO Ballotiral that produced additional insights by approaching the subject from different angles. Firstly, it allowed me to observe the interactive dimension and the dynamics of conflict that are difficult to reconstruct from interviews. Secondly, the Ballotiral play not only utilized but palpably illustrated the popular discourses and ethnic stereotypes commonly associated with farmer–herder conflict.

As I argue, there is a tendency among Grassfielders, Mbororo and administrators to draw on established discourses in describing farmer–herder disputes and cattle theft, and to frame both issues as conflicts between ethnic groups. Yet in taking a closer look at actual incidents in the Misaje area, it becomes apparent that the situation is much more complex, and that popular discourses of farmer–herder conflict and cattle theft should not be taken at face value, but as idioms of economic rivalry rooted in their respective historical and regional contexts.

Farmer–Herder Disputes in the Cameroon Grassfields

Farmer–herder disputes have been a common feature of the coexistence of Grassfielders and Mbororo in northwest Cameroon. Particularly in the densely populated Bamenda Highlands, incidents of crop damage, the blockage of water points and mutual encroachment have been frequent and have strained the relationship between the two groups. At the root of these conflicts is a complex interplay of ecological, demographic, economic and political factors.

The Bamenda Highlands are fertile and support agriculture as well as cattle husbandry. Grassfielders and Mbororo both practise extensive economic systems that require access to large plots of land and are hardly compatible with a system of mixed farming. Thus, with increasing population density, competition over land has increased as well. As several authors have argued, gender differences within Grassfields society are a crucial factor promoting farmer–herder conflicts (Chilver 1989; Kaberry 1952; Ottiger 1996).[10] Moreover, they have largely been ignored by policy makers who effectively, though inadvertently, contributed to the deterioration of farmer–herder relations. Since the colonial period, economic programmes, such as the introduction of cash crops and mixed-farming schemes, have generally been addressed to the male population, who are also in charge of almost all political decisions. Conversely, women, who are the main food producers within Grassfields societies, have been sidelined, and their need to secure farmland has been ignored. As a consequence, competition over natural resources has increased both within Grassfields societies and between Grassfielders and Mbororo. In addition, with the institution of the farmer–grazier commission, administrative procedures have been further complicated, if not obfuscated. Moreover, farmers and herders have become frustrated with widespread practices of corruption, court delays and pending cases. Grassfields farmers have reacted to this situation with public protest, demanding that the administration limits Mbororo graziers' access to land. Occasionally, demonstrations have culminated in violent altercations (Ritzenthaler 1960; Westermann 1992). There are, however, regional differences in the degree of conflict between Grassfields farmers and Mbororo graziers (Harshbarger 1995).

In the Misaje area, farmer–herder conflicts have been less frequent and severe than in most parts of the Bamenda Highlands. Factors supporting a lower rate of crop damage and land disputes are primarily ecological and demographic. Compared to the Bamenda Highlands, the population density in the Misaje area is relatively low, and as informants generally asserted, there is abundant land for farmers and herders. Moreover, the cultivation of dry season crops, which due to the seasonal scarcity of fresh grass are prone to be eaten by cattle, is limited. As a consequence, farmer–herder disputes centre mainly on riverine areas that are of interest to both economic groups.

In my work with Andreas Dafinger (Dafinger and Pelican 2002, 2006), we suggest that the spatial separation of farmers and herders may contribute to the intensification of farmer–herder conflict, as it limits social interaction and the mutual integration of the two population groups. Considering regional differences within the Cameroon Grassfields, this situation applies mainly to the Bamenda Highlands. Conversely, in the Misaje area, Grassfielder and Mbororo compounds are interspersed, and their proximity favours the settlement of farmer–herder disputes at an interpersonal level.

Established Discourses of Farmer–Herder Conflict
Despite regional variations in the frequency and intensity of actual farmer–herder conflicts, ethnicized discourses of farmer–herder dispute are popular throughout the Grassfields. These discourses are characterized by the deployment of formulaic arguments and ethnic stereotypes that are rooted in the colonial period and widely shared among the region's inhabitants as well as government agents.

In the following I explore discourses of farmer–herder conflict on the basis of a play scripted and performed by Ballotiral. Ballotiral was a partnership organization operating between 1998 and 2003 that focused on the improvement of the socio-economic and political situation of Mbororo in northwest Cameroon. It involved the collaboration of three regional NGOs, including MBOSCUDA, and counted among its staff individuals of both Mbororo and Grassfields background, many of whom were experienced in using 'theatre for development' techniques in their community work.

The benefits of basing my analysis on staged role play, rather than exclusively on observational or interview data, are rooted in the nature of drama and performance. Drama as a theatrical form uses the expression of conflict as a way of communicating its content. Moreover, in contrast to everyday life, a staged performance allows for mockery, criticism and the candid expression of conflicting views and practices, as it has no immediate effect on actual social relations. Finally, in assessing the accuracy of a staged performance, it is important to take into account the presenters' intentions and the context in which the play is performed. Thus, in addition to analysing the play, I will also discuss Ballotiral's aims and the audience's responses to the event.

In January 2001, Ballotiral convened a one-day seminar, 'Farmer–Grazier Conflict: Awareness and Transformation'. The event was held in Nkambe, the divisional headquarters and neighbouring town to Misaje, and representatives of the administration and the different population groups were invited. The initiative was not motivated by any particular event but by a general desire to improve interethnic relations by alerting farmers, herders and civil servants to their rights and duties. Just over a hundred participants attended the seminar. More than 60 per cent of the workshop participants were officials, representing government services and non-governmental organizations, roughly 25 per cent were representatives of the Mbororo community and nearly 15 per cent represented local Grassfields communities. The meeting included a number of instructional speeches by administrators and development practitioners, a staged performance by the Ballotiral drama group, general discussions and the formulation of resolutions.

For the purpose of the meeting, the Ballotiral staff devised a play in which they portrayed a farmer–herder dispute in its most simplistic form, pitting Mbororo graziers against Grassfields farmers and state officials (Figure 4.1).

The first act portrays the complaint of a Grassfields woman whose crops have been destroyed by trespassing cattle. We see the woman farmer arriving at the Grassfields chief's palace in tears, claiming that cattle have destroyed her entire farm and that she has been attacked by the Mbororo herdsman. The news of the incident reaches the local schoolmaster, who attempts to reconcile the two parties.

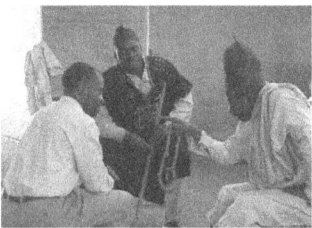

The second act focuses on the attempted resolution of the conflict by representatives of the two parties, the Grassfields chief (*fon*) and the Mbororo leader (*arDo*), mediated by a schoolmaster. The *fon* claims that his people came first and hence are the landlords of the place. Mbororo herders arrived only later, he says, but now they want to occupy the land so that nothing will be left for the farmers and their future generations. The *arDo*, on the other hand, argues that his family has stayed in the area for many decades. They have always tried to maintain good relations with the Grassfields chief, supporting him with gifts. He cunningly asks the schoolmaster, 'Would you bring your bicycle to the petrol station?'

Dissatisfied with the schoolmaster's mediation, in the third act the *arDo* seeks legal redress with a higher institution, the state counsel. The latter promises to send the farmer to jail, but concurrently warns the *arDo* of potential consequences if he does not reward the state counsel for his services. The *arDo* is scared, but gains self-confidence in view of his wealth in cattle. The *arDo* leaves the scene with the words, 'I have you all in my pocket!'

While the play could be analysed in various ways, I here concentrate on the cultural logics and ethnic stereotypes deployed by the actors. Ethnic and cultural difference is also conveyed in everyday life, yet it is in the fictitious context of a piece of educational

Figure 4.1: The enactment of farmer–herder conflict: play by the Ballotiral staff, Nkambe, 29 January 2001. Photographs by Michaela Pelican.

This play was approximately 30 minutes in length. An edited video of the event is accessible via the virtual archive of the Max Planck Institute for Social Anthropology in Halle/Saale (http://corpora.eth.mpg.de/), see M. Pelican. 2002. *Farmer–Herder Conflict: Role Play of the Ballotiral Staff* (Nkambe, 29 January 2001). Video clip, 2.46 mins, with English subtitles. File name: Conflict_RolePlay.mpeg.

theatre that it is expressed most pointedly. The stereotypes elucidated in this play include the hysterical Grassfields woman farmer, the aggressive Mbororo herdsman, the opportunistic Grassfields chief, the conceited Mbororo leader, the well-intentioned but ineffectual headmaster and the corrupt state counsel. Furthermore, the play reflects the different stages entailed in farmer–herder disputes: negotiations at the interpersonal level, at the group level and at the level involving government officials.

The first act deals with the stereotype of over-emotional and over-reactive Grassfields women. Women farmers are generally reputed to exaggerate and dramatize damage done to their farms. This assessment suggests underlying gender issues within Grassfields society (Chilver 1989; Ottiger 1996). A second stereotype refers to the allegedly aggressive behaviour of Mbororo herdsmen, who are regularly blamed for unjustly attacking Grassfields farmers. However, the Mbororo reputation of being rough refers predominantly to youths whose unruliness is also regretted by their elders.

In the second act, the matter is brought to the next higher authority, namely community leaders. The case has thus advanced to a political matter, in which not only personal but group interests are at stake. The staged confrontation between the Grassfields chief (*fon*) and the Mbororo leader (*arDo*) replicates the formulaic charges commonly exchanged between representatives of the two parties. The *fon* claims political and economic ascendancy on the grounds of his group's anteriority and his ancestral links with the land. Conversely, Mbororo leaders are generally viewed as arrogant, flaunting their economic and political influence. In the Ballotiral play, the *arDo* is portrayed as a shifty and sly person. He responds to the *fon*'s claims not by querying Grassfielders' claims to anteriority, but by emphasizing Mbororo herders' lengthy presence and their significant economic contribution to the chiefdom's development. The *arDo* thus reminds the *fon* that his power rests on Mbororo financial support, in exchange for which he should consider Mbororo interests. Thus the *arDo*'s wily question to the schoolmaster 'Would you bring your bicycle to the petrol station?' could also be interpreted as, 'Would you invest in good relations with the *fon* if he cannot offer you anything in return?'

The *arDo* is also portrayed as speaking only rudimentary Pidgin English, the lingua franca in anglophone Cameroon. Grassfields informants and administrators often interpret Mbororo individuals' lack of mastering Pidgin English as a sign of their contempt for Western education and as an impediment to progress. The headmaster, finally, represents members of an educated, liberal elite who attempt to bring the two community leaders together in order to facilitate a viable solution. This is the role administrators and NGOs like Ballotiral seek to fulfil. Yet in the view of many civil servants and NGO workers, the rural population – in their seeming backwardness and unwillingness to collaborate – frustrate all attempts at conflict resolution and economic progress.

In the last act of the play we observe a further dimension of negotiating farmer–herder relations by appealing to external institutions, namely state officials, here represented by the state counsel. It is a popular conviction that Mbororo herders prefer bribing civil servants over compensating farmers. Conversely, it is known that the backing of state officials is conditional on their generous remuneration. They are thus widely suspected of corruption and extortion, and are held responsible for exacerbating farmer–herder conflicts. The play ends with the Mbororo leader's triumphant words, 'I have you all in my pocket!' Yet everyone in the audience is aware of the decline of Mbororo wealth and the *arDo*'s self-delusion, which benefits third parties like government officials, while the occurrence of farmer–herder conflicts is perpetuated.

While Ballotiral's piece of educational theatre provides a good idea of the formulaic exchanges and ethnic stereotypes that characterize public discourse on farmer–herder conflict, there are also alternative perspectives. Here it is helpful to disaggregate the herder category and distinguish between Mbororo and native graziers. Observational and interview data suggest that native and Mbororo graziers tend to differ in their cultural logics regarding appropriate strategies in response to farmers' complaints. While native graziers tend to favour a reconciliatory approach by seeking pardon and compromise, Mbororo prefer evasive or confrontational strategies.

Many native graziers argued that farmers were more willing to compromise and reach an amicable solution if they felt that the herder sympathized with their losses. From the perspective of Grassfielders, arguing and negotiation are part of a standard process that renders the two parties equal; concurrently, they perceive refutation as insulting and as rendering them powerless. Conversely, many Mbororo and some native graziers have a different understanding of appropriate responses to farmers' complaints. They argued that farmers generally think graziers are rich, with their capital vested in cattle, and thus should pay dearly. Moreover, some Mbororo interlocutors considered it beyond their dignity to dispute publicly with agitated Grassfields farmers, arguing that the latter tended to demand outrageous sums of money for damage whose perpetrator was not clearly identified.

Yet in actual conflict situations, both Mbororo and Grassfielders may apply not only different but changing conflict strategies. For example, in a farmer–herder conflict I was able to witness in a location close to Sabga in 2009, the Mbororo herd-owner alternated between confrontation and compromise. When he was informed by his herdsman that his cow was found dead after having damaged the crops of neighbouring Grassfields farmers, he was determined to go straight to the gendarmerie and press criminal charges. Yet after sleeping on the matter, he opted for inspecting the site together with his herdsman, the farmer and the local Grassfields chief, and he invited me along. We came to understand that the cow was not killed intentionally, but had died accidentally when driven away from the damaged farm. The parties then decided to settle the issue in the palace of the Grassfields chief. During the negotiations, the Mbororo herd-owner sympathized with the Grassfields farmers, but stood firm on his claim for speedy reimbursement for the loss of his cow. Eventually, the Grassfields chief endorsed the herder's claim and ordered the farmers to reimburse him within a feasible time frame. The Mbororo herd-owner later congratulated himself for keeping a cool head and pursuing a strategy of compromise – an approach that he and many others considered useful but uncommon for Mbororo. This critical self-reflection brings us back to the ethnic stereotypes enacted in the Ballotiral play that have long informed and continue to inform public perception and policy – even in spite of divergent or much more complex everyday practices.

Ballotiral's objective was to entertain and, more importantly, to educate its audience by confronting it with its own stereotypes and predicaments in order to generate reflection and discussion about possible solutions to the farmer–herder problem. Ballotiral only partially succeeded in its endeavour. On the one hand, spectators responded to the play with laughter and affirmation, and several speakers acknowledged their own contribution to the perpetuation of farmer–herder disputes. On the other, participants tended to reiterate stereotypical allegations, giving little room to reconciliation. The resultant discussion of possible solutions remained on a hypothetical level and ended in administrative resolutions with limited practical implications.

In their work on reconciliation after violent conflict in Ghana, Kirby and Shu argue that peace building is not just a matter of discussion and negotiation but requires that both sides undergo some kind of 'cultural conversion' (Kirby and Shu 2010: 150). They see 'culture-drama' as an effective tool to experience each other's ways of thinking and acting, and posit role reversal as the crucial technique for achieving full understanding of divergent cultural pathways (Kirby and Shu 2005, 2010). In the Ballotiral play, such role reversal did not take place. Despite ambitions to the contrary, by reproducing rather than reversing popular stereotypes and discourses of farmer–herder conflict, Ballotiral may have contributed to their reinforcement.

Cattle Theft in Misaje Sub-Division

In the Misaje area, graziers and administrators seemed more concerned with frequent incidents of cattle theft than farmer–herder disputes. Cattle theft firstly became an issue in the 1980s and was one of the factors that contributed to the socio-political split between Nchaney and Mbororo graziers. In the 1990s the scale of cattle theft increased significantly, not only in Misaje but in the Grassfields in general, as well as in other parts of Cameroon (see Moritz et al. 2002, 2011). This development is largely related to the nationwide economic crisis of the late 1980s, followed by the process of political liberalization in the early 1990s. This period of radical economic and political change, accompanied by the decline of the civil state, led to an upsurge in criminal activities of which cattle theft is just one expression.

In the following I will first examine the extent to which Mbororo and native graziers in the Misaje area have been affected by cattle theft. Secondly, I will analyse popular discourses of cattle theft and their apparent ethnicization. I will base my elaborations on an administrative meeting organized by the divisional officer (DO) for graziers in Misaje Sub-Division. In addition, I will complement my analysis with information obtained from conversations with graziers and administrators.

In January 2001 the DO was alarmed by the frequency of cattle theft reported for the period over Christmas and New Year. He invited herders and civil servants to a public meeting to deliberate on possible causes and solutions. The meeting was attended by 103 people, and it was established that 223 animals had been stolen from 29 victims. Participants were invited to contribute their perspectives on the problem, and a set of recurrent arguments crystallized. The first speaker, a Mbororo man in his early forties, stood up in rage and laid blame on Mbororo, Grassfielders and state agents. He called Mbororo youths thieves, blamed local Grassfielders for collaborating with the thieves by demanding and buying stolen meat, and accused palace hierarchies and law enforcement officers of complicity by accepting bribes and releasing thieves. As I later learned, he was an alleged cattle thief himself who had been caught and imprisoned in the early 1990s. Subsequent speakers bought into his argument, stressing one or the other side's responsibility.

When the statistics of cattle theft were established during the meeting, no distinction was made between Mbororo and native graziers. On the basis of my notes, however, I was able to group victims along ethnic lines: out of the 29 victims, 11 were native graziers who had experienced a total loss of 157 cattle; 18 were Mbororo graziers who had lost 66 animals.

It is generally acknowledged that native graziers tend to experience higher losses through cattle theft than Mbororo herders. Pertinent explanations refer to interethnic rivalry between Mbororo and native graziers, intra-ethnic solidarity among Mbororo and the frequent maltreatment of hired herdsmen by native graziers. Many native graziers are convinced that Mbororo herders are envious of their success and view them as rivals over shared resources. Grassfields interlocutors complained about Mbororo herders' reluctance to assist them in pursuing stolen animals, and accused them of encouraging theft from native graziers. Moreover, they assumed that Mbororo youths felt morally and socially less restrained from robbing native graziers than their own ethnic fellows.

Mbororo interlocutors agreed with these suppositions to some extent. Yet, even within Mbororo society, solidarity is limited to the family group and social control is relatively weak. If Mbororo cattle are stolen, only close relatives and friends are expected to assist in following up on this. A number of Mbororo in the Misaje area are known or suspected cattle thieves and, apart from denouncing them to the gendarmerie, there are no internal social institutions or mechanisms to discipline and restrict them. Furthermore, Mbororo interlocutors explained that cattle theft has become a means of settling interpersonal animosities and competition between Mbororo. As they pointed out, even better-off graziers partake in cattle theft – motivated not just by a desire to enrich themselves but by jealousy, anger and a desire for vengeance against 'their own brothers'.

Another explanation for the higher losses of cattle to native graziers referred to the bad treatment of hired herdsmen. It is generally assumed that hired herdsmen show less commitment to their animals than herd-owners. Thus graziers who employ herdsmen run a higher risk of being robbed than those who take care of their animals themselves. Besides, the low payment and maltreatment of hired herdsmen further increase their frustration and may prompt misdemeanours. Native graziers and Mbororo herders differ in the way they remunerate hired herdsmen. Mbororo herders usually employ a herdsman to take care of fifty to eighty animals. The standard salary for five months work ranges between 40,000 and 60,000 CFA (€60 to €90), in addition to feeding and housing. Most native graziers have fewer cattle, which they entrust to a herdsman who joins them with his own animals. They remunerate the herdsman according to the number of cattle, paying a standard rate of 1,000 CFA (€1.50) for each animal for a period of five months. In addition, they provide catering on a weekly basis, that is, either a bucket of maize and additional food items or 1,000 CFA. Comparing the two remuneration systems, it becomes clear that the salary paid by native graziers constitutes only a supplementary income for hired herdsmen and is insufficient to live on. Thus hired herdsmen who have no alternative to augment their income may be tempted into cattle theft.

The argument that native graziers promoted the occurrence of cattle theft by maltreating their herdsmen was also raised during the administrative meeting on cattle theft in Misaje Sub-Division. In addition, blame was laid on anxious Mbororo parents, ravenous Grassfielders and corrupt state agents for preventing the successful prosecution of cattle thieves.

Ethnic Stereotypes and Discourses of Cattle Theft

Administrators and meeting participants conceived of cattle theft as involving a well-organized chain of individuals who fulfil complementary functions, from the ringleader to the thief, and then on to the middleman, the butcher, the trader and the consumer. All these roles are considered complementary and essential for the functioning of cattle theft in the Misaje area and are ascribed to different population groups. While the act of stealing is generally attributed to Mbororo youths, Grassfielders are associated with the consumption end, and state agents with facilitating illegal transactions.

Participants elaborated on the various ways Mbororo are thought to partake and contribute to the occurrence of cattle theft. Mbororo youths are generally held responsible for the act of stealing, as they are perceived to possess the required skills. Mbororo adults are blamed for failing in their parental duties and thus facilitating cattle theft. Furthermore, participants blamed Mbororo parents for the practice of posting bail for their relatives caught in the act of stealing in order to prevent disgrace to the family. These complaints against Mbororo involvement in cattle theft implied a lack of social control within Mbororo society, a concern shared by both Grassfields and Mbororo interlocutors.

In addition, Grassfielders criticized Mbororo for their reluctance to integrate into the local community; that is, to pay due respect to Grassfields authorities and to treat their neighbours as equals. Arguably, these failings have facilitated the occurrence of cattle theft. Village heads argued that they are unable to distinguish between resident Mbororo and strangers or potential thieves, as most Mbororo failed to properly introduce themselves. Moreover, many Grassfields interlocutors interpreted cattle theft as a corollary of unsettled farmer–herder problems, and native graziers accused their Mbororo neighbours of instigating cattle theft out of envy and contempt.

At the other end of the imagined producer–consumer chain are butchers, traders and clients who are thought to instigate acts of cattle theft by buying cheap meat, obviously from stolen cattle. As it was pointed out during the meeting, Grassfielders have the reputation of being voracious meat-eaters. For example, unlike Muslims, many Grassfielders do not hesitate to eat the meat of dead animals. Thus, when a cow dies accidentally, its Mbororo owner often gives the cadaver to his Grassfields neighbours or the local *fon*, who are happy recipients. Particularly during important festivities, the demand for beef is generally high, as each family group and voluntary association aims at sharing a good meal to celebrate the respective occasion. Not coincidentally, the rate of cattle theft increases cyclically, with its highest peak at Christmas and New Year. Other occasions triggering an increase in cattle theft are Islamic celebrations, when Mbororo youths may be tempted into illicitly selling their parents' or stolen cattle, as they need money for entertainment. The DO cautioned the Grassfields chiefs who attended the meeting to be alert to illegal transactions. Moreover, he emphasized that traders and butchers who did not inquire about the origin of animals or intentionally concealed the provenance of the meat they sold were considered liable of collaboration.

The third party that participants identified as collaborators in the business of cattle theft are law enforcement officers who fail to ensure the punishment of culprits, and allegedly enrich themselves by extorting money from victims as well as thieves. The native grazier Bruno, for example, was robbed of eleven animals, some of which were recovered at Ndu. He was asked to come to the gendarmerie in Ndu to identify the thief and make a statement.

> After the statement I went to eat. When I came back, the commandant told me the boy had escaped. When I received the news, death was at my hand. If I had [had] a knife or a rope, I would have killed myself. Can this be true that the brigade has only one chain [hand cuffs]!? How can that boy escape!? Now, as I am here, the person who killed me [figuratively] was the commandant of the brigade. He allowed the thief to run away. How can he catch a man who stole cattle for a million and something CFA francs and just leave him carelessly!? I would have killed myself, and my family would have been informed that I died in the brigade.[11]

While this report is rather melodramatic, it gives a fair idea of victims' desperation about the malfunctioning of state services, in particular the gendarmerie. However, not all civil servants comport themselves in the same way; often they do not support the venality of their colleagues. For example, the DO of Misaje Sub-Division tried hard to get cattle theft under control. Yet he, too, was said to accept 'gifts' of cattle and money from Mbororo whose sons were suspected cattle thieves. The DO compared the organization of cattle theft in Misaje to the Italian mafia, with individuals being threatened with having their cows stolen if they did not collaborate. During the meeting the DO emphasized that, if cattle theft were to be eliminated, it required cooperation at all levels of society, including the assistance of Mbororo herders, native graziers, traders, butchers, meat consumers, Grassfields and Mbororo leaders and civil servants. He recommended a number of measures: herders should keep their animals in paddocks overnight and check them regularly; herdsmen should not move at night; and *fon*s and *arDo*s should set up vigilante groups. The DO claimed that he was close to dismantling the Misaje cattle mafia. He also came up with administrative measures to reduce cattle theft, such as limiting cattle movement to daytime only. For their implementation, however, he needed funds which were not available. Finally, before the DO succeeded in realizing his plans, he was transferred to another sub-division. His successor was less concerned with cattle theft and focused on other issues, such as the containment of witchcraft.

As my analysis of the administrative meeting on cattle theft indicates, there is a tendency among administrators and the local population to perceive cattle theft in terms of established discourses and ethnic stereotypes. Yet, unlike in the case of farmer–herder disputes, there is no clear distinction of victims and perpetrators along ethnic lines, as both Mbororo and native graziers have been affected. Instead, cattle theft is imagined as an organized chain of criminal activity in which each group fulfils a distinct function; while Mbororo youths count as potential thieves, Grassfielders count as potential instigators and clients. In addition, corrupt state agents are thought to function as auxiliaries and to frustrate all attempts at prosecution. Thus, in the case of cattle theft and farmer–herder disputes, state agents are seen as playing a crucial role and as contributing to the perpetuation of existing conflicts.

From Complementarity to Competition?

In concluding this chapter, I address the question suggested by its title: in the course of economic diversification, have relations between Grassfielders and Mbororo evolved from complementarity to competition? Moritz (2006) asked a similar question and based his analysis on the existing literature. He concludes that the overall effect of the agro-pastoral conversion, widespread among pastoralists across Africa, on farmer–herder conflict remains unclear. With my case material I cannot offer a general answer to this question. Yet my detailed analyses of changing economic practices and intergroup relations in the Grassfields suggest that processes of economic diversification have intensified rather than reduced the potential for conflict, as competition over natural resources, particularly land, has generally increased. It would be simplistic, however, to describe farmer–herder relations as having developed from economic complementarity to competition. As outlined earlier, the relationship between the two economic groups has been overshadowed by incidents of crop damage and arguments over access to land from the moment cattle were introduced into the Grassfields. Thus, even in the early phase, when Mbororo and Grassfielders occupied distinct economic niches, their relationship was complementary only in terms of their products (meat and crops) and not with respect to their economic practices and land-use patterns. We may contend, however, that Cameroon's economic crisis and its political ramifications have contributed to economic competition within and between ethnic groups, and to what we may term competitive ethnicity.

A significant feature of farmer–herder relations in the Cameroon Grassfields is the apparent disjunction of corresponding discourses and practices, and the general tendency to frame economic conflict in ethnic terms. Similar to my distinction of discourses and practices, Breusers et al. (1998) proposed differentiating front-stage (public) and backstage (private) discourses in emic descriptions of socio-economic relations between Mossi and FulBe in Burkina Faso. There, many Mossi farmers are also cattle owners and entrust their animals to FulBe herdsmen, with whom they often entertain friendly relations. While in private they may acknowledge these relationships, in public they generally conceal any social and economic relations with FulBe herders and endorse negative ethnic stereotypes. A similar argument is made by Dafinger (2013: 144–156) regarding the relationship between FulBe and Bisa in Burkina Faso's central south, where both farmers and herders tend to conceal their social and economic relations. Dafinger here speaks of 'concealed economies [as] the hidden dimension of conflict and cooperation' (Dafinger 2013: 136).[12] A similar situation also exists in the Grassfields, though to a lesser degree and more on the side of the Mbororo than native graziers. Yet discourses on farmer–herder conflict and cattle theft in the Grassfields include a relevant third party, namely corrupt state agents.

Here we return to a point stressed before, concerning the impact of changing administrative frameworks on farmer–herder relations. By elevating farmer–herder conflict to a pertinent administrative problem, while failing to provide efficient strategies of conflict resolution, the British colonial and more so the postcolonial administration have contributed to framing the relationship between Grassfielders and Mbororo in terms of competition over natural resources, even in regions where this is actually less of a problem. Moreover, by endorsing complex ethno-occupational identities rooted in the early colonial period, governmental and non-governmental agents have contributed to the strengthening of the ethnic stereotypes which lie at the heart of discourses of farmer–herder conflict and cattle theft.

In my reading, farmer–herder conflict and cattle theft will remain an unresolved issue as long as Grassfielders, Mbororo and administrators continue to frame economic relations between the two groups in terms of established discourses and ethnic stereotypes that leave little scope for alternative approaches.

Notes

1. A similar perspective is adopted by Ndudi Umaru in assessing local farming communities in northern Cameroon (Bocquené 2002: 137).
2. For a detailed analysis of the generational division of labour among pastoral FulBe, see Boesen (1996).
3. Among the examples of problematic farmer–herder relations are case studies of FulBe pastoralists who migrated southwards into the humid areas of Ghana, Côte d'Ivoire, Nigeria and Cameroon (Bassett 1988; Blench 1994; Boutrais 1996; Diallo 1996; Harshbarger 1995; Mimche 2014; Tonah 2002; Vabi 1991; Waters-Bayer and Bayer 1994).

4   Despite historical differences, state agents and NGO representatives have become influential players in shaping farmer–herder relations in most African countries. See Bassett (1988) and Diallo (1996) on Côte d'Ivoire; Beeler-Stücklin (2009) on Mali; Dafinger (2013: 160–80) and Hagberg (1998, 2005) on Burkina Faso.
5   For example, in March 2001 I met two Grassfielders working a plot on a Mbororo grazier's farm for which they jointly were to be paid 32,000 CFA (€50) and which would take them approximately eight to nine days. Before that, they had earned 70,000 CFA (€105) working in a Mbororo neighbour's farm for three weeks. In comparison, the standard rate for a labourer's daily income is 1,000 CFA (€1.50), i.e. nearly half of the amount paid by their Mbororo employers.
6   The term 'native grazier' is based on the colonial categorization of Grassfielders as 'natives' of the Grassfields. The term is commonly used both by administrators and the general public in referring to Grassfields graziers. I will henceforth use it in the text with the same meaning.
7   The Pinyin polity is located south of the provincial capital, Bamenda. There is a considerable number of Pinyin people that have been drawn to other parts of the Grassfields, including Misaje, due to their active involvement in the cattle trade.
8   Similarly, Frantz (1981: 216) reports close socio-economic relationships between Mbororo pastoralists and rural Mambila farmers in Nigeria, which include the fostering of farmers' children.
9   While livestock raids have long been part of social and political relations between pastoral groups in East Africa, and constitute an established strategy of accumulation (Greiner 2013; Schlee 1997), there is no such understanding of cattle theft in Cameroon. Here, the abduction of animals is generally considered a criminal act.
10 Similarly, in his play 'Lake God', the Cameroonian playwright Bole Butake (1999: 14–23) dramatized conflicts over crop damage between women farmers, Mbororo herders and Grassfields chiefs. In the play, women farmers report a Mbororo herdsman to the *fon* because of crop damage. Yet the *fon* sides with the herder, as he is the original owner of the cattle he has entrusted to the Mbororo herdsman.
11 B.K., Nfume, 3 March 2002.
12 Guichard (1996, 2000) observed similar strategies of concealment among FulBe in Benin regarding their socio-economic relations with their Bariba neighbours.

5

On Being Hausa

Consolidation of the Hausa Ethnic Category in the Grassfields

Hausa presence in the Grassfields is a subject largely neglected in the scholarship on this region. The two authors who have written on the subject are the Cameroonian historian Nicodemus Awasom (1984) and the French geographer Jean Boutrais (1996), both of whom focus on the colonial and early postcolonial period. Drawing on Abner Cohen's (1969) classic study of Hausa migrants in Yoruba towns, Awasom attributes the early dispersal of Hausa settlements to their engagement in long-distance trade and their role as middlemen in the cattle business. Boutrais's primary interest is in Mbororo pastoralists and their establishment in the region; in this context, he elaborates on the close socio-economic relations between Mbororo and Hausa in the Grassfields.

In this chapter I wish to expand on these preliminary works by highlighting gendered experiences and contemporary meanings of Hausa ethnicity in the Grassfields. Furthermore, I propose considering the Hausa ethnic category not as a discrete ethnic group but as a residual category that comprises the descendants of early Hausa traders as well as individuals who for structural or personal reasons have opted out of their original community and have assumed Hausa identity. As I will show in this and the next chapter, close socio-economic relations with Mbororo pastoralists, intermarriage with Grassfields partners, and the integration of Muslim converts have been constitutive of the consolidation of the Hausa ethnic category and the formation of a Muslim moral community in the Misaje area. Thus, Hausa ethnicity in the Grassfields is composite in nature and only conceivable in relation to Mbororo and Grassfields societies.

Right from the beginning of my research it became clear that 'Hausa' is a broad and ill-defined category that comprises members of various ethnic and cultural backgrounds. The ethnonym Hausa is popularly employed as a generic

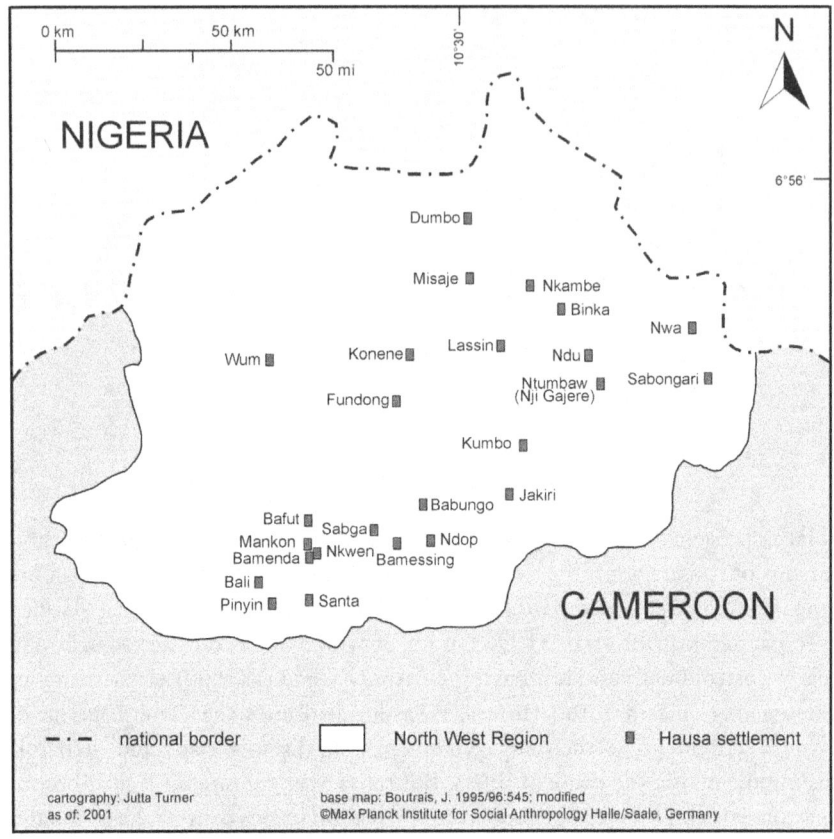

Figure 5.1: Current Hausa settlements in the North West Region. Reproduced by kind permission of the Max Planck Institute for Social Anthropology, Halle.

term for Muslim village dwellers and is also used by the latter in their ethnic self-identification. In the Grassfields, the Hausa category came into being at the beginning of the twentieth century with the arrival of traders and Muslim scholars from northern Nigeria. In time, members of other ethnic groups, such as Huya (Town FulBe) from northern Cameroon, Grassfielders who married Hausa, Huya or Mbororo partners and converted to Islam, as well as Mbororo individuals who adopted an urban lifestyle, intermingled with the descendants of early Hausa traders. They formed Muslim communities throughout the Grassfields that soon became known as Hausa quarters. Nowadays, Hausa settlements are found in more than twenty locales in the North West Region, including Misaje and Dumbo (see Figure 5.1). While on a regional scale, Hausa residents may account for less than 1 per cent of the population, they are well represented in the Misaje area, where they comprise 5 to ten 10 cent of the population of the sub-division.¹

As Hausa and non-Hausa informants frequently noted, only a few of the so-called Hausa in Misaje are of actual Hausa descent, that is, individuals who can trace back their origin to the Hausa homeland, in particular to Kano. Most were identified as Town FulBe from northern Cameroon or as Grassfielders who converted to Islam. These statements provoke two questions. Firstly, which factors have been conducive to the emergence of the Hausa ethnic category? And secondly, what does it mean to be Hausa in a Grassfields context? To answer these questions, I will draw on the existing scholarship on Hausa ethnicity and relate it to the historical trajectories and contemporary political strategies of Hausa in the research area.

Theoretical Debates on Hausa Ethnicity

The literature on Hausa speakers is substantial, as they constitute a widely dispersed linguistic and ethnic category. Firstly, they are the main population of the Hausa homeland in northern Nigeria and southern Niger. Secondly, Hausa migrant communities are found throughout West and Central Africa. The subject of Hausa identity was widely discussed in the 1960s and 1970s, particularly in studies of the Hausa diaspora in Nigeria, Ghana and Chad.² Best known is the work of Abner Cohen (1969) on Hausa migrant communities in the urban centres of southern Nigeria. Yet ethnicity also emerged as a topic in the literature on Hausaland (e.g. Adamu 1976; Barkow 1976; Nicolas 1975; Paden 1970). The following quote pointedly illustrates the difficulties researchers generally faced in delineating Hausa identity:

> There can be no cut-and-dry definition of a Hausa person. This is because different criteria were, and still are, used by different people at different times to define who was or should be regarded as Hausa. Some people used purely historical claims to Hausa ethnicity, others used cultural traits and social values as their yardstick, while others still used religion plus language. There are also people who on very rare occasions prefer to use occupational specialization in commerce. (Adamu 1976: 5)

Researchers diverge in their assessment of the Hausa ethnic category. Anthropologists who have studied Hausa in their homeland tend to characterize them as a linguistic group with a particular cultural system or civilization (e.g. Barkow 1972; Smith 1952; Sutton 1979; Wall 1988). Conversely, researchers working on the Hausa diaspora tend to comprehend them as political and economic interest groups that are organized along the criteria of religious affiliation, occupational organization, settlement pattern and language (e.g. Cohen 1966, 1974; Salomone 1975c). Upon reading an early draft of this chapter, the

Hausa historian and anthropologist Murray Last commented as follows on the relevance of Hausa ethnicity in Hausaland and in the diaspora:

> My guess is that terms like *hausawa* [Hausa people], *bahaushe* [Hausa man] matter more in the peripheries of Hausaland and beyond – and your study is therefore fascinating for its care and skill in that context; for ethnicity matters in your world [the Cameroon Grassfields]. It matters too in some wider political contexts. But it is a different world from Hausaland itself, and the day-to-day talk of farmers and their wives and children in, say, the Kano or Katsina countryside. It is in the periphery that notions like 'becoming Hausa' (used by Salomone at a particular political conjuncture) become important. The current trend in the Nigerian middle belt is marked more by 'ceasing' to be Hausa.[3]

Furthermore, Last pointed out that, in identifying themselves, individuals in Hausaland – now and in the past – use terms that refer to their regional background – for example, Kanawa (people from Kano), Katsinawa (people from Katsina), or Zazzagawa (people from Zazzau, present-day Zaria). Similarly, Nicolas (1975) has argued that Hausa ethnicity may comprise a number of sub-ethnicities on the basis of members of other population groups being integrated into the Hausa category; he names the examples of Hausa-Fulani, Hausa-Kanuri and Hausa-Buzu. Similar sub-ethnic categories also exist among the Hausa in the Cameroon Grassfields and are mirrored in emic distinctions of 'real' Hausa, Huya and Grassfields converts (that is, Muslim converts of Grassfields background).

Nicolas (1975) further contends that the heterogeneity of the Hausa category defies popular understandings of ethnic groups as closed and bounded units. His finding has been endorsed and extended by the seminal contributions of Cohen (1969, 1974, 1981), who interprets the Hausa case as a prime example for a constructionist and instrumentalist model of ethnicity. At more general level, similar considerations have been raised by Brubaker (2002, 2004), who argues against the reification of ethnic groups as entities or collective actors, and advocates consistently distinguishing between 'groups' and 'categories', so as to problematize the relationship between them. As I will show below, this distinction is illuminating with regard to the Hausa population in the Grassfields, whose strategies of political participation and representation suggest a limited degree of 'groupness' as compared to their Mbororo and Grassfields neighbours.

Modalities of Hausa Historiography

As in Chapters 2 and 3, I will tackle the question of Hausa identity using a historical and interactionist approach. My elaborations on the Hausa community in the Grassfields, and more specifically in the Misaje area, are based on interviews with local Hausa informants, and also draw on colonial reports and scholarly accounts (Awasom 1984; Boutrais 1996; Newton 1935). Many conversations produced rich life histories with relevant information on diverse subjects, including Hausa history, identity, economy, interethnic relations, religion and married life. While the latter will be central to the next chapter, here I focus on the factors that have contributed to the consolidation of the Hausa ethnic category in the Grassfields, Hausa relations with neighbouring groups, as well as Hausa strategies of participation in community development and political representation.

Hausa approaches to historiography differ significantly from Nchaney attitudes and come closer to Mbororo modalities. Similar to the latter, they have not come up with a collective historical narrative. Rather, informants' accounts are limited to the individual or family unit and hardly extend beyond two generations. In-depth knowledge is accredited to elderly and experienced community members who spent large parts of their lifetime in Misaje. Moreover, Hausa society in general is characterized by significant gender segregation, which finds expression in a duality of life worlds, visions and socio-economic goals (Barkow 1972; Callaway 1984; Schildkrout 1982; Smith 1959; Werthmann 1997). This was also recognized by Hausa interlocutors who recommended I interview both men and women, whose historical perspectives are seen as complementary.

Hausa history also diverges from Nchaney and Mbororo history with regard to its content and orientation. While Nchaney history is primarily a reconstruction of political relations, and Mbororo history a composite of migration and settlement histories, Hausa history is largely a recollection of economic and social trajectories. Outside interview situations, the topic of Hausa history rarely emerged, and Hausa informants expressed little interest in their history's codification. For example, when an earlier draft of this chapter was sent to Misaje, responses were generally appreciative, yet no critical discussion emerged. I would like to stress, however, that this finding is specific for Hausa settlements in the Grassfields where their presence only dates back to the early twentieth century. Conversely, long established Hausa communities in northern Nigeria have produced elaborate traditions of oral and written historiography (Hassan and Shuaibu 1952; Smith 1961).

Hausa in the Grassfields: A Historical Reconstruction of Socio-economic Trajectories

Before engaging with Hausa informants' historical accounts, I will provide a more general sketch of their establishment in northwest Cameroon. As the subsequent narrative will show, Hausa history is best understood as a history of specific socio-economic practices. In addition to describing the economic trajectories of Hausa immigrants in the Grassfields during the colonial period, I will elaborate on their relationship with their Grassfields and Mbororo neighbours and the colonial administration.

Hausa Establishment in the Cameroon Grassfields

Hausa migration both southward and westward from northern Nigeria was embedded in pre-colonial long-distance trade and was stimulated by the FulBe *jihad*. Similar to Jaafun and Aku migration, it gained momentum in the course of the nineteenth century. While early Hausa traders reached the Cameroon Grassfields in the late nineteenth century, settling there became feasible only after the German colonial powers had pacified the area. The incentives to settle in the Grassfields were of a political and economic nature. German and British colonial administrators offered their assistance and protection to Hausa merchants. The villages that Hausa chose to settle in were either rich in trade goods or large enough to provide a market. A basic requirement for their establishment, however, was an agreement with the village head to guarantee the settlers' safety. This was not always achieved. Particularly in the areas on the western fringes of the Bamenda Plateau, while rich in trade goods like palm oil and palm kernels, turned out to be dangerous and unsuitable for Hausa settlement.

The first and hitherto most important Hausa hamlet was founded around 1903 at Bamenda, where the Germans had established a military base known as 'the Bamenda Station' (Awasom 1984: 33–65). Most early Hausa migrants worked as guides, carriers and servants for German colonists. Subsequently, more Hausa migrants were attracted, most of whom engaged in long-distance trade in kola, textiles and salt. Within a few years, the initial group of approximately thirty male bachelors rose to more than one hundred individuals, including men, women and children. Subsequently, the first off-shoots of the Bamenda community were set up in Bali, Nso, Ndop and Sabongari, whose rulers welcomed the stranger population for economic and political reasons. Conversely, the chiefs of Mankon and Bafut were reluctant to receive Hausa settlers, whom they saw as allies and prospective spies of the Germans.

After the downfall of German colonial power, Hausa communities in the Grassfields scattered. Some transferred to Foumban, others repatriated to Nigeria. When the British assumed control over Southern Cameroons, they encouraged the return of Hausa migrants. By 1918 the Hausa settlement at Bamenda again numbered nearly one hundred inhabitants. Subsequently, more Hausa migrants were attracted, and within less than two decades more than twenty Hausa hamlets were established in the Grassfields, including Misaje (Awasom 1984: 53–55).

Hausa Long-Distance Trade between Nigeria and the Grassfields

Hausa merchants were widely involved in long-distance trade, in which the Misaje area – alongside many other locales in the Grassfields – featured as a station of supply and demand. During the pre-colonial and colonial periods, the Grassfields constituted a rich and vibrant area of regional and long-distance trade (Chilver 1977; Rowlands 1979; Warnier 1985). A wide range of locally produced goods including palm oil, iron, agricultural products, small livestock and craft products were exchanged within the area. Long-distance trade relations connected the Grassfields with trading centres along the Benue River and in the Adamaoua Highlands. Trade items comprised kola and cattle (in pre-colonial times also slaves and ivory), which were sold or exchanged for goods like cloth, garments, salt and potash from the northern areas. Below, I will focus on Hausa involvement in the long-distance trade in kola in return for garments and salt.

Kola nuts were one of the main export products from the Grassfields to the Muslim north, where demand for this stimulant was high. The indigenous species, *Cola anomala*, had been cultivated in many parts of the Grassfields since pre-colonial times. By the 1920s, Grassfielders had expanded their kola plantations significantly, as trading activities were facilitated by the region's pacification. Kola trees currently found at Nkanchi were most likely introduced during that period (Hassert 1917). The most dynamic phase in the kola trade lasted from 1916 to the early 1930s and involved both Hausa and Grassfielders. Among the latter were traders from the Nso and Bum chiefdoms, which constituted crucial stations along the kola trade routes (Boutrais 1996: 636–37). Merchants did not solely rely on kola, but supplemented their trade with additional goods. These included textiles, salt and minor merchandise, such as spices, beads, tools and household items imported from the Benue region and Adamaoua Highlands (Figure 5.2).

Textiles have been a prominent trade item in West Africa since the pre-colonial period. Hausa garments, in particular, have been popular because of their rich design, embroidery and quality (see also Adamu 1978). In the Grassfields, textiles were relatively uncommon until the 1930s. Commoners and women were clad simply: women dressed with a wisp of grass fibre, while men wore a loin cloth of bark fibre or fabric. Grassfields notables, on the other hand, had the prerogative of dressing in textiles. According to Warnier (1985: 141–42), Hausa gowns were already available before the German conquest, and popular among Grassfields notables. Even nowadays, certain fabrics and garments classified as 'Hausa style' are much appreciated across a wide section of the Grassfields population and constitute a significant trade good imported from Nigeria. The trade in textiles was the monopoly of Hausa merchants. The main centres of cotton cultivation and cloth fabrication were in Hausaland

142 *Masks and Staffs*

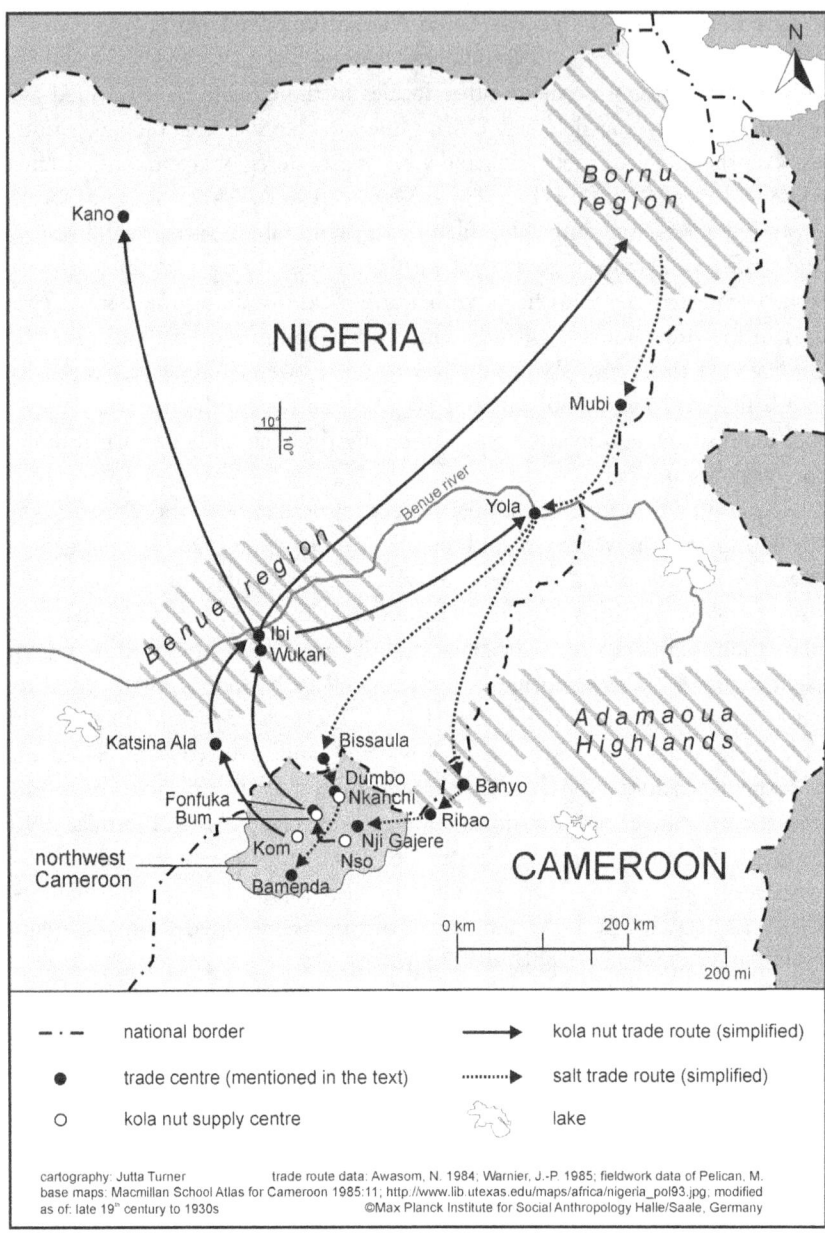

Figure 5.2: Hausa long-distance trade between Nigeria and the Grassfields. Reproduced by kind permission of the Max Planck Institute for Social Anthropology, Halle.

and the Benue region. Moreover, as Chilver (1977: 158) notes, the import of European textiles was also handled by Hausa traders stationed near Banyo.

Another relevant item of long-distance trade in the Grassfields was salt (sodium chloride) for human consumption, gained and imported from salt springs in the Benue region. Additional supply came from minor salt springs in the Cross River area, and small quantities of maritime salt were imported from the coast. A second type of salt (sodium bicarbonate), used for animal treatment and commonly known as *kanwa* (Pidgin English: potash), was imported from the Bornu region and was in high demand among Mbororo for their cattle herds. While Mbororo graziers in the southern areas of the Bamenda Highlands benefited from local salt springs, those in the northern parts depended entirely on salt imports. The salt trade route from the Bornu region to the Cameroon Grassfields extended a considerable distance (some 800 to 1,000 kilometres) and involved a number of stations where the goods changed hands, as well as a variety of means of transport, including manpower and donkeys (Figure 5.3). As the trade with salt constituted a lucrative business, Hausa merchants competed with local traders from Nso, Nkambe and Ndu (Boutrais 1996: 99–101).

Figure 5.3: Donkey caravan, 1930s. Source: Basel Mission Archives / Basel Mission Holdings, E-30.85.164. Reproduced by kind permission Basel Mission / Basel Mission Holdings.

The photograph was taken by Wilhelm Zürcher sometime between 1932 and 1939, and the original caption reads 'Haussas on trek with donkeys'.

In the early 1930s, administrative, economic and ecological circumstances changed and caused disruption among Hausa merchants (Awasom 1984: 109–12). With the partitioning of the German protectorate of Kamerun into British and French administered zones, new national boundaries emerged. Consequently, trading activities across the border were discouraged, and trade routes were altered to remain within the boundaries of the respective colonial empires. Secondly, by the early 1930s the effects of the Great Depression had trickled down to markets in Africa. Prices of export products to Europe and America dropped considerably, and the subsequent shortage of cash impacted on long-distance and regional trade. Finally, a locust plague affected the Grassfields. Over a period of four years (1930 to 1934) the insects devastated food crop and kola cultivation. Kola production dropped to a quarter of its initial amount.

Consequently, itinerant traders as well as settled businesspeople were forced to explore alternative domains. Many Hausa in the western Grassfields intensified already established economic and social ties with Mbororo pastoralists and engaged in cattle trade, a noted economic niche of Hausa migrants in other areas of West Africa (Cohen 1965, 1969).

Cattle Trade and Hausa–Mbororo Relations

Socio-economic relations between Hausa and Mbororo were one of the primary factors facilitating Hausa establishment in the Grassfields. With both groups originating from northern Nigeria, they share socio-cultural affinities, such as being Muslims and generally being conversant in each other's languages (Fulfulde and Hausa).[4] These commonalities constituted the basis for business relationships between Mbororo and Hausa, from which the latter largely derived their living (Awasom 1984: 122–24; Boutrais 1996: 636–41).

Coming from Nigeria and northern Cameroon, Mbororo were used to food and clothing habits different to those that they encountered in the Grassfields. They soon became the main customers for goods imported from the north, and their demand for salt, garments, spices and household items shaped Hausa trading activities. Rural Hausa hamlets turned into focal meeting points for Mbororo graziers, who acquired many of their supplies from Hausa merchants. While Hausa women prepared ready-made food items that were in high demand by Hausa and Mbororo customers, Hausa men provided services as specialized craftsmen (such as tailors, saddlers) or as Islamic scholars (Hausa: *mallamai*). At that time, only a few Mbororo had undergone Islamic training, while many Hausa had at least basic knowledge of the Koran. Thus Mbororo largely relied on Hausa *mallamai* to teach their children, fulfil ritual functions and produce amulets and medicine.

Mbororo herdsmen, on the other hand, offered Hausa entrepreneurs the opportunity to engage in cattle trade, which under British colonial rule became an important economic sector and a lucrative source of income. In 1921 the British imposed a cattle tax (*jangali*) on the Mbororo, which obliged them to sell some of their animals to meet their fiscal requirements. Cattle markets only existed in urban centres, such as Viktoria (Limbe), Tiko and Douala to the south, and Abakiliki and Enugu to the north of the Grassfields. As Mbororo graziers preferred to concentrate on pastoral activities, they handed over the task of driving animals to distant markets to Hausa middlemen. The latter capitalized on this opportunity and realized considerable profits (Awasom 1984: 115–20). In the 1940s, however, the British administration deliberately challenged the involvement of Hausa intermediaries, which they viewed as exploiting Mbororo herders (Awasom 1984: 121–24). They introduced cattle markets and alternative cattle cooperative schemes, and by the 1950s the cattle business was no longer in Hausa hands. Consequently, Mbororo individuals began to undertake the marketing of their own cattle, and Grassfields businessmen with substantial capital entered the trade (Njeuma and Awasom 1990: 229). Particularly successful among the latter were entrepreneurs from Pinyin, some of whom established themselves in Misaje and remain involved in raising animals and trading cattle to this day. Moreover, with the disruption of the close relationship between Mbororo and Hausa, the latter were compelled to reassess their economic strategies. Today, many are involved in a variety of professions, often focused on the service sector but no longer limited to commerce or the cattle trade.

Historical Memories of Hausa Establishment in the Misaje Area

Having given out a general portrait of Hausa establishment in the Grassfields, I will enliven it with personal narratives of Hausa informants in the Misaje area. While so far my focus has been on early Hausa traders from northern Nigeria, I will broaden the account by including the perspectives of Hausa of different sub-ethnic backgrounds, both men and women. For this purpose I will introduce the narratives of three individuals of Hausa, Huya and Grassfields descent who provide a complementary and gendered idea of Hausa history and identity in the Misaje area. The first narrative is a composite of the historical memory of Mallam Mudi who, at the time of my fieldwork, was an elderly man in his seventies and the *sarkin hausawa* (Hausa: head of Hausa settlement) of Misaje. Mallam Mudi died in 2008 and was followed by his son Bala as head of the Hausa community. His account focuses on the early years of Hausa settlement in the Misaje area and largely agrees with the descriptions of Awasom (1984) and Boutrais (1996). The second narrative is based on the recollections of Salamatu, a woman of Huya (Town FulBe) background who has lived in Misaje for approximately fifty years. Her contribution introduces a female perspective, so far omitted in earlier writings on Hausa history in the Grassfields. Thirdly, I will introduce the case of Amina, a woman of Grassfields origin who was Mallam Mudi's wife and an eminent personality within the Hausa community of Misaje. Her example will illustrate the relevance of marriage with Grassfields (and Mbororo) women, and will shed light on the process of ethnic transition.

Early Hausa Establishment in the Misaje Area: A Male Perspective

The first Hausa settlement in the Misaje area evolved in Nkanchi. It was established in the 1920s, during the rule of Fon Fuma, who welcomed the Hausa newcomers because of their commercial activities. Two decades later, the Hausa community of Nkanchi transferred to Misaje under orders of the colonial administration. There, they were given the area now known as Unguwa Rogo (cassava quarter), which became the Hausa neighbourhood of Misaje. In his historical recollection, Mallam Mudi recounted his family's migration and establishment at Nkanchi, their economic activities and subsequent relocation to Misaje.

Mallam Mudi was one of the few 'real' Hausa who was able to trace back his ancestry to the Hausa homeland. As he recounted, his mother was from Kano. His father was a man from Gora, south of Kano, and belonged to the sub-ethnic group of the Buzaye.[5] His father's occupation as a *mallam* (Koranic teacher) took the family to many places in Yorubaland as well as to Jos, Bauchi and the Adamaoua Highlands, and to Garoua and Maroua in northern Cameroon. They came to the Grassfields and later settled at Nkanchi, where his father engaged in the cattle trade. Mallam Mudi was born in Nkanchi during one of his parents' earlier trips to the area. During his early adult years he collaborated with one of his father's friends in trading *kanwa* (potash) between Nigeria and Cameroon, using donkeys for transport. When his capital was depleted, he went to stay with his father's brother, who was the *sarkin hausawa* (Hausa chief) in Nkanchi. He began to work as a *mallam* and later engaged in cattle trading, a venture that attracted more Hausa immigrants to the Misaje area.

Mallam Mudi estimated the size of the initial Hausa community at approximately fifty families who congregated under the leadership of his paternal uncle. Many Hausa settlers made their living from trading goods like salt, textiles, spices and beads which they acquired from Umuahia, a commercial centre in southern Nigeria. Others worked as Koranic teachers and supplemented their income with farming. Based on his personal experiences, Mallam Mudi elaborated on the trade with cattle, salt and textiles, and the relationship between Hausa and their Mbororo neighbours.

I have been trading for more than twenty years, mainly in cattle. We bought them one by one from the Mbororo. When all the cattle were joined together to consolidate a herd we would bring them to Umuahia. We were many cattle traders. The traders came from places like Binka, Nkambe, Lassin, Konene, Bafmen etc. All of us followed one route to Kashimbila [Nigeria]. Some traders travelled with their wives. We would carry food along or buy corn flour on our way. There were fixed points along the route. From here we had forty-four stations before we reached Umuahia. The traders did not go to one market only. They went to Wukari, Umuahia, Onitsha and other places. We bought women's and men's garments to take back. We also bought *kanwa* [potash] and other things. We tied the goods in bundles and paid people to transport them. I used to carry things on my head.[6]

As Mallam Mudi and other informants explained, the area around Dumbo, Nkanchi and Fonfuka was the main transhumance area for Mbororo from the adjacent highlands. While spending three to four months in the lowlands with their cattle, the herdsmen relied on their Hausa neighbours and the local Grassfields population for food, clothes and other items of daily use, as well as salt for their animals. Many Hausa at Nkanchi and Dumbo bought cattle from Mbororo graziers on credit to sell at Umuahia (in Nigeria) or Kumba (in southwest Cameroon).[7] In return, they brought goods demanded by Mbororo and Grassfielders.

Beyond business relations, the Hausa benefited from social and religious commonalities with their Mbororo neighbours. According to Mallam Mudi, Mbororo often supported their Hausa acquaintances with alms (*sadaka*) and religious tax donations (Hausa: *zakka*; Fulfulde: *jakka*). Today Islamic charity is still practised, but amounts to less than in the past, when – at least in informants' memory – economic growth and generosity prevailed.

In the 1940s, a few years after the customary court had been established at Misaje, the Hausa community transferred from Nkanchi to Misaje. Mallam Mudi recounted the visit of four colonial administrators from Bamenda and Buea (the British headquarters) who invited the Hausa community to relocate to Misaje. They agreed to transfer within a year. Upon their arrival in Misaje, they met Mallam Ibrahim with his congregation from Dumbo, and who was installed as Hausa chief. He died after three years and was followed by Audu Awaria, the former *sarki* of Nkanchi, from whom Mallam Mudi eventually took over.

Men's and Women's Economic Strategies: A Female Perspective
While Mallam Mudi's account focused on the economic activities of Hausa men, I will now complement this picture with the perspective of Salamatu, a woman of Huya (Town FulBe) descent. As her story shows, the flourishing cattle business in the Misaje area attracted migrants from northern Cameroon in search of

economic opportunities. Moreover, not only men but also women were drawn to the busy areas of transhumance to make a living or find a husband.

Salamatu traced her origin to Maroua, a town in northern Cameroon dominated by Town FulBe. Her father was a Muslim cleric who worked for the *laamiiDo* (FulBe: paramount chief) of Banyo. Her mother was a female chief's daughter from the area of Ganye, where allegedly only women became chiefs. Her father had two children, two slaves, two concubines and many cattle. Subsequently, one concubine left, one slave escaped and the cattle were entrusted to a caretaker who squandered them all.

Salamatu's life and marriage history entails detailed information which I can only summarize here. She was married at least eight times, these lasting from two months to eight years. For the most part of her married life she led a secluded life. Yet two of her husbands were herdsmen, and they lived with their cattle 'in the bush'. The periods between marriages she spent with her relatives on the adjacent Nkambe Plateau from where she frequented Nkanchi, Dumbo and Misaje. About this phase she told me that she was stubborn, enjoyed the life of a *bordel* (Pidgin English) or *karuwa* (Hausa), smoked and supported herself by selling kola nuts and ginger.[8]

Eventually, Salamatu settled in Misaje with her sixth husband, a man from Yola whose occupation, she explained, was to play cards or gamble. With the profits he bought cattle and later operated a store selling miscellaneous goods. When Salamatu first came to the Misaje area, the Hausa community resided at Nkanchi. She recalled a few Hausa elders, including the *sarkin hausawa*, the *sarkin pawa* (Hausa: chief of the butchers) with three butchers, the *imam* (religious leader of a Muslim community) with one *mallam* and three merchants trading cattle and kola. Salamatu also recalled her early encounters with Mbororo in the area.

When Mbororo herdsmen took their cattle to the temporary grazing grounds around Nkanchi and Dumbo, they were followed by 'free women' who made a living by selling food items and offering their services. These were predominantly Huya women, and their customers were Mbororo herders or paid herdsmen, most of them being Huya from northern Cameroon. As Salamatu explained:

> We used to go to the transhumance area [grazing grounds] at Dumbo. There were so many people. Everyone had his own woman. So the women followed the herdsmen to Dumbo, because there was nobody left on the highlands. We prepared food to sell. The women without husbands fried *makala* and *masa* [snacks]. They sat and made their market. When the men came to greet their girlfriends they bought what the women were selling. A man would tell his girlfriend that he loved her. Some men even promised marriage. The woman agreed. If she had a brother, she informed him that this man wanted to marry her. They would discuss before

the marriage was tied. Not all women were free. Some who stayed at Dumbo were married. They sold *coBBal*,[9] *makala*, *masa* [snacks]. They just made their business.[10]

Salamatu's narrative describes women's economic activities and their changeable lives. While Hausa men were drawn to the Misaje area by trade goods and cattle, women likewise were attracted by socio-economic incentives. Married women had no choice but to follow their husbands, but benefited from the herdsmen's demand for prepared food items, which they sold via their children. 'Free women' were drawn by the opportunity of being able to support themselves by selling snacks, offering sexual services and the likely chance of finding a husband. At the time, the status of *karuwa* ('free woman') was not considered permanent but transitory. Moreover, women were exposed to switching between life in the village and in 'the bush', depending on their husband's occupation. Today, Hausa women in Misaje still practise similar economic activities. At the same time, it has become more frequent and socially tolerable for Hausa women to stay unmarried and support themselves. Yet in Salamatu's view, the situation of 'free women' in Misaje was dire when compared to earlier days. As she explained, 'nowadays it is the *bordel* of hunger. Women only receive *sadaka* [alms]'.[11]

Salamatu's account also reflects her sub-ethnic background as a Huya (Town FulBe) woman. Her description of her father's property (concubines, slaves, cattle) illustrates the earlier lifestyle of the FulBe aristocracy of northern Cameroon. Since Huya and Mbororo belong to the FulBe ethnic category, they share narratives of a pastoral past. Huya men were attracted to the Grassfields mainly to work as paid herdsmen for wealthy Mbororo. Some returned to northern Cameroon after amassing enough capital to build up their own herds or start a business. Others settled in the Grassfields and were integrated into the Hausa ethnic category, while retaining their sub-ethnic identity.

Today, the Hausa-Huya category of the Grassfields also includes Mbororo individuals (both women and men) who, as a result of economic or social pressure, have given up their pastoral lifestyle and have settled in Hausa quarters or married Hausa partners. In Misaje their number is relatively small and they retain allegiance to both Mbororo and Hausa communities. Yet, as the subsequent example of Amina and her children shows, the process of ethnic transition is fluid and tends to be completed only in the second generation.

Interethnic Marriage and the Consolidation of the Hausa Ethnic Category
As we learned from Mallam Mudi, early Hausa traders formed the nucleus of the current Hausa community in the Misaje area. While some travelled with their wives and children, many were either single or had left their families behind. Thus, upon settling in the Grassfields, they were reliant on local

women as marriage partners. It is against this background that we may read Fon Richard's earlier statement that, while Hausa traders brought kola nuts, Hausa caps and salt to the region, 'the Nchaney had palm oil, traditional caps and wives to offer in exchange'. Consequently, the majority of Hausa today have at least partial Grassfields parentage. This also applies to Hausa of Huya descent, many of whom have married Hausa, Mbororo or Grassfields partners.

At the time, marriage between neighbouring chiefdoms was a common practice among Grassfields societies. According to Warnier's (2007: 148) calculation, at the end of the nineteenth century 30 per cent of women in Mankon originated from neighbouring polities. Moreover, marriage was a strategy employed by Grassfields rulers to engender political alliances and to secure the support of their neighbours (Nkwi 1987: 43–49). Today, marriage between people of different ethnic backgrounds is still accepted and widely practised in the Misaje area. Although Grassfields parents tend to argue in public against marrying their daughters to Hausa or Mbororo men, they are generally pragmatic and accept their children's choice. Marriage to a Hausa or Mbororo partner is usually tied to conversion to Islam, a topic discussed in the next chapter.

At this point I wish to take up the case of Amina, the wife of Mallam Mudi, so as to highlight the structural significance of interethnic marriage as well as the relevant contributions of committed individuals to promoting Hausa identity and community in the Misaje area. Moreover, she and her children's example will provide us with an insight into the process of ethnic transition.

Mallam Mudi's first wife was a Hausa woman from northern Nigeria, with whom he had four children. After her death, he married Amina, a young woman from the neighbouring Mbembe chiefdom. As Amina recounted, Mallam Mudi was the first person she met when visiting her father, who had just moved to Misaje. Mallam Mudi was startled by her appearance and began to court her from the very moment of their first encounter. At the time, Amina was in her late teens and in an unhappy marriage with a young and rowdy Bessa man. She eventually quit her husband and accepted Mallam Mudi's proposal on the assumption that she would receive better treatment by a man who was considerably older and who, being the head of Misaje's Hausa community, held a position of social responsibility.

Gradually, Amina grew into her role as the wife of the *sarkin hausawa*. For the purpose of their marriage, she converted to Islam and was supervised by the *imam* in learning the relevant Muslim teachings and practices. Within the first six years of their marriage, she gave birth to a son and a daughter. Having a gift for languages, she was quick to learn Hausa. With the help of female Hausa elders, she became conversant with the religious and cultural practices associated with childbirth, marriage and widowhood. Concurrently, she familiarized herself with the responsibilities of her husband's office and gained the reputation of being a sociable and generous woman who welcomed visitors of all ethnic backgrounds, be they Hausa, Mbororo or Grassfielders. At the time of my research, Amina was in her forties and recognized as a female Hausa elder. Besides taking care of her own children, she had raised two of her siblings and cared for the children of Grassfields acquaintances, all of whom she tried to bring up as 'good Muslims'. Furthermore, she facilitated marriages between Hausa and Grassfields partners, and served as a religious and social guide for several Grassfielders who had converted to Islam.

Amina's case illustrates the crucial role of interethnic marriage as a process by which women with a Grassfields background contribute to the biological and social reproduction of Hausa society in the Misaje area. While this process has been ongoing since the settlement of Hausa traders in the Grassfields, at the time of my fieldwork in the early 2000s a generational shift was imminent. As several interlocutors outlined, only a few Hausa elders with direct family relations in Nigeria and northern Cameroon were still alive. Moreover, they were soon to be replaced by members of the younger generation, mostly Hausa with Grassfields parentage. In subsequent years this has come to pass, with Amina's son, for example, becoming *sarkin hausawa* in 2008. At the same time, Amina's example also demonstrates the capacity of individuals to embrace a different ethnic identity and promote the Hausa cause. With her hospitable manner and her efforts at bring people closer, she contributed to fostering interethnic marriages and enhancing the Hausa reputation in Misaje.

In our conversations, Amina freely talked about her background as a Grassfields woman and her experiences of religious and ethnic conversion. Conversely, her children fully identified themselves as Hausa, assuming their father's language and ethnicity. Following the example of their parents, they too married across ethnic lines, choosing Grassfields and Mbororo partners. Amina's son married a Grassfields woman who converted to Islam for the purposes of their union. Amina's daughter was first married to a Hausa man in Misaje, but was later remarried to a wealthy, settled Mbororo man in the neighbouring town of Nkambe. While Amina's two children were firm in their identity as Hausa and Muslims, her younger siblings were rather unsteady. Both grew up in Mallam Mudi's compound, were raised as Muslims and married Muslim partners. Some years later, however, they moved to southwest Cameroon to make a better living. Faced with a non-Muslim environment, they eventually gave up their Muslim faith and decided to play on their Grassfields identity and social networks.

The examples of Amina, her siblings and her children are illustrative of the process of ethnic transition. In the first generation, individuals tend to retain allegiances to their community of origin as well as the society into which they have married. They can claim belonging to both and may choose or switch between them, as illustrated in the case of Amina's siblings. In the second and subsequent generations, the process of ethnic transition is generally accomplished. That is, following the principles of a patrilineal system, children take after their father's ethnicity, language and religion. Consequently, the children of Amina and Mallam Mudi identify themselves and are identified as Hausa.

Taken together, the three narratives of Mallam Mudi, Salamatu and Amina have provided a differentiated account of Hausa history and identity in the Misaje area. They exemplify the social situation Hausa traders faced when they first established themselves in the Grassfields, as well as the processes that facilitated the integration of individuals of varied backgrounds into Hausa society. These processes include the adoption of a settled lifestyle, marriage with a Hausa partner and conversion to Islam. At the same time, their accounts demonstrate the relevant contributions of Grassfields and Mbororo individuals to the lasting consolidation of the Hausa category in the Misaje area.

Taking into account the composite and relational character of Hausa identity, the question emerges of what exactly it means to be Hausa in this context. To tackle this question, we may look into the mechanisms that promote 'groupness' (Brubaker 2002, 2004) or a sense of community as the basis for collective action and self-understanding.

The Hausa as a Moral Community?

The criteria on which contemporary Hausa identity in the Grassfields rests are threefold: Islam, spatial congregation in so-called Hausa quarters, and at least superficial mastery of the Hausa language. These correspond to the core elements of Hausa identity in other parts of West Africa, where Hausa constitute an immigrant minority (see Cohen 1966, 1974; Salomone 1975c). While these criteria are relatively easy to attain, their fulfilment is embedded in a set of shared social, cultural and religious practices which engender a feeling of belonging that goes beyond mere identification with the Hausa ethnic category.

For men, it is religious and social practices – such as Friday prayers, socializing with Muslim elders in front of the Hausa chief's compound and offering charity and alms – by which they uphold a spirit of togetherness and solidarity. Among women, it is social and cultural activities in the context of childbirth, marriage and widowhood, as well as frequent visits and the exchange of gossip that contribute to a tightly knit social community. A sense of togetherness is also conveyed in the Islamic educational system, when children meet in the private classroom of their *mallam* or, more recently, when attending the Islamic primary school in Misaje. A further supporting factor is the spatial pattern of Hausa compounds, which is conducive to community activities, particularly as compared to the dispersed nature of Mbororo settlements.

To better understand the process of 'group making' or community formation, I wish to draw a comparison with Cohen's notion of the Hausa as a 'moral community' (Cohen 1966). Based on his analysis of the kola trade in southern Nigeria, Cohen interprets membership in the Hausa moral community as the prime mechanism of channelling individual strategies and generating group conformity. He defines moral community as follows:

> By a moral community in this context I am referring to the multiplicity of informal, face-to-face, essentially non-contractual relations which link and cross-link members of the community and which impel men to act in accordance with intrinsic values and norms, without much consideration for specific gain [...] The intimate relations which make up the texture of such a moral community can arise only between men who can easily and effectively communicate with each other, by using the same language and sharing the same cultural symbols, customs, and traditional values. Within a multi-tribal society they can arise mainly between members of the same tribe. (Cohen 1966: 25–26)

In Cohen's understanding, shared ethnicity is a basic precondition for the emergence of a moral community. Yet, my case material from northwest Cameroon suggests otherwise. In line with Cohen's definition of a moral community, Hausa interlocutors perceive of the Muslim community as one that is governed by religious norms and binding obligations. At the same time, the Muslim community goes beyond the narrow confines of the Hausa ethnic category and includes Mbororo and Grassfielders who have converted to Islam. Thus, from a Hausa perspective, it is not shared ethnicity but religion that provides the moral grounds for community formation. Moreover, their conception of the Muslim community as one that integrates Hausa, Mbororo and Grassfielders echoes the composite and relational nature of Hausa history and ethnicity in the Grassfields.

In terms of political representation, Hausa prefer to rely on good relations with their Mbororo and Grassfields neighbours rather than claiming resources on the basis of an exclusive Hausa ethnicity. As the subsequent examples show, Hausa actors tend to pursue their individual and collective interests via reference to superseding units, such as Misaje town, the Muslim community or the Nchaney chiefdom.

Hausa Strategies of Political Participation and Representation

Probably more than any other population group in the Misaje area, Hausa men and women have been affected by the economic decline of the past decades. Being mainly involved in the service sector, their subsistence is closely tied to good socio-economic relations, in particular with the Mbororo. Yet unlike the latter, they have not responded to the political changes of the 1990s by forming an ethnic elite association. As we will see, they largely rely on their Mbororo and Grassfields neighbours for political representation and participation in community development.

Access to Community Development

At the time of my fieldwork, Hausa access to community development was mediated in two ways. Firstly, via residence and active participation in the development of Misaje town; secondly, via membership of the Muslim community. The Hausa strategy of associating with politically and economically more influential groups thus entails an appeal to common denominators (Eriksen 1998), such as shared location and religion.

Among the projects benefiting Hausa residents of Misaje town was the provision of public water taps. In 1999, the *fon* of Nkanchi and the divisional officer of Misaje encouraged the population of Misaje to embark on a community development project proposed by SIRDEP (Society for Initiatives in Rural Development and Environmental Protection), a Cameroonian NGO. The project's goals were to demarcate a water catchment area, to provide public water taps and to train individuals in the maintenance of the provided infrastructure. The Hausa community, alongside other population groups, contributed their share in cash, kind and labour, and participated in the water committee. Later, when the public taps were installed, the *sarkin hausawa* took responsibility for managing the tap in the Hausa quarter. Thus, the Hausa community benefited from this project on the basis of actively contributing to the development of Misaje town. Conversely, Mbororo did not take part in the project, as they did not consider themselves residents of Misaje town.

Projects geared to the Muslim community attracted both Hausa and Mbororo support. Most significant was the establishment of an Islamic primary school in Misaje, which was realized with the sizeable financial assistance of Mbororo individuals. At the time, the introduction of Islamic schools was relatively new and an important step towards extending formal education to Mbororo and Hausa children. The school began in 1994 as an informal venture that subsequently expanded in ambition and size. In 1998 it was registered as a formal educational institution within the Islamic educational framework of the Cameroonian government. In 1999 a school compound was constructed, as more than 110 students were enrolled and proper teaching facilities were required. Many individuals supported the endeavour. The *fon* of Misaje offered the site, Hausa and Mbororo individuals contributed in cash, kind and labour. Moreover, the school received teaching aids, books and prizes from external bodies, such as the Cameroonian government, the national Islamic Association based in Yaoundé, the Swiss development association Helvetas and Mafor

University Women, an association of female university graduates. Moreover, the Islamic primary school in Misaje was not the only one of its kind. In 2001 there were six registered Islamic schools in Donga-Mantung that provided primary school education in English as well as instruction in Arabic language and Islam.

As these two examples illustrate, in pursuing their collective interests, Hausa tend to prioritize their local and religious identity over their ethnicity. Similarly, making the choice to participate in local self-help groups is guided by the criterion of membership in the Muslim community rather than ethnic identity.

Both Hausa men and women commonly participate in Muslim voluntary associations, such as the Islamic Youth Association and a variety of rotating credit associations. The Islamic Youth Association was formed by young Hausa men in the late 1980s as a self-help group and was officially registered in 1995. By 2002 it had more than fifty members, including Hausa and Mbororo as well as Grassfielders interested in the Muslim faith. During their weekly meetings, members operate a savings group, advance their Islamic education, organize social activities and fulfil community duties, such as cleaning the mosque, clearing the graveyard or helping out in the Islamic primary school. The Islamic Youth Association in Misaje is a local organization with equivalents in many places across the Grassfields and Cameroon. Yet despite occasional contacts and exchange visits, no attempts were made to cooperate or form a trans-local umbrella association. Moreover, members of the Islamic Youth Association in Misaje are aware of the existence of international Muslim organizations based in Egypt, Saudi Arabia and Oman. As visiting scholars from Egypt and Cameroonian individuals who have benefited from their programmes have made clear, these organizations offer Islamic educational schemes and assistance for Muslim community projects, such as the construction of mosques or health centres. As yet, the Muslim community in Misaje has no intention of applying for assistance from international Muslim organizations. That they exist is well known, however, and this has influenced Hausa strategies of pursuing their community interests by identifying with the wider Muslim community in Cameroon.

While young Muslim men in Misaje are organized in the Islamic Youth Association, many Hausa women and men engage in rotating credit associations. During the time of my research, five Muslim rotating credit associations existed, most of which included Muslim and non-Muslim members. Many Hausa women participated in one or more of these savings groups, which fulfil financial and social functions.[12] Most exceptional among the Muslim groups in Misaje town is the group Kawtal Pulaaku (Fulfulde: FulBe meeting). It was formed in the late 1990s on the initiative of the NGO Ballotiral. Its activities include an adult literacy programme, a basic savings scheme and occasional training in income-generating activities. Initially, the group was planned as being for Mbororo women exclusively, but after requests from Hausa women, it was opened up to Hausa members.

Hausa attempts to partake in Mbororo development projects are a common phenomenon in Misaje and reflect the primary self-identification of Hausa as members of the Muslim community. Hausa generally stress their close relationship and socio-cultural interrelatedness with their Mbororo neighbours. Mbororo reluctance to integrate Hausa into their programmes of community development and political self-representation was met by Hausa interlocutors with incomprehension:

> The Hausa and the Mbororo understand each other [...] The only difficulty we have been facing is that they say they have their own cultural organization. They do not want to invite us, the Muslims. They say, it belongs to the Mbororo only [...] They say MBOSCUDA [the Mbororo Social and Cultural Development Association] is only for the Mbororo. It is only now, really at the running hour, that they have invited us and that they mix with some of our Hausa. Really, we are happy now for that. Everything has come together.[13]

The issue of whether or not Hausa should be integrated into the activities of MBOSCUDA or Ballotiral, both of which were aimed at promoting Mbororo interests in particular, was contentious on both sides. From the perspective of MBOSCUDA leaders, their success in representing Mbororo claims to the state and accessing its resources rested on the marginal situation of the Mbororo as a distinct ethnic group. Thus, opening the association to Hausa members would be contrary to the idea of an ethnic elite association. For Ballotiral as a localized programme, integrating Hausa individuals in their activities was more feasible, as long as it did not affect Mbororo welfare. Conversely, from a Hausa perspective, a strict separation of Mbororo and Hausa interests was odd and not well received. The eventual solution of integrating Hausa individuals into the activities of the Ballotiral, while retaining MBOSCUDA as a national organization exclusively for Mbororo, was acceptable to all parties.

Membership of the Nchaney Chiefdom

As well as emphasizing their social and religious linkages with Mbororo, Hausa also claim political representation in the Nchaney chiefdom. As the Hausa community in Misaje resides on Nchaney land, they are administratively and politically subordinated to the *fon* of Nkanchi. This arrangement dates back to their establishment in the area in the 1920s and has been endorsed by the colonial and postcolonial administrations. Today, they see themselves as local citizens and members of the Nchaney chiefdom.

Grassfields and Hausa interlocutors equated the political status of the *sarkin hausawa* to the position of a sub-chief or quarter head who represents the interests of a faction of the Nchaney population, in this case Hausa residents on Nchaney territory. The assistant (*wakiili*) of the Hausa chief in Misaje, described the political hierarchy between Hausa and Nchaney leaders as follows:

> The *sarki*[14] is like the *nji* [Grassfields sub-chief, advisor] of the *fon*. Since we are all in the land of the *fon*, he is our overall ruler. The *fon* is the head of all the people living on his land, including the FulBe and the Hausa. The big men representing the Hausa are the *sarki* and his assistant, the *wakiili*.[15]

Both Hausa and Nchaney informants portrayed the relationship of their community leaders as characterized by mutual respect and cooperation. While the *fon* is generally perceived as a father to all subordinates, the *sarki*, Mallam Mudi, was regarded as his elder because he surpassed Fon Richard in age and life experience. The *sarki* is expected to advise the *fon* on matters concerning the Hausa population and is responsible for communicating administrative orders to his community. Furthermore, he attends to exclusively Hausa matters such as marital disputes and the organization of Muslim rituals. Occasionally, the *sarkin hausawa* represents not only the Hausa population but Muslims in general, including Mbororo; for example, when participating in the traditional council.

In comparing Hausa and Mbororo regarding their socio-political integration into the local and regional community, a number of significant differences emerge. While Hausa generally accept a subordinate position in the local political system, Mbororo tend to contest the *fon*'s political supremacy and demand autonomous representation vis-à-vis the state. Similarly, during the conflict surrounding Fon Richard's investiture ceremonies (see Chapter 1), the two groups differed in their approaches. While most Hausa aimed at mediation and reconciliation, many Mbororo favoured an aggressive approach. Although the two groups eventually pursued a common strategy, the Hausa remained apprehensive about damaging social and political relations with their Nchaney neighbours.

The reasons that account for the differing approaches of Mbororo and Hausa are varied and include historical factors as well as economic considerations. Firstly, compared to the Mbororo, the Hausa community in Misaje has apparently never achieved the same level of groupness required to engender and sustain a politicized ethnicity. This may be explained with reference to the composite character of Hausa ethnicity in the Grassfields and its manifold entanglements with both Mbororo and Grassfields societies.

Secondly, the small size of the Hausa population and its relative economic weakness are relevant. That is, while the Hausa constitute less than 1 per cent of the population of North West Region, the Mbororo comprise approximately 15 per cent. Moreover, Hausa economic assets are minor when compared to the capital vested in Mbororo livestock. Accordingly, the colonial and postcolonial administrations largely ignored the Hausa population, while they took interest in mediating farmer–herder relations and in endorsing Mbororo strategies of political representation.

Finally, Hausa apparently find it easier to insert themselves into the local political hierarchy than do Mbororo, who aspire to autonomous integration in the overarching regional unit. Thus, Hausa informants rejected the idea of forming an ethnic elite association, arguing that they have successfully pursued their interests by drawing on their relations with Grassfields and Mbororo neighbours.

Comparing Hausa, Mbororo and Grassfields Ethnicities

The specific character of Hausa ethnicity in the Grassfields comes to the fore when compared to Mbororo and Grassfielder conceptions of their ethnic identities. As I argue, the three groups differ considerably in the ways they view themselves and their relationship with each other. They may thus be described as having different kinds of ethnicity as well as being different ethnic groups.[16] To illustrate this argument, I will briefly recapitulate the findings of this and earlier chapters.

The Nchaney conception of ethnicity is inclusive and multilayered, and accounts for the capacity of Grassfields societies to accommodate internal as well as ethnic and cultural 'others'. Conversely, Mbororo self-understanding is rather exclusive and essentializing, and puts emphasis on both internal and external boundaries. Different again, the Hausa conception of ethnicity is composite and relational in nature, and highlights interconnections with Mbororo and Grassfields societies.

All three ethnicities have been shaped by the historical conditions of their emergence and consolidation in the Grassfields, and importantly by their encounters with other population groups and colonial and postcolonial administrations. There is, however, a crucial difference that distinguishes the Hausa case from that of Mbororo and Grassfields societies, and that relates to Schlee's argument about group size (Schlee 2008). Thanks to their numeric and economic strength, Grassfields and Mbororo ethnicities have not been reliant on the integration and support of ethnic 'others', which – as I have argued – has been constitutive of the lasting establishment of the Hausa ethnic category in the Cameroon Grassfields. Furthermore, at the time of my research, both

Mbororo and Grassfielders had attained a higher degree of groupness in a political sense (Brubaker 2004), which is mirrored in their strategies of representation, such as the formation of ethnic elite associations.

Yet groupness does not only refer to the political domain but may as well materialize in other fields. In the Hausa case, group-making processes have concentrated on the religious and social domain. That is, membership of the Muslim or Hausa community provides individuals with a familiar social environment and a social security network. These are also vital incentives for Grassfielders to consider when contemplating religious and ethnic conversion, a subject explored in the subsequent chapter.

Notes

1 According to the census of 1953, the Hausa population of the western Grassfields comprised approximately 3,500 persons out of a total of 420,000 (Awasom 1984: 1; Boutrais 1996: 636). Later censuses indicated 2,700 Hausa for 1964, and 3,100 for 1968 (Boutrais 1996: 636–37). Subsequent censuses did not differentiate between ethnic groups. It is unlikely that the Hausa population has increased proportionally more than the Grassfields population.

2 Researchers who have worked on the Hausa diaspora in West and Central Africa are Paden (1970), Salomone (1975a, 1975b, 1975c, 1980), Sanjek (1977), Winchester (1976) and Works (1976).

3 Murray Last, e-mail communication, 9 September 2005.

4 In other regions where FulBe and Hausa co-reside, different patterns of language adoption have evolved. While in northern Nigeria Hausa has become the dominant language, in northern Cameroon and the Blue Nile region (Sudan) Fulfulde has gained ground at the expense of Hausa (Abu-Manga 1986, 1999).

5 Possibly, the sub-ethnonym Buzaye used by Mallam Mudi is equivalent to Bugaje, a Hausa term that, according to Nicolas (1975: 418–22), is used to refer to Hausa of Tuareg slave origin (Hausa-Buzu). They are represented mainly in the region of Zinder (Niger).

6 Mallam Mudi, Misaje, 19 December 2001.

7 The current cattle markets at Misaje and Dumbo were established in 1969. Before then, traders frequented Mbororo hamlets to inquire about trade animals.

8 The terms *bordel* (Pidgin English) and *karuwa* (Hausa), as used by Salamatu, refer to 'free women' or 'women between marriages' who are searching for a new partner. *Bordel* is also used in northern Cameroon with regard to prostitutes (Eguchi 1973: 72) and is probably derived from the French term *bordel* for brothel, but used to denote both a place and a person. Kapfer (2005: 131) names a number of possible origins of the term 'free woman' or *femme libre*. It may have been a legal term used in the Belgian Congo for those women who were given papers to move around freely in settlements normally restricted to Africans (Little 1973: 113).

9 *CoBBal* is the Fulfulde term for maize or millet dumplings; in Hausa they are called *fura*.

10 Salamatu, Misaje, 3 December 2001.

11 Salamatu, Misaje, 26 November 2001.

12 Rotating credit associations are a well-known and long-established institution in many areas of Cameroon (Ardener 1964; Ardener and Burman 1995). On rotating credit associations among Hausa in the Hausa homeland, see Hill (1972: 203).
13 P., Misaje, 25 November 2001.
14 Following Hausa grammar, the nominative form is *sarki*; when followed by a genitive, it becomes *sarkin*, as in *sarkin hausawa*.
15 I., Misaje, 18 December 2001.
16 A similar argument has been put forward by Dereje Feyissa (2011) in his study of Anywaa-Nuer relations in western Ethiopia, where he describes the Anywaa as having an emic primordialist conception of ethnicity, while the Nuer have an emic constructionist interpretation.

6

Grassfielder by Birth, Muslim by Choice

Religious and Ethnic Conversion

Compared to northern Cameroon, where Islam has attracted many members of local non-Muslim populations, Muslim conversion is rather limited in the Cameroon Grassfields. Here, the majority of the population are Christians and/or practitioners of African local religions, and it is mainly in areas with a strong Hausa and Mbororo presence that Grassfields individuals have been attracted to the Muslim faith and religious community. For example, in Misaje town, 19 per cent of all compounds are Muslim, and twenty-one compounds or 4 per cent of all households belong to converts of Nchaney, Bessa, Nso or Wimbum backgrounds. Taking into account the relative numerical, political and economic insignificance of the Muslim community in the Cameroon Grassfields, it is noteworthy that Grassfields individuals are attracted to Islam.

As I will argue, it is both positive and negative incentives that motivate individuals to change their faith and integrate themselves into a different social environment. For many converts of a Grassfields background, it is personal rewards as well as structural constraints, such as disadvantageous gender roles and the fear of witchcraft, that prompt them to opt out of their own society and adopt another religion and identity. I will base my elaborations on participant observation and interviews with Grassfields, Mbororo and Hausa informants. For comparative dimensions I draw on similar research in northern Cameroon. Most pertinent are the studies of Burnham (1972, 1996) and Schultz (1979, 1980, 1984), which focus on the interplay of migration and religious and ethnic conversion. A number of subsequent studies have addressed related themes, and special attention has been paid to gendered perspectives (e.g. van Santen 1993).

Closely linked to the subjects of religious and ethnic conversion, and by extension interethnic marriage, are the questions of how individuals and collectives deal with shifts in identity and belonging, and how this impacts on their social relations. According to Elwert (1997, 2002), people may belong to different reference groups simultaneously, and may thus situationally stress different affiliations and identities. Moreover, some identities may include a polytactic potential, meaning a latent multiplicity of order and identifications. My interest here is in identity discourses relevant to interethnic marriage and religious conversion; that is, I am concerned with the ways individuals switch between religious and ethnic identities, in particular Muslim, Grassfields, Mbororo and Hausa identities.

As will be discussed in more detail below, in most parts of the Grassfields, Muslim and Hausa identities are widely seen as congruent and interchangeable. Thus religious conversion comes close to ethnic conversion. On the other hand, while Muslim converts count as members of the Hausa community, they partially retain their Grassfields identity. As several interlocutors explained, they understand themselves as Muslims or Hausa by choice and Grassfielders by birth. Thus, while they have the opportunity to switch their allegiance from one group to the other, they also face the predicament of managing their loyalties and liabilities to both communities.

Finally, I will bring my findings to bear on the debate concerning the integrative or dissociative faculty of cross-cutting ties, which was initiated by Gluckman (1955) and further refined by Hallpike (1977) and Schlee (1997, 2000, 2004). Allegiances between Grassfielders, Mbororo and Hausa resulting from historical, cultural, political and economic commonalities have been discussed in earlier chapters. Here, my focus is on social bonds, in particular those created through interethnic marriage and religious conversion. I posit that in the Grassfields, as compared to other parts of Cameroon, the occurrence of such cross-cutting ties is relatively limited, and that the individuals embodying these linkages vitally contribute to facilitating communication and interaction across ethnic boundaries. In conflict situations, however, they may find it difficult to retain an integrative role.

Religious Conversion in Northwest Cameroon: General Considerations

In the following I will briefly outline the approaches of Grassfielders, Mbororo and Hausa to religious identity and conversion. These elaborations provide a general background to the individual cases of Muslim conversion that will be subsequently analysed.

As my Grassfields, Mbororo and Hausa interlocutors argued, religion is an important spiritual source that provides moral guidelines for a successful and good life. Active membership in a religious community is seen to yield emotional support and social security. Moreover, the choice of one's faith is generally considered an individual freedom. Yet religion occupies different positions in the self-understanding of Grassfielders, Mbororo and Hausa. Whereas for the latter two, being Muslim is an inseparable part of their ethnic and cultural self-understanding, for Grassfielders their religious identity is not constitutive of their ethnic identity. Many Grassfielders are Christians, others practice African local religions and some are Muslims. Besides, many families are 'mixed', with their members belonging to different religious denominations.

While among Grassfielders religious conversion is relatively common, interlocutors emphasized that sequential conversion is not desirable, and that once people have chosen their faith, they should be serious and remain with it. Conversely, among Hausa and Mbororo, conversion to Christianity or alternative religions is rare. Although there are a couple of American missionaries in Nkambe and Sabga working towards this aim, their success rate is low.

Hausa and Mbororo generally welcome conversion to Islam by Grassfielders, as it supports the spread of the Muslim faith and concurrently strengthens the Muslim community and its political and economic influence in the Grassfields. As outlined in the previous chapter, Hausa society is particularly receptive to the integration of Grassfields spouses and Muslim converts, who constitute a vital part of contemporary Hausa society.

While a person's religious choice is generally respected during their lifetime, religious differences and competing claims are occasionally played out in the context of converts' funerals. Grassfielders and Muslims differ significantly in their eschatological beliefs and burial practices. For Grassfielders, the dead continue to exist in a parallel though invisible world, to which the funeral is the gateway. If the burial rites are not performed properly and according to the deceased's social status, they may turn into a roaming spirit.[1] Muslims and Christians, on the other hand, believe in the existence of paradise and hell. Christian burial practices are still compatible with Grassfielders' traditional funeral rites, but Muslim practices differ so much that Grassfielders tend to take offence when their converted sons or daughters are buried in a Muslim manner. Such an instance occurred during my research in 2001 when Musa, a convert with a Nchaney background and a protégé of the Hausa chief, died.

Musa had a government job and was considered a member of the local elite. Upon his death, both his Nchaney relatives and his chosen Hausa family claimed the right to bury him according to their respective religious traditions. Eventually, it was agreed that Musa considered himself a Muslim and wished to receive a Muslim burial. His corpse was covered with a white cloth and laid out in the Hausa chief's compound before it was buried in the Muslim graveyard on the outskirts of Misaje. A close relative to the deceased summarized Grassfielders' reservations over Musa's Muslim burial as follows:

> The women complained that it is not good to keep somebody on the ground [on the floor]. They compared it with their own fashion to keeping the dead person on a bed and to coming and seeing the person. I saw it the first time with important personalities like Abacha.[2] I decided that if they do the same thing with important people in Nigeria, it is really their fashion. That is why I was not too angry. Also, they only allowed the family members to see his face; that is not the same with our tradition. They kept the corpse in a separate house and also separated the Muslim and the other mourners. I would have preferred them to join the two groups, because we are all the same people. But the Hausa do not like to cry, although it is a normal thing when you lose a person. We know it is their fashion and you cannot force them to cry. It is not because they do not feel the loss, it is just their fashion.[3]

Hausa informants, on the other hand, stated that by no means could they have allowed Musa's relatives to bury him. As they argued, the latter suspected that Musa had been killed by witchcraft, and they wanted to put magical potions in his grave that would find and punish his murderer – a practice they considered irreconcilable with Islamic doctrine. Moreover, Hausa women argued that the Grassfielders' expressive style of mourning was incompatible with the Muslim etiquette of bereavement, and hence it was necessary to separate the two groups of mourners. In the end, Musa's burial passed without serious incident and no lasting grievances remained between his Nchaney and Hausa relations.

As this example illustrates, funerals occasionally become a site of contention where religious differences and competing claims over an individual's identity are played out.[4] Similar incidents have been documented by researchers working on religious conversion in northern Cameroon. Gausset (1999), for example, mentions disagreements over burial rites between Muslim and non-Muslim Wawa in Adamaoua, which took quite a different turn than those in the Grassfields. Elder Wawa were shocked that their Muslim sons no longer participated in funeral masquerades and feared that they would refuse to bury or mourn them. As a consequence, they abandoned the masquerades and adopted Islam.[5]

Two Portraits

In order to examine the ways in which Grassfielders are enticed and socialized into the Muslim faith and community, I will now introduce two portraits of Muslim converts from the Misaje area, one woman and one man. The portraits are based on interviews with each convert and reflect their respective perspectives.

Fadi: Forever Muslim

Fadi is the daughter of a Nchaney man and a Bessa woman. Her father died when she was still young, and her mother is a practising Presbyterian. Fadi went to the Presbyterian Church until she fell in love with Abdu, a Hausa man. At the time, she was in her late twenties and already had two children out of wedlock. They stayed together for one year, before Abdu had to serve a prison sentence for two years. Fadi waited for him, but after some time she got pregnant and gave birth to her third child. When Abdu got out of prison, he wanted her back. Abdu approached Fadi's uncle and asked to marry her and make her a Muslim. Her relatives agreed but left the final decision to her, as she had to choose herself if she wanted to convert to Islam. Fadi agreed, and Abdu gave her uncle 7,000 CFA (approximately €11) as bridewealth, which he accepted.[6]

Although many men had come to ask for Fadi, she had refused all earlier marriage offers from local Grassfielders. In her view, Grassfields men cause too much trouble. They beat their wives and often provide insufficiently for them. A Muslim husband, on the other hand, is more responsible and only in exceptional cases batters his spouse.

Fadi was instructed in Muslim practices and ideology by her husband, who is a *mallam* (that is, he has completed reading the Koran). She learned how to pray and to observe Ramadan, the Muslim month of fasting. Initially, she and her husband communicated mainly in Pidgin English, but gradually she learned Hausa, though not from her husband but from her children. Her son refused to communicate in Nchaney, his mother's original tongue, but only responded in Hausa. For some time, Fadi resisted and scolded him. Eventually, she gave in and made the effort to learn Hausa.

While staying at her parents' compound, Fadi used to drink *shah* (maize beer). As she recalled, at times, they drank maize beer in the market until they were drunk and even slept there. But when she became a Muslim, she gave it up. It was not hard for her. She pointed out that while she may tolerate relatives and friends drinking *shah*, she no longer considered it good for herself. However, many of her Grassfields friends no longer visit her, as she spends most of her time in the company of Hausa women. Some of her former friends were angry because she left the Presbyterian Church; others felt offended by Hausa women who resented them for drinking *shah*. Throughout her marriage, Fadi insisted on cultivating her own farm, although this contradicts the Muslim ideal that married women should not be seen in public or do heavy work. She explained to Abdu that it was important that she and her children had enough food to eat, and eventually she had her way.

By the time of my research, Fadi and Abdu had been married for more than twenty years. Together they had five children, and Abdu made a living by building fences and washing clothes. When I asked Fadi why she converted to Islam, she answered:

> Only the marriage. Since I like him, am I not supposed to enter his faith? And it is all the same thing. But now I am inside the Muslim Church [religion], direct. Now I cannot change my Church again. Even if I leave this marriage, I cannot change the Church. I will stay in it until I die. This Church is good. It is very good. It has truth inside. It does not lie. The Church is like that, you sit down and you see the food. God sends it to you. I tell you the truth. Now that we sit here, we will see the food coming. God sends it. That is why I agree that this Hausa Church is good. And I will die in this Church. Even if the man leaves me, I will still stay. I will not change and go back to our own Church.[7]

Karimu: A Man of Two Worlds

Karimu was born a Bessa, but grew up as a Hausa. His father was a soldier in the Nigerian army and a close friend of the husband of Aisha, a popular but childless Hausa woman. When Karimu was five years old, his parents sent him to stay with Aisha. He explained that, while growing up with Aisha and her husband in Bamenda, he completely forgot about his initial home, his parents and siblings. At the age of twelve, Aisha took him back to Misaje to his family, who had called for him under the pretence that his grandmother had died. They had heard that he did not attend school in Bamenda, and planned to send him to school in Misaje. As Karimu explained: 'I got used to them, but not as much as my foster parents. It was also because the cultures of the Muslims and Bessa differ. I did not have an interest in the Bessa culture, because I had already gone deep into the Muslim culture'.[8]

His birth parents did not want Karimu to remain a Muslim and engage with Muslim friends. They wanted him to learn the language, customs and religious practices of the Bessa. But Karimu resented his Bessa background and environment. He refused to learn the Bessa language and instead socialized with Nchaney friends. As soon as he was old enough to be independent, he moved to Douala, and there he took up Islamic education again. At first, he stayed with a *mallam*. Later he rented his own flat, and after prayers attended the lessons of the *imam* (prayer leader) who taught them the Arabic script. He read many religious texts in English and in Hausa translation.

As Karimu explained, studying the Muslim faith also helped him to accept his dual identity as a Bessa and a Muslim. He began to ask himself how he could reject his natural parents and his culture, although the Koran prescribes that a Muslim should respect his biological parents – even if they are not Muslims – but should not follow those customs that contradict the Muslim faith. He began to understand that nobody is born a Muslim but instead joins the faith;

that is, even Hausa have both an ethnic and a religious identity. He came to see himself as 'a man of two worlds'.

While in Douala, Karimu worked a number of odd jobs. He was employed at a bank, later by a German road construction company. Subsequently, he ran an import–export business between Nigeria and Cameroon. Finally, he ended up as a bus driver. He began to look for a wife in Douala, but eventually decided to ask his foster mother Aisha to find him a suitable wife. As he explained, he completely trusted her and she did everything she could to the best of her ability, treating him as her own son. Karimu's natural parents were not involved in the marriage arrangement, nor did he ask them for financial support.

Karimu pointed out that he was aware of his dual responsibility towards his natural parents and his foster mother Aisha, and that he supported both equally by sending letters and money. Moreover, being an active member of BECUDA (Bessa Cultural and Development Association), he began to cultivate his knowledge of Bessa culture and language. Yet ultimately he felt that he shared a stronger bond with his foster mother Aisha and with Muslim religion and Hausa culture than with the Bessa side of his identity.

Incentives for Muslim Conversion

The cases of Fadi and Karimu are representative of Muslim conversion among Grassfielders in Misaje, and exemplify a variety of factors that inspire and facilitate the process. Among them, Muslim reputation plays a significant role and has both attracted and deterred local Grassfielders.

Grassfields interlocutors often interpreted the leisurely and sociable lifestyle of Muslim villagers in terms of their piety and solidarity. Muslims are admired for their 'sense of togetherness', their affability towards strangers, their generosity and their concern for the needy. These are all qualities promulgated by Muslim faith and bolstered by institutionalized forms of charity, such as alms (*sadaka*) and levies (*zakka/jakka*), which are thought to add to the donor's happiness and fortune. Moreover, Muslims are admired for their respectful way of interacting with each other, their calmness and abstinence from alcohol and other kinds of intoxication. But the same features of self-control and sociability that here are valued positively also give rise to criticism. Occasionally, Hausa are viewed as lazy, Mbororo as conceited, and Muslims' distaste for *shah* (maize beer) is seen as an impediment to their socializing with Grassfielders. Thus Muslim reputation among Grassfielders is ambiguous and, taken on its own, cannot fully account for an individual's conversion. In most cases the prospective convert's social context is a vital factor.

As the portraits of Fadi and Karimu illustrate, friendship, marriage and foster parenting are additional factors facilitating religious conversion. Most villagers have friends, acquaintances and relatives from different social and religious backgrounds. Youths and children in particular tend to breach ethnic, religious and social divides, and are interested in learning about each other's religion and culture. Furthermore, the Islamic Youth Association offers opportunities for Muslims and interested Grassfielders to socialize and familiarize themselves with the Muslim faith. As one leading member explained, it is difficult to assess the number of individuals attracted to Islam as a result of the association's activities. However, over the past few years, they counted five new converts alone in Misaje.

Marriage is a strong incentive for religious conversion for both genders. For Grassfields women who aspire to marry a Muslim, conversion is a precondition. Grassfields men also envisage religious conversion when seriously planning to marry a Muslim girl.[9] For example, for many years Paul (a Bessa man) befriended a Hausa girl, and together they had two children. But as he refused to convert to Islam, the girl's family did not agree to their marriage. Eventually, the relationship broke up and the two lost contact. It was only many years later that Paul linked up with his one-time girlfriend, who in the meantime had married a Muslim. While Paul had remained firm in his Christian faith and had finally married a Nchaney girl, he occasionally regretted that, at the time, he was not decisive enough to become a Muslim and establish a family with his first great love. As with the initial decision, the longevity of the act of conversion is contingent on the individual's experiences and commitment. While Fadi is convinced that her devoutness will endure, others may revert to Christianity, as illustrated by the trajectories of Amina's siblings, discussed in the previous chapter.

Probably the most effective way of socializing a Grassfields individual into the Muslim community and faith is foster parenting. The Arabic term for foster parenting is *kafala*, which is derived from the verb 'to feed' and may be translated as sponsorship. According to Islamic rules, a foster child retains the name of their biological parents, and inherits from them rather than their foster parents. Moreover, members of the foster family are not considered blood relatives and thus count as possible marriage partners. The Islamic concept of foster parenting emphasizes the foster parents' role as trustees and caretakers of another person's child. It is thus different from adoption, which implies the legal change of a child's identity and inheritance rights (cf. Goody 1971; Alber 2013). The fostering of children of relatives and friends is a relatively common practice among Hausa in the Grassfields and elsewhere (cf. Smith 1965). Foster parents thus contribute to disseminating the Muslim faith and show charity to those facing difficulties in the upbringing of their children. At the same time, foster parenting is also a way of increasing the economic potential of one's household. Muslim women greatly rely on the assistance of their children, as they are restricted in their movements by social norms informed by Islamic ideology (Hill 1969; Schildkrout 1982). Childless women, in particular, depend on relatives or friends to give them a child which they then treat as their own. Aisha, for example, fostered two of her relatives' children and Karimu, the son of her husband's Bessa friend. As she explained, she benefited from her foster children, who supported her in her economic activities and cared for her in her old age. Moreover, by educating Karimu to be a good Muslim, Aisha gained spiritual redemption.

Conversely, foster parenting is less common among Mbororo. As Mbororo women commonly practise parent–child avoidance in the case of their firstborn child, the latter is often raised by their grandparents. With regard to subsequent children, however, the bond between parents and children seems more intimate than among Hausa. With the establishment of an Islamic school in 1995, a 'modern' system of custody emerged in Misaje. Mbororo pupils from distant compounds stay with relatives or family friends who live nearby the school. A few stay with the Hausa chief and his family during term time and receive basic accommodation, food and care. In turn, the Hausa chief is presented with gifts in cash or kind.

Among Grassfielders it is not uncommon to entrust children to friends or respected individuals (Awasom 1984: 108). Conversely, to find Hausa or Mbororo children entrusted to Grassfields foster parents is rare, as Muslim parents generally do not allow their children to grow up in a non-Muslim environment.

Discomfort with Grassfields Societies

When asked about the benefits that they have gained from Muslim conversion, informants in Misaje stressed three features: participation in Muslim solidarity networks, genial husband–wife relations, and a general 'peace of mind' which also entails a detachment from witchcraft beliefs. I argue that these features not only refer to the rewards of a Muslim lifestyle, but they mirror the structural constraints that, in the first place, may have motivated these individuals to opt out of their society of origin. These include discomfort with discourses of occult aggression and with gender relations. With this interpretation I go beyond the perspective of my interlocutors, who portray their religious conversion as a response to external incentives rather than being a conscious act of distancing themselves from their original society.

Solidarity and Occult Aggression

Among the incentives frequently mentioned by Grassfields informants were the opening up of economic opportunities and converts' access to Muslim support networks. This is reflected in the following statement by a Nchaney man, commenting on a distant relative's conversion:

> He joined these people because he was sure that they would contribute money and help him. The style of the Hausa people is like that. They assure you that if you join their faith everything could be possible for you. They will buy you clothes, contribute money, and buy you suitcases. Even if you wanted to marry, they could give you a wife for free and you could continue in your own way. He was attracted, accepted the conditions, and joined them. That is how he came about being a Hausa man or a Muslim.[10]

Likewise, Fadi's statement, that members of the Muslim community receive food freely, refers to the benefits of Muslim solidarity networks. These networks, however, function on the basis of reciprocity. If there are few wealthy individuals who contribute, there will be little to share among the poor and needy. As one informant put it, looking back on his Muslim life, he had thought that, 'being a Muslim is enjoyment and wealth at one's disposal'. However, with the on-going economic recession the situation has changed.

In the long term, this downturn may be a factor reducing incentives for Grassfielders to convert to Islam. Yet at the same time, there is an underlying aspect to the argument of Muslim support networks that deserves further attention. The values of solidarity and generosity attributed to the Muslim community are often said to be lacking in Grassfields societies. Here, unconditional support is inconceivable, and social proximity tends to be overshadowed by fears of witchcraft and occult aggression. Thus, only by converting to Islam may one be able to cultivate these values and reap their benefits.

Similarly, interlocutors noted that becoming Muslim had impacted on their mindset in several ways. For example, it has helped them to overcome negative habits, such as drinking, smoking or bad temperedness, as reflected in Fadi's statement. According to Amina, the wife of the *sarkin hausawa*, it is the daily routine of five prayers that urges Muslims to take a break from daily issues, reflect on their comportment and improve their self-control. It also prevents them from working themselves up into a rage.

> MICHAELA: What helped you most in the Muslim faith?
> AMINA: What I have seen with the Muslims, I can say is good. I can say I liked fighting. I used to find palaver. But since I started *salla* [Hausa: praying], when I see something coming which is bad, I like to run from the thing. And I like to make the thing cool down. Then, something like *mimbo* [Pidgin English: alcohol], I was fond of drinking. Whenever I drank a little, it worried me, but I forced myself to drink. I stopped it. I smoked cigarettes at my [previous] husband's store where I was the saleswoman. I learned to smoke when I was still little. But when I came here and stayed for a while, and began to understand what was said in the

book [Koran], I decided to leave those things. Yes, things have really been planted in me. Like the five prayers; if I wanted to do something bad, I would remember something recited there and become weak. Those are the things, I can say, I gained from it.

MICHAELA: That is, the book [Koran] itself helped you to calm down?

AMINA: Yes, it helped me to calm down my temper. At first, if they said anything about fighting, I would start to fight. It lasted for about a week and I would not get tired. It would just be as if I should continue to fight. And if I argued with somebody, it would just be as if each time that we met we should continue quarrelling. But since I have come here, all those things have gone off my mind. I do not have those things again. Secondly, at first, when they were doing something like *ngambe* [Pidgin English: soothsaying], we would just go and stand. You know, certain things like *ju-ju*s [masquerade, medicine], my heart has come out of it. But at first, the least thing that occurred, we would go to the *ngambe-man* [soothsayer] or to make 'country-fashion' [sacrifices, witchcraft]. But these things are no longer in my heart. So when they are doing these things, I no longer feel it. Or if they say, there are witches in that house, I am not afraid. I will just go, enter and come out. At first, I was afraid of going to places like the one we just came from [where a woman suspected of witchcraft had been present]. In the time of my grandmothers, they would say, if you go there, you will be caught by witchcraft. Today, I am no longer afraid; all that was nonsense. Now I no longer have that fear. I think it is the Muslim faith that helped me. That is what I believe.[11]

Amina's statement clearly voices her initial anxiety about witchcraft, which she was able to overcome by converting to Islam. Beliefs in the occult and concomitant practices and discourses are a subject widely dealt with in the anthropological literature on Cameroon and a feature of Grassfields societies that cannot be ignored (e.g. Ardener 1970; de Rosny 1985; Geschiere 1997, 2013; Nyamnjoh 2001). At the same time, in the Misaje area their impact on interethnic relations is relatively limited (Pelican 2006: 352–92).

Here, it is local Grassfielders who seem most troubled and afflicted by perceived occult aggression. Suspicions are raised against potential perpetrators on the basis of wealth disparity and sudden individual success. The majority of allegations are directed against members of Grassfields societies, including local Grassfielders as well as migrants from neighbouring and distant Grassfields chiefdoms. Only very recently have Mbororo and Hausa been suspected of related practices, such as the purported trade in human body parts, an example of which will feature in the next chapter.

More generally, however, Muslims are thought to be immune from occult aggression. This conviction is endorsed by Hausa and Mbororo, who tend to distance themselves from occult practices by stressing their Muslim identity, thus employing a rhetoric of cultural difference. They frequently present themselves as informed by 'rational' thinking in contrast to the 'superstition' of Grassfielders. Moreover, they claim immunity on account of their lack of belief in occult forces, but also on account of the efficacy of Muslim protective medicines. The rhetoric of Muslim superiority in occult matters seems convincing, as many non-Muslims both in Misaje and beyond enlist the services of Muslim scholars and healers.[12] At the same time, we learn from Amina's statement that Muslim practices and ideology can engender a certain mindset that may help converts to master their fears and dissociate themselves from witchcraft beliefs. In this sense, Muslim conversion may appeal to those discomforted by discourses and practices of the occult prevalent in their society. Yet, as the low rate of Muslim conversion suggests, the majority of Grassfielders tend to rely on alternative ways of controlling occult activities (e.g. Fisiy and Geschiere 2001; Pelican 2009b).

Transforming Gender Relations

Gender relations have been a contentious issue in Grassfields societies, where control of political and economic resources is generally in the hands of male elders (Argenti 2007; Chilver 1989; Kaberry 1952; Warnier 2007). It is against this background that we ought to consider women's emphasis on congenial husband–wife relations as a vital factor motivating their conversion to Islam.

According to the Muslim ideal, women are supposed to show deference and obedience to their husbands, who in turn should act as their caretakers and provide them with everything necessary for their material and spiritual well-being. Women are not supposed to move around freely and should be exempt from strenuous tasks, such as fetching water or cultivating food (Ogunbiyi 1996: 48–49; van Santen 1995: 186–87). Due to pragmatic and financial constraints, however, many Muslim families in the Grassfields do not strictly adhere to this ideal. Nonetheless, the vision of a leisurely lifestyle is still a strong incentive to marry a Muslim husband. This has to be seen against the idea that women married to a Grassfields husband face harsher treatment and greater economic responsibilities. According to the gender model practised by Grassfielders, women are responsible for the subsistence of the family by cultivating food crops. They cannot expect much financial support from their husbands and largely have to fend for themselves and their children. One of my interlocutors, a Bessa woman married to a Mbororo man, assessed the two gender models as follows:

> I was married to a 'country-man' [Grassfielder] before I left him and married this one [Mbororo husband]. The reason is that, if you stay with a 'country-man', you have to suffer before you eat; but with this man you will only eat [enjoy]. With the 'country-men' you have to suffer, you have to work and sell crops before you can buy oil, Maggi [seasoning] etc. But with this man, if things get finished, he will bring them. It is God who has given me this marriage. Otherwise I would not be

here now. If you never get a Mbororo man who takes good care of you, you only have to 'tie heart' [Pidgin English: persevere]. But if you get one, you only thank God.[13]

A second difference highlighted by several of my interlocutors refers to the attitudes of Muslims and Grassfielders to violence in gender relations. Among Mbororo and Hausa, self-control is a valued social quality and violence against women and children is tacitly disapproved of. Conversely, among Grassfielders, physical punishment is an accepted and common practice. Moreover, women fight back and, coupled with the extensive consumption of maize beer (*shah*), disputes between spouses may turn into serious brawls. Hence, for Fadi, her apprehension about mistreatment by a Grassfields husband was a valid and motivating factor for marrying Abdu, despite their protracted relationship due to his prison sentence and his relative poverty.

Thirdly, from the perspective of Grassfields women, polygyny is handled more sensibly in Muslim households. According to Islamic norms, men are allowed to marry up to four wives with the condition that they are capable of providing equally and sufficiently for them and their children. Among Grassfielders, on the other hand, it is acceptable to marry as many wives as possible as long as the first wife agrees to a polygynous arrangement. As there is no social or moral imperative to treat all wives equally, women tend to be exposed to their husband's tastes and preferences. Under these conditions, some of my interlocutors recommended opting for marrying a Muslim husband and converting to Islam rather than being integrated into a polygynous Grassfields household.

Practicalities of Being a Muslim

Becoming a Muslim also has its downsides. It entails a number of divergences from a person's previous lifestyle, such as abstaining from alcohol, observing Ramadan and learning Hausa. Some of these changes collide with Grassfielders' proclivities, and so the practical part of being a Muslim may entail some difficulties.

Converts occasionally face problems in keeping up with Muslim doctrine and in reconciling their Grassfields and Muslim identities, a process that may even result in occasional re-conversion. To facilitate this transition, the Muslim community in Misaje offers a number of auxiliary institutions. Individuals who have firmly taken the decision to convert to Islam are required to undergo a period of formal instruction in everyday Muslim practices, which may take several months. They are encouraged to choose a *jagora* (Hausa) or *kollitowo* (Fulfulde), meaning a guide or helper. The English term that describes this role most pointedly is godparent. Although it is a term borrowed from Christianity, informants occasionally used it in referring to the Muslim convert's spiritual and social guide. The *jagora/kollitowo* facilitates the convert's socialization into the Muslim community and acts as a confidant. The *jagora/kollitowo* normally also takes care of the convert's burial, as in the case of Musa discussed above. Most often, it is learned and respected community members who are approached to assume the responsibility. Their benefit is more ideational than material, as it is a Muslim's duty to assist others on their religious path.[14]

It is common that converts are instructed in basic practices and doctrines, such as ablution, prayers, fasting and sexual duties, by their *jagora/kollitowo* or their partner. Frequently a *mallam* (Muslim teacher) is hired to broaden a person's education. Informants pointed out that Christian and Muslim ways of teaching differ considerably. While Christian doctrines are promulgated in English, Pidgin English and Grassfields languages, Muslim teaching is mainly done in Hausa, Fulfulde and Arabic. Several interlocutors mentioned their initial inadequate understanding of Muslim doctrine as a challenge. Yet, as the case of Karimu illustrates, some literate converts make an effort to read the Koran and other Muslim writings in English or Hausa translation.

Moreover, being a Muslim or being married to a Muslim partner requires learning the language of the community in which the convert aspires to integrate. Multilingualism is an essential feature of the Cameroon Grassfields. Each individual speaks or understands at least three languages, including their mother tongue, Pidgin English and the language of at least one neighbouring group. Hence learning another language as a result of Muslim conversion is perceived as no more an obstacle than the normal requirements of living together. In a multi-ethnic or multilingual household, the question of the dominant language is often resolved pragmatically. Since Mbororo, Hausa and most Grassfields communities are patrilineal, primary importance is placed on the father's language and culture. Yet as the cases of Fadi and Karimu show, often it is the children themselves who decide which language they want to speak.

Many Grassfielders face difficulties in keeping up with Muslim doctrine and practices. While some welcome the structure provided by the five daily prayers, others experience their performance as a disruption to their usual routines. Most challenging, however, is the fasting of Ramadan, during the twenty-eight days of which Muslims are only allowed to eat and drink before sunrise or after sunset. Generally, learning to adhere to religious requirements takes time and dedication. As Amina, the Hausa chief's wife explained, it took her four years to become firm in the Muslim faith and to perform the fasting correctly.

Such practical difficulties, as well as the personal dislike of specific Muslim practices, occasionally prevent inclined individuals from converting to Islam.

Female informants, for example, mentioned that they disliked the reluctance of many Muslim parents to send their children to (a secular or a Christian) school, and that they could not accept marrying their daughters off into a forced arrangement at an early age. The same concerns, however, were shared by many Hausa and Mbororo mothers, and parents' attitudes were gradually changing.

Some Muslim converts only subsequently realized – and often under the influence of an urban, non-Muslim environment – that the religious impositions on their lives were too burdensome. Evidently, living in a predominantly non-Muslim setting puts converts' conviction to the test.

Juggling Multiple Identities and Social Liabilities

Conversion to Islam may be interpreted as a strategy for opting out of one's social and cultural environment. This move, on the one hand, can free converts of their social and ritual liabilities; on the other, it can deprive them of their social network and sense of belonging. Yet, from a Muslim perspective being a Muslim does not require the exclusion of other, ethnic or social identities, though it implies a hierarchy of identities. A Mbororo acquaintance clarified this point as follows:

> While in theory it is possible to be a Muslim and keep your ethnicity or culture, in practice it is difficult, because Islam seeks to be an entire way of life, a government with laws for all aspects of life. It is also said that you are a Muslim first before anything else. So, Islamic identity precedes any other.[15]

Grassfielders who convert to Islam are faced with the quandary of managing their belonging to two partly overlapping, partly exclusive social contexts. Some converts have difficulties in accepting their Grassfields background alongside their chosen Muslim identity. The most glaring example is Karimu, from whose case we can see that, while being socialized into the Muslim community in Bamenda, he developed disdain for his birth community. Upon his return to Misaje, he deliberately refused to reintegrate socially and culturally into the Bessa community. Only as an educated adult did he begin to reconcile the two sides of his identity, and came to see himself as 'a man of two worlds'. Most converts understand themselves as Grassfielders by birth and Muslims by choice. They experience the partial incompatibility of their ethnic and religious identities as a pragmatic issue.

With conversion to Islam, a number of practices and social liabilities that are vital to Grassfields social organization become untenable, as they contradict Islamic doctrines. These include ritual duties with regard to land and ancestors, burial rites, the consultation of a diviner and the indispensable consumption of *shah* (maize beer) during social activities. As a result of neglecting or refusing to engage in these practices, converts may face social and cultural estrangement. Several interlocutors noted that their circle of friends changed after they converted, and that both sides developed mutual contempt.

Even more significant than the loss of friends is the impact of religious conversion on the relationship between parents and children. For example, a Grassfields woman who intends to marry a Muslim husband cannot expect financial support from her parents, as marriage among Grassfielders involves the payment of bridewealth, while the Mbororo and Hausa furnish their daughters with a dowry. Instead it is her *jagora/kollitowo* (social guide) who may assist in accumulating a woman's dowry, or she may provide for it on her own or with her husband's support.

Conversely, by converting to Islam, Grassfields individuals also free themselves from liabilities vis-à-vis their birth parents and relatives. Since many of the required services and ritual duties conflict with Muslim doctrine, Grassfields parents cannot expect the full support of their Muslim children. The Hausa elder Aisha described Muslim impositions on the obligations of Grassfields parents and their children as follows:

> Her mother [of a female convert] who is a Christian cannot send her to buy *mimbo* [Pidgin English: alcohol] for her, and she too cannot give money to the mother to buy *mimbo*. She cannot eat or buy the meat of a dead animal to give to her parents. Also, if any of her relatives die, she can only send money. She is not supposed to perform the traditional rites of the 'country-people' [local Grassfielders]. The husband can also give money, but will not take part in the celebrations. The parents of the girl have to accept that she should become a Muslim. Therefore they should not get angry that she does not respect the tradition any longer.[16]

Among the Muslim converts I met in the Misaje area, none made the ultimate decision to sever relations with their birth family. Both women and men considered it important to keep up good relations with their parents and to assist them as much as they could. They tended to interpret religious restrictions laxly and support their relatives by giving them money, ignoring the fact that it may be used to buy alcohol or to consult a diviner. By doing so, they were able to reconcile their social liabilities with their religious conviction and to do justice to their dual identity as Grassfielders by birth and Muslims by choice.

Comparing Muslim Conversion in Northern Cameroon and the Grassfields

The subject of religious conversion is also a pertinent feature of the literature on northern Cameroon (Burnham 1972, 1991, 1996; Gausset 1999; Schilder 1993, 1994; Schultz 1979, 1980, 1984; Regis 2003; van Santen 1993, 1995,

1998). Here, Muslim conversion is portrayed as an urban phenomenon related to labour migration. Moreover, men and women are said to be attracted to Islam for different reasons. In comparing motivations and processes of religious conversion – and by extension marriage with a Muslim partner – in northern Cameroon and the Grassfields, a number of similarities and differences emerge.

In northern Cameroon – the Adamaoua, North and Far North Regions– Muslim identity has been associated with political power, social status, urban lifestyles and civilization. Since the colonial period, members of local non-Muslim groups have been attracted to Muslim conversion and marriage with FulBe as a way of upward social mobility. These incentives were further enhanced when the northerner Ahmadou Ahidjo became the first president of Cameroon and granted Muslims privileged access to government jobs and business licences. While these social, economic and political incentives have mainly facilitated the conversion of non-Muslim men, women have been attracted to Islam and marriage with Muslims for different reasons. According to van Santen (1993, 1995, 1998), whose research focuses on Mafa women in Cameroon's Far North Region, women's motivations include the suggested link between Islam (in particular the Muslim marriage system) and civilization and improved gender roles. Moreover, Mafa women without sons to care for them in their old age are attracted to Muslim conversion by the prospect of fostering Muslim children, and thus attaining social security, an opportunity they lack in their own society.

In northwest Cameroon the situation is a bit different. Firstly, the structural incentives that facilitate Muslim conversion in northern Cameroon are largely absent in the Grassfields, where the Muslim population does not constitute a politically or socially dominant group. Here, as outlined earlier, individuals may be enticed into Muslim conversion by discomfort with aspects of their society of origin, such as fears of occult aggression or gender relations. Secondly, individuals also choose to marry and become Muslims in rural areas. That is, more important than an urban environment is the presence of a substantial Muslim community that assists the converts in their religious duties. Finally, male and female converts' motivations are similar. Some divergence is observable with regard to Muslim gender roles, which tend to be favoured by women more than men. However, critical views of Muslim injunctions on women's economic activities were expressed by both male and female informants.

Besides these differences, there are also a number of similarities. The prospect of a social security network provided by the Muslim community is a vital incentive for aspiring converts in northern Cameroon as well as in the Grassfields. While according to van Santen (1993, 1998) many elderly Mafa women are attracted to Islam by the option of fostering children, this argument was never mentioned by Grassfields interlocutors, probably because child fostering is also practised among non-Muslim Grassfielders. Nonetheless, as outlined above, foster parenting plays a significant role in facilitating Muslim conversion by integrating Grassfields children (instead of Mafa mothers) into a Muslim environment.

While I have so far centred my analysis on religious conversion and switching between ethnic and religious identities, I will now examine the potential correlation of religious and ethnic conversion as it is observable in the Grassfields and other parts of Cameroon.

Correlations of Religious and Ethnic Conversion

In the Cameroon Grassfields, Muslim and Hausa identity are seen as largely congruent and interchangeable. Analogously, Grassfielders who convert to Islam are seen as becoming Hausa. However, the correlation of religious and ethnic conversion is not a necessary given. Alternatively, new ethno-religious categories could emerge, such as in the Nso area, where Muslim converts identify themselves as Nso Muslims rather than Hausa.

Similar processes of religious and ethnic conversion have been described for northern Cameroon and northwestern Nigeria, and have been termed 'Fulbeization' and 'Hausaization' respectively (e.g. Burnham 1991, 1996: 48–56; Gausset 1998, 1999; Salomone 1975b; Schilder 1994: 213–16; Schultz 1979, 1980, 1984; van Santen 1993: 47–57). In the following I will outline some of the main findings on Fulbeization in northern Cameroon and draw comparisons with the Grassfields.

Fulbeization in Northern Cameroon and Hausaization in the Grassfields

In northern Cameroon, the FulBe have been the politically and economically dominant group since the early nineteenth century. Consequently, the FulBe ethnonym has come to represent urban Muslim culture. Many local non-Muslim groups opposed the political and cultural hegemony of the FulBe. Others cooperated and were inclined to adopt FulBe lifestyle and religion (Gausset 1999; Schilder 1993). As a consequence, a system of ethnic ranking emerged with the primary distinction between Muslim and non-Muslim groups. While all Muslims were associated with FulBe identity, all non-Muslims were lumped together under the category of *haaBe*, the antonym to FulBe (e.g. Regis 2003). Even Mbororo were seen as inferior to Town FulBe and were stigmatized as backward and only superficially Islamized.

Two leading anthropologists in the study of Fulbeization in northern Cameroon are Schultz (1979, 1980, 1984) and Burnham (1972, 1991, 1996). Both have demonstrated that in their region of study ethnic change was possible within one generation, the preconditions being the convert's use of Fulfulde as their principal language, open adherence to Islam and overt consensus with FulBe norms and ideals (Burnham 1996: 48; Schultz 1984). According to Schultz (1979: 240–75), many ethnic groups in northern Cameroon define ethnicity not in terms of descent, but on the basis of social and cultural practices (language, religion and lifestyle). Thus, Fulbeization is only one process of ethnic change among others that have existed. Its particularity is that it involves an ideology of cultural and ethnic superiority. Because emic concepts of FulBe identity include descent as an important criterion, local converts have to conceal their original ethnicity so as to count as 'proper' FulBe. Moreover, Schultz (1979: 290–92) shows that, at the time of her research, the town of Guider provided a particularly supportive environment for religious and ethnic change. Since ethnically 'authentic' FulBe were few, they welcomed the integration of converts as a strategy for enlarging their community. However, in other towns of northern Cameroon, such as Maroua, where 'ethnic' FulBe were more numerous, the situation was different and FulBe identity could not be claimed so easily.

In comparing religious and ethnic conversion in northern Cameroon and the Grassfields, a number of similarities but also striking differences become apparent (Table 6.1). One of the major differences regarding ethnic conversion in northern Cameroon and the Grassfields concerns converts' attitudes to their

Table 6.1: Comparing religious and ethnic conversion in the Grassfields and northern Cameroon.

	Cameroon Grassfields	Northern Cameroon
reference group of religious and ethnic conversion	Hausa	FulBe
political status of reference group	marginal minority	ruling class
incentives for religious and ethnic conversion	discomfort with society of origin affinity for Muslim faith and community social security network improved gender relations	upward social mobility political and economic advantages social security network improved gender relations
features of religious and ethnic conversion	superficial mastery of Hausa or Fulfulde open adherence to Islam refusal to participate in Grassfields customs that conflict with Muslim ideology	use of Fulfulde as the principal language open adherence to Islam overt consensus with FulBe norms and ideology
attitude to original identity	Grassfielders by birth, Muslim/Hausa by choice	tendency to hide non-FulBe ancestry

original identities. Muslim converts in northern Cameroon are keen to portray themselves as FulBe exclusively and to distance themselves from their community of origin. Conversely, Hausa identity in the Grassfields allows for multiple identifications and social liabilities. Moreover, while in northern Cameroon ethnic conversion can be attained within one generation, in the Grassfields it takes two generations for an individual to fully count as Hausa.

When analysing these processes of religious and ethnic change in terms of switching identities (Elwert 1997, 2002), Muslim converts in the Grassfields are more flexible in switching back and forth between different frames of reference when compared to Muslim converts in northern Cameroon, who tend to switch once and forever.

Religious and Ethnic Conversion Disentangled

Recent studies on ethnicity in northern Cameroon indicate that the findings of Burnham and Schultz, which are mainly based on research conducted in the 1970s, are not applicable to the same extent to all communities in northern Cameroon. Moreover, they show that over the past few decades alternative notions of religious and ethnic conversion have emerged.

As Schilder (1993, 1994) argues, among Mundang in Cameroon's Far North Region, religious conversion has not become as popular as proposed by Schultz in the 1970s. In Schilder's reading, it was mainly the chiefs who converted to Islam as an act of political opportunism to Ahidjo's regime, while the majority of the population continued to adhere to their original religious system. Schilder clarifies matters, stating that those Mundang chiefs who converted to Islam did not take up FulBe ethnicity, but constituted a new category of Mundang Muslims known as *juulBe*, a Fulfulde expression meaning 'those who pray'. Likewise, van Santen (1993) notes in her study on Muslim conversion among Mafa women in Mokolo (in the Far North Region) that none of her informants claimed FulBe identity. She groups the population in her research area into three categories, namely FulBe, *juulBe* (Muslim converts) and *haaBe* (non-Muslims).

In the Grassfields too, religious conversion is not always and everywhere equated with ethnic conversion. Muslim converts in Nso, for example, constitute a distinct ethno-religious category: they are Nso Muslims. The Nso chiefdom in the eastern part of the Bamenda Highlands has been exposed to Muslim influence for more than a century through the settlement of Hausa traders and FulBe herders, as well as of Muslims from the neighbouring and related Bamoun chiefdom. The late *fon* of Nso was a practising Muslim, and the chiefdom's capital, Kumbo, has a large Muslim quarter inhabited by Hausa and FulBe. The majority of the Muslim population of Nso consider themselves Nso Muslims rather than Hausa, as is the case in Misaje.

Moreover, Kumbo has two mosques and is the only town in the Grassfields with a secondary and high school in Islamic or Anglo-Arabic education (Ndze 1998).

As the example of Nso Muslims shows, the popular equation of religious and ethnic conversion does not result from the incompatibility of Grassfields and Muslim identities and social practices. Rather, it reflects the historical context of Muslim presence and the nature of socio-political relations between Grassfielders and Muslims in their respective area. While initially, the Muslim community in Nso was largely associated with the presence of Hausa and FulBe, the situation has changed over time. With increasing economic wealth and political influence, Muslim converts in Nso redefined their identity and generated the category of Nso Muslims. However, the few Nso and Wimbum Muslims living in Misaje are perceived by the local population as Muslim converts and subsumed under the category of Hausa. Apparently, the distinct notion of Grassfields Muslims has not established itself outside the Nso area, although individuals are aware of the long-standing history and strength of the Muslim community in Nso.

Religious Conversion, Interethnic Marriage and Cross-cutting Ties

To conclude, I will apply the concepts of identity switching and cross-cutting ties to my material on religious conversion and interethnic marriage in the Misaje area, drawing on this and the previous chapter.

In the Grassfields, switching ethnic identity is linked to religious conversion and interethnic marriage. As outlined above, it is mainly Grassfielders who engage in such processes by converting to Islam, marrying a Muslim partner and consequently adopting Hausa identity. Yet Hausa identity in the Grassfields is composite and relational, and permits individuals to retain their original identity at a sub-ethnic level. Thus, Muslim converts have ample opportunity to switch between different frames of reference and to explore their links with both Hausa and Grassfields communities.

Moreover, Muslim converts and Grassfields spouses of Hausa or Mbororo partners personify cross-cutting ties. Due to their familiarity and loyalty to both groups, they often act as conduits and facilitate communication and interaction between Grassfielders, Mbororo and Hausa. Yet their integrative capacities are largely confined to the interpersonal level and to times of peaceful coexistence. In conflict situations their dual loyalties may become untenable. They may need to take sides and, by doing so, run the risk of becoming targets of criticism. To illustrate this argument I will take the example of Amina, the wife of the *sarkin hausawa*, and discuss her role in the investiture conflict described in Chapter 1.

For many Grassfielders in Misaje who aspired to marry a Muslim partner or to convert to Islam, Amina served as a model. She enjoyed a good reputation and the general support of members of both the Muslim and non-Muslim population of Misaje. In the investiture conflict, however, Amina was faced with the predicament of siding either with Grassfielders or Muslims. When the issue arose about Muslims refusing to take off their caps, and Grassfielders threatened to bring out their dangerous *nggumba ju-ju*, Amina was personally confronted by Nchaney individuals. As she explained, they appealed to her Grassfields background and asked her to mediate on their behalf. Yet being the wife of the Hausa chief, she was bound to side with the Muslim community. Consequently, local Grassfielders accused her of endorsing Muslim aggression and treated her as a traitor. As we know, in the end the conflict was contained through the divisional officer's intervention, and both parties laid aside their hostility in order to restore peaceful coexistence. At the time of my fieldwork, three years after the event, Amina was no longer discredited by my Grassfields interlocutors, but entertained good relations with Grassfielders, Hausa and Mbororo.

Similarly, as discussed above, the funerals of Grassfields converts may arise as a site of contention where religious differences and competing political claims are played out. Thus, as the case of Amina and other examples illustrate, there is no noticeable correlation between the existence of cross-cutting ties generated through religious conversion and interethnic marriage, and the instance or intensity of conflict. These findings support the conclusion of Schlee (2000: 73; 2004: 114) that cross-cutting ties in themselves have no active effect, but may be used as raw material for political rhetoric. Their integrative propensity, however, may be applicable in the aftermath of conflict by facilitating the reinstitution of social relations between members of the conflicting parties.

Notes

1. On notions of death and burial rites in the Grassfields, see e.g. Haaf and Fondö (1992: 175–91), Koloss (1980; 2000: 329–46) and Ritzenthaler and Ritzenthaler (1962: 62–73).
2. Sani Abacha was president of Nigeria from 1993 to 1998.
3. M.B., Misaje, 8 January 2002.
4. Similar examples have been provided by Cohen and Odhiambo (1992) concerning the burial of a prominent politician in Kenya, and by Geertz (1973: 142–69) for eastern central Java, where the burial of a boy became the centre of a conflict between rival political factions. Geschiere (2005, 2009) engages with burial rites as a site of contention over belonging.
5. Similarly, van Santen (1993: 228–44) compares funeral rites of non-Muslim and Islamized Mafa in northern Cameroon. She states significant differences, but does not report any emerging conflict.

6   In comparison, my Bessa host settled the bridewealth for his Nchaney wife at 40,000 CFA (€60), while my Hausa neighbour contributed 150,000 CFA (€230) for the indirect dowry of his Hausa wife.
7   Fadi, Misaje, 26 November 2001. This conversation was held in Pidgin English, and Fadi used the expression 'Church' to refer to both the Muslim and Christian faiths as well as their respective prayer houses.
8   Karimu, Misaje, 16 November 2001.
9   According to Yamani (1998: 154), Islam permits Muslim men to marry non-Muslim women provided they are 'people of the Book' (Jewish or Christian). Muslim women, on the other hand, are prohibited from marrying non-Muslim men; their relationship would be considered illegal and their children illegitimate.
10 B.J., Misaje, 24 December 2001.
11 Misaje, 13 January 2001.
12 Muslim scholars, commonly known as *mallam*, provide a variety of mystico-religious services, such as performing prayers or preparing Koranic amulets (Burnham 1996: 58–59). They combine Islamic techniques taught in the Koran and other holy books with alternative methods like herbal treatment and divination. Alternatively, there are Mbororo and Hausa healers whose proficiency is based on their knowledge of medicinal plants and their personal connection to the spirit world. Both categories of Muslim religious specialists are widely respected for their knowledge of the occult, including its positive and negative applications.
13 H.G., Misaje, 24 November 2001.
14 While in the Koran the concept of a spiritual and legal guide (Arabic: *murshid*) is acknowledged, their responsibility does not extend to the social domain. Conversely, the *jagora/kollitowo* in the Grassfields is mainly concerned with the integration of their convert into the Hausa community, while spiritual guidance is often provided by a *mallam*. Thus, the role of the *jagora/kollitowo* seems to be adapted to the particularities of this region, where Muslim conversion implies integration into a distinct social environment.
15 S.S., e-mail communication, 25 June 2003.
16 Aisha, Misaje, 16 October 2001.

7

The Murder of Mr X

Legal Pluralism and Conflict Management in the Early 2000s

In Chapter 1, I presented the case study of the investiture conflict of 1997. As I have argued, the incident was shaped by the socially destabilizing effects of the country's political liberalization, and it reflected a heightened tendency towards violent forms of conflict resolution. By the time of my fieldwork in the early 2000s, local approaches to conflict resolution had changed. Individuals and groups tended to adopt procedural strategies, such as political lobbying and litigation. These strategies, while having existed before, gained popularity in the light of global discourses on human and minority rights and the activities of NGOs, in particular human rights and ethnic elite associations.

It is my aim in this chapter to situate current strategies of conflict management in their political and legal context and to examine the degree to which they contribute to social cohesion in the Cameroon Grassfields. By way of example, I will analyse a conflict that emerged in 2001 over the occult murder of a Bessa man of which a wealthy Mbororo grazier was suspected. My analysis will not centre on the murder and its actual exposition, but on the ensuing conflict between the Bessa and Mbororo communities. Finally, I will relate the incident – henceforth referred to as 'the murder conflict' – to Cameroon's plural legal system.

Procedural Strategies of Conflict Resolution

Elwert (2001, 2004, 2005) developed a model in which conflicts are ordered by a field of four poles, namely destruction, warring, procedure and avoidance. These poles are situated along the two axes of more or less violence and stronger or weaker social embedding (Table 7.1).

Table 7.1: Elwert's field of four poles. Source: Elwert (2001: 2544).

	More violence ˅	Less violence ˅
Stronger embedding >	warring	procedure
Weaker embedding >	destruction	avoidance

In analysing the investiture conflict of 1997, I concluded that the main strategies employed by Grassfielders, Mbororo and Hausa in managing interethnic conflict were avoidance and destruction. By the early 2000s these were no longer preferred strategies. Individuals and groups reverted to approaches that in Elwert's model belong to the pole of procedure. Drawing on Luhmann (1969), Elwert defines procedure as follows:

> A procedure is distinct from daily interaction by its form and ordered sequence of action. Elections, court cases, and auctions have also been seen as conflict resolution procedures. During a procedure some power differentials are suspended. It may, for example, be excluded that a stronger person physically harms a weaker person during the procedure. A procedure has an outcome with consequences in action. Who will profit from the outcome is, in principle, open. It should be called a procedure only when it ends in a conclusion which has meaningful consequences for action. (Elwert 2001: 2544)

Elwert further distinguishes between conclusive and pending procedure. While a pending procedure may have the ritual form of procedure, it does not result in consequential conclusions. 'Thus, the pending procedure is not a way of conflict resolution but a way of conflict perpetuation. Pending procedures can have a high annoyance potential and are rather forms of warring with reduced violence' (Elwert 2001: 2544).[1]

Elwert's distinction between conclusive and pending procedure will be instrumental in analysing the integrative or dissociative potential of current procedural strategies of conflict management used in the Misaje area. We may remember that the colonial and postcolonial administrations instituted a number of procedures to resolve farmer–herder conflicts. Yet, as these procedures never resulted in constant and consequential conclusions, they had no lasting effect, but contributed to the perpetuation of conflict and corresponding discourses.

I would like to add a cautious note concerning my application of Elwert's conflict model to the Cameroonian case. I fully agree with Bierschenk (2004) – and my case material supports this – that neither of the conflict categories suggested by Elwert refers to exclusive or alternative strategies; rather, they should be seen as complementary and combinable. Accordingly, by describing avoidance and destruction as the dominant conflict strategies of the 1990s, and procedure as a popular strategy in the early 2000s, I do not indicate absolute categories but a historical and regional trend. Moreover, I acknowledge the possibility of actors exploring multiple and situationally changing strategies, as happened in the investiture conflict when individuals alternated between strategies of avoidance and confrontation.

The procedural approaches I am concerned with are political lobbying and litigation. Both strategies have been applied by individuals and groups in the murder conflict. The recent popularity of these strategies is related to global discourses on human and minority rights, the political and legal measures of the Cameroonian government, and the regional and local activities of NGOs.

The Cameroonian government favourably responded to the demands of the UN, World Bank, IMF and other international organizations to introduce a democratic system, to respect human and minority rights and to adjust its legal frameworks accordingly. Among other measures it introduced press freedom, enabled the registration of political parties and 'socio-cultural and development associations', and incorporated the rights of minorities in the revised Cameroonian constitution. Furthermore, the government ratified human rights conventions. For example, as one of the gendarmes in Misaje proudly pointed out, it adopted regulations condemning the use of torture by state functionaries.[2]

In the same way that the Cameroonian government responded to global discourses and international pressure, local population groups and individuals reacted to the upsurge of new political and legal avenues. As outlined in previous chapters, a number of NGOs emerged, many of which adopted programmes advocating human rights and civil society. In the Misaje area, the organization most active in the field of legal counselling at the time of my fieldwork was Ballotiral. Although Ballotiral does not figure prominently in the murder conflict, I will briefly outline its paralegal programme, as its activities provide a fair idea of the ways in which the local population has gradually been familiarized with procedural strategies of conflict resolution.

The Ballotiral programme 'Access to Justice' was initiated in 1998 and was run by a qualified lawyer in collaboration with his Ballotiral colleagues. They trained Mbororo individuals as paralegals (community-based resource persons) and provided legal counselling to Mbororo community members. For example, from March 2000 to October 2001, the Ballotiral team assisted in twenty-three cases. These included eleven cases of abuse of office by state functionaries, six farmer–herder disputes, three cases of alleged cattle theft, two offences against women and one case of legal interference in a case handled by the Muslim *alkali* court. The Ballotiral staff supported their Mbororo clients by discussing possible legal strategies and by submitting depositions and petitions to the relevant legal bodies. Mbororo individuals who decided to pursue a lawsuit were required to engage a legal counsel.

The primary aim of the Ballotiral paralegal programme was to inform the Mbororo population about their civil rights and to encourage them to challenge the extortionist practices of public officials. While many Mbororo have been the targets of extortion and abuse due to their lack of literacy and relative poverty, most have shied away from exploring legal avenues because they lack the necessary familiarity with the state legal system. This predicament is not particular to the Mbororo, but is widely shared by the rural population of the Grassfields. One of Ballotiral's main achievements in the Misaje area in 2001 was the demotion and transfer of the then commandant of the gendarmerie, whom they repeatedly reported to the divisional court for false accusations, unlawful detention and extortionist practices. While Ballotiral centred its assistance on cases against government functionaries, it largely refrained from intervening in disputes between Mbororo individuals and between Mbororo and members of neighbouring communities. Nonetheless, many Mbororo have been enthusiastic about political lobbying and litigation as effective strategies of conflict resolution, and have applied them to other conflict situations, such as land disputes and leadership rivalries. While the growing inclination for procedural strategies has been most evident among Mbororo, other population groups have explored similar strategies, as the case of the murder conflict will show.

Legal Pluralism in Northwest Cameroon

In order to assess current procedural approaches to conflict resolution and their impact on interethnic relations, it is important to analyse the legal framework to which they relate. Here the concept of legal pluralism is relevant (e.g. Galanter 1981; Griffiths 1986; von Benda-Beckmann 1994; von Benda-Beckmann et al. 2009). It refers to the coexistence of plural normative orders and also points to the different origins, interpretations and applications of laws within these normative systems. In the following I will briefly delineate its connotations in the Cameroonian context.

The Cameroonian legal framework includes a number of parallel, partly overlapping, partly rival normative systems. As a consequence of the legacies of French and British colonial administration, Cameroon simultaneously operates two systems of state law, namely English Common Law and French Administrative Law, which are applied in the anglophone and francophone regions respectively. Furthermore, institutions of customary and Islamic law are integrated into state law and operate alongside local normative forums.

Keebet von Benda-Beckmann (1981) introduced the notion of 'forum shopping and shopping forums' in referring to clients choosing between legal forums and the competition for cases between these forums. This notion also applies to the Cameroonian context, where clients have a wide choice of different forums of negotiation, mediation and adjudication. They tend to base their choice on their familiarity with the respective normative order applied in that forum and on their socio-political or economic ability to influence adjudicators in their favour. Besides, they frequently change course or pursue parallel avenues. Conversely, the forums also compete for cases. The examples I know best concern land and farmer–herder disputes (see Fisiy 1992). The forums that are officially entitled to resolve land and farmer–herder disputes are the land administrative board and the farmer–herder commission respectively. Both are administrative institutions composed of members of the sub-divisional administration and representatives of local communities. Other institutions that claim responsibility to adjudicate land and farmer–herder disputes are the traditional council (the primary legal institution of Grassfields societies) and the forces of law and order (police and gendarmerie). The latter tend to label such cases not as land or farmer–herder disputes but as criminal offences, such as 'trespassing' or 'destruction'. The reasons for competition between these forums over land and farmer–herder disputes are of a political and economic nature: control over land implies power, and each negotiation entails the opportunity to extort a bribe. In reviewing administrative files on farmer–herder and land disputes, I came across cases in which several legal avenues were pursued in parallel, leading to contradictory judgements, procedural confusion and considerable expense for claimants and defendants.

It is important here to note that – more often than not – clients are not fully aware of all available legal forums, their respective requirements and procedures. Similarly, mediators and adjudicators frequently ignore the possibility of multiple applications of Cameroonian legislation. In this context, NGOs with paralegal programmes (such as Ballotiral) have a strong impact. They advise forum shoppers in their choice of legal alternatives. Furthermore, by highlighting irregularities and failures, they induce mediators and adjudicators to be aware of legal developments and to fulfil their responsibilities.

The following illustration gives a rough idea of the plural legal avenues that are open to forum shoppers in northwest Cameroon (Table 7.2). I should clarify, however, that not all forums are equally applicable to all conflict situations, and that their jurisdictions vary, ranging from mediation to arbitration and adjudication. The table is complemented with brief descriptions of the forums' primary liabilities.

The legal authority contacted first is normally the community leader, who assumes the role of a mediator in family and matters internal to the community, such as marriage disputes, power struggles, witchcraft allegations and land disputes. If an agreement cannot be achieved at this level, the case is taken further, often to the traditional council, the main adjudicative institution of Grassfields chiefdoms. Its members are village elders and notables who

Table 7.2: Schematic illustration of legal forums operative in northwest Cameroon.

Levels		State law		Local law	Muslim law
	administrative institutions	*judiciary*	*law enforcement agencies*		
national		Supreme Court			
regional		Appeal Court	military tribunal		
divisional		High Court			alkali court
sub-divisional	divisional officer, land administrative board, farmer-grazier commission		gendarmerie, police	customary court	
village				traditional council	
community				Grassfields (sub-)chief	Mbororo and Hausa leader

convene their meetings under the chairmanship of the local Grassfields chief (*fon*). Muslims tend to eschew the traditional council and to report cases to the Muslim *alkali* court. The *alkali* court and the customary court were introduced by the British colonial administration and their jurisdictions are limited to marital, inheritance and contract matters.

Individuals frequently opt to consult the divisional officer (DO) in a wide variety of conflict matters. The DO only provides a forum for negotiation and mediation, while legal adjudication within the state system entails reporting the case to the judiciary. Matters reported to the gendarmerie assume the character of a criminal offence and are supposed to be prosecuted at the level of the High Court. From here, cases may be taken further to the Appeal Court and Supreme Court for final judgement. In exceptional cases, a criminal offence may be judged by a military tribunal. This happened for example in 2002, when four Mbororo were arrested and condemned to ten years imprisonment on the basis of participating in a collective attempt to recover community territory. The solicitors for the accused Mbororo claimed that the procedure was inappropriate, and with the support of international human rights organizations they succeeded in reversing the judgement.

Another factor complicating Cameroon's plural legal system is corruption, which many informants and authors have described as an integral feature of the Cameroonian state. It is important here to clarify my use of the term corruption, as references to allegedly corrupt government officials and local chiefs have been made throughout the study. Interlocutors (including farmers, herders, journalists, academics, politicians and government officials) frequently invoked corruption as one of the main reasons for the malfunctioning of the Cameroonian state. The features they referred to include bribery, extortion and the misappropriation of public resources. Furthermore, corruption comprises transactions of money as well as the exploitation of socio-political networks. It is difficult, however, to assess the degree to which the frequent rumours and allegations of corruption are based on actual fact, as corrupt practices are generally characterized by an aura of secrecy. This also applies to the conflict studied in this chapter, in which a number of actors were suspected of corruption.

The subject of corruption has been popular in the literature on Cameroon and West Africa more generally (e.g. Bayart et al. 1999; Bierschenk 2004; Blundo and de Sardan 2001; Chabal and Daloz 2002; Fombad 2000). Best known is Bayart's work, where he describes the Cameroonian state as a rhizome (or neo-patrimonial) state that is characterized by actors' exploitation of networks of family ties and patron–client relationships (Bayart 1993). In describing the political logic supporting this system, he uses the Cameroonian expression 'the politics of the belly', which has numerous equivalents throughout sub-Saharan Africa:

> It [the politics of the belly] denotes at the same time the accumulation of wealth through tenure of political power (implied in the proverb 'the goat grazes where it is tied'), the symbolic reference to family lineage and to witchcraft, and the physical corpulence which is felt to be appropriate in 'big men' or powerful women. (Bayart et al. 1999: 8)

As Bayart (1993) points out, the politics of the belly is a complex mode of government with roots in the past and the present. Corruption is thus not a new phenomenon. However, it became an issue of public contention in the second half of the 1990s, when the Cameroonian government officially addressed the subject in response to demands by the international community. In 1997, a group of Cameroonian scientists, the Groupe d'Etudes et de Recherche en Démocratie, Développement Economique et Sociale (GERDDES), carried out research on corruption in Cameroon, the results of which were published two years later (GERDDES 1999). In 1998, the government launched a sensitization campaign as part of the national governance programme. In the same year as well as the year following, Cameroon was ranked first in the corruption perception index of Transparency International, a German-based NGO.

Today, Cameroon is no longer at the top of the world's purportedly most corrupt countries. Nonetheless, the government's attempts at eradicating corruption were seen critically (e.g. Eboussi Boulaga and Zinga 2002).

In 2000 the government instituted an anti-corruption observatory which, six years later, was replaced by the Commission Nationale Anti-Corruption (CONAC), still in operation today. In 2004 the judicial and disciplinary anti-corruption campaign *Opération Epervier* (Operation Sparrowhawk) was initiated with the proclaimed goal of prosecuting the misappropriation of public funds (Mebenga et al. 2007). As a result, a considerable number of high-ranking government officials were put on trial and imprisoned. However, public opinion has it that punitive action was taken selectively against the president's political adversaries.

In the view of many interlocutors and international donor organizations, corruption is a negative factor that impedes the successful functioning of the state. Conversely, some authors – such as Bierschenk (2004) with regard to the judiciary in Benin – argue that corruption may also have positive implications and actually enable the operation of state sectors that otherwise would collapse due to a lack of resources and personnel. Similarly, the Cameroonian anti-corruption observatory reported upon their visit to the Ministry of Public Services that the lack of office equipment endorsed acts of corruption, as clients freely offered to pay for some of the services that otherwise could not be accomplished. According to the national survey of GERDDES (1999: 31), 31 per cent of their informants admitted to freely offering gifts, money and other things to state functionaries in order to obtain services to which they were entitled. As GERDDES concludes, '[f]or these people, corruption has ceased to be considered a social evil, it has become a way of life, a social act that has become so much a part of them that they perform it spontaneously' (GERDDES 1999: 31).

By embedding corruption in the framework of legal pluralism, I interpret it as part of an institutionalized practice that is structured by certain rules and that provides alternative avenues to official administrative and legal procedures. Moreover, by relating corruption to the conflict model of Elwert, we may see it as a factor that undermines the legitimacy and effectiveness of legal procedural strategies. In many cases it results in pending procedures and promotes the perpetuation of conflict rather than its resolution.

Having sketched out procedural approaches to conflict management and Cameroon's plural legal framework, I will now turn to the murder conflict of 2001, which will provide further examples of local actors' strategies in dealing with conflict and legal pluralism in the Misaje area.

The Murder of Mr X

At the time of my research, the murder conflict was still ongoing and no single, consistent account had yet been established. The version presented below is a composite of different informants' accounts, and is intended to depict the major events as well as the responses of individuals and groups. To help the reader understand the murder conflict in its complexity, I have integrated a number of explanatory and analytical statements. At a later stage I will introduce the standpoints of some of the key actors in order to clarify the multiple layers of conflict and the diverse strategies of conflict resolution that characterize this social situation.

Dramatis Personae

The dramatis personae in the murder conflict are individuals and collectives. The main collective actor is the Bessa Cultural and Development Association (BECUDA), whose activities have been described in Chapter 2. The individual actors are members of the Bessa and Mbororo communities living on the territory of one of the three Bessa chiefdoms situated within Misaje Sub-Division. At this point I will concentrate on three key figures, namely the victim, the alleged murderer and the latter's prime opponent. Other players, such as the suspected murderer's accomplices, the local *fon* and the outgoing and incoming DOs, will be introduced in the course of the story. For obvious reasons I will keep individuals and places anonymous.[3]

The victim of the alleged murder was Mr X, a Bessa farmer. While living at a considerable distance from the village, he regularly visited the market to sell farm produce and palm oil. Mr X was generally considered a social outsider. He allegedly smoked marijuana, repeatedly harassed his relatives and was known as a notorious palm nut, sheep and cattle thief.

Alhaji Y was the prime suspect in the murder case. He is a Mbororo pastoralist and the son of an *arDo* (Mbororo leader). His father settled in the area in the 1930s and was installed as *arDo* in the late 1940s. Alhaji Y controls a large cattle-grazing area, part of which adjoined the farm land of Mr X. He is one of the few highly educated Mbororo in the region. He attended primary and secondary school in Cameroon, studied business administration in Nigeria and had worked for the Ministry of Industrial and Commercial Development for more than fifteen years. Alhaji Y is married to a European who spent some time in his compound and eventually returned to her home country. They have a child together and pay each other sporadic visits. Alhaji Y was generally described as a proud and difficult person.

Mr Z was said to be one of Alhaji Y's key opponents. He is a member of the Bessa elite and works at the legal department. In the context of the murder case he acted as a spokesperson for the Bessa community and facilitated the case through his connection with the legal department. The enmity between Alhaji Y and Mr Z was said to be rooted in earlier incidents. They competed for a political post in the regional branch of the ruling party (CPDM sub-section president), which was eventually given to Mr Z. Furthermore, the younger brother of Alhaji Y and the daughter of Mr Z had a love affair that culminated in the birth of an extramarital child, a development disapproved of by both Mr Z and Alhaji Y.

The Course of Events

In describing the murder conflict I will distinguish three major phases, each of which includes a series of events and actions that relate to the initial incident. I will depict these in chronological order, starting in July 2001, and end by summarizing the state of affairs in 2004.

Before doing so, I wish to discuss a particular feature of the murder conflict, namely its conflation with discourses on occult aggression which relate to the victim's decapitation. The murder at the heart of this conflict was not perceived as a simple case of manslaughter but as entailing an additional, polluting act of violence, namely the removal of human body parts for the purpose of self-enrichment.

This was not the first case of its kind in the Grassfields or in Cameroon. Rumours about 'cut-head' – occult murder and the trade in human heads – have been present in the Misaje area since the 1950s and 1960s. They gained momentum in the course of Cameroon's democratic transition and economic crisis of the 1990s, when cases of occult murder were frequently publicized in the media. Informants identified human heads as lucrative contraband goods, trafficked by African suppliers to Western buyers. The heads' assumed uses were of a practical and magical nature, and these uses were associated with technological innovation and the production of modern consumer goods. Similarly, their trafficking was perceived as requiring extraordinary skills, thus rendering the trade in human body parts part of the realm of the occult (Pelican 2006: 352–92).

A growing preoccupation with the occult over the past decades has been documented for many parts of Africa, including Cameroon. However, the surprising element in this particular murder case is the apparent transgression of ethnic and cultural boundaries. As informants explained, it has long been assumed that witchcraft and related occult activities are a feature of Grassfields society, while Mbororo and Hausa – on the grounds of their cultural and religious difference – were thought to abstain from such practices. Yet over the past few years, this perception has changed, as exemplified by the murder conflict. Thus, as an expression of their complex integration, members of all ethnic groups represented in the Misaje area may be suspected of participation in occult activities. However, as the reaction of Alhaji Y will illustrate, Mbororo and Hausa do not voluntarily submit to this kind of integration but decidedly distance themselves from occult activities, attributing them to non-Muslims.

It is not my intention here to prove or disprove the possibility of Alhaji Y's involvement in occult aggression and the alleged trade in human body parts. Rather, I am interested in informants' assessments which help us understand the social position of Alhaji Y within the local community. What actually happened to the head of Mr X, if it was removed intentionally, if it was carried away by the river, if it was sold or hidden, will most probably remain a secret. With these considerations in mind, we now turn to the details of the murder conflict.

Phase 1: The Discovery of the Corpse

On 19 July 2001, a corpse was found on the bank of a river in the Bessa area. The corpse lacked a head, and as various accounts indicated, the genitals and heart had been removed and veins extracted from the legs. The corpse was in a state of progressive decay and had been lying there for approximately two weeks. The people who found it were from a nearby village. Since nobody was missing in their area, they sent news to the neighbouring village. A group of men went to the riverbank to examine the corpse, which was soon identified as the body of Mr X. They reported the case to the gendarmerie in the divisional capital Nkambe, and the following day a gendarme was sent to investigate the scene of the crime.

Circumstantial evidence pointed to Alhaji Y who, more than two weeks earlier, had reported the theft of cattle to the local *fon*. He also informed the *fon* of his plan to send his herdsmen to find Mr X, whom he suspected of the act. This was not the first incident of this kind, and Alhaji Y seemed committed to hunting down the suspected thief. As his herdsmen did not know the exact location of Mr X's compound, they were guided by a Bessa man who had occasionally worked for Alhaji Y.

The day the corpse was found, Alhaji Y was absent from his home. He had gone to the capital Yaoundé to arrange his papers, since he planned to visit his wife in Europe. In his absence, the herdsmen he had sent to investigate the theft were arrested and imprisoned, together with their Bessa guide. As a relative of Alhaji Y explained, the herdsmen were severely tortured and eventually confessed that they had found Mr X in his hut and may inadvertently have beaten him to death in an act of self-defence. Yet they strongly repudiated the accusation of having molested and dragged the corpse to the riverbank so that traces of their crime would be washed away.

A few days after the herdsmen's detention, Alhaji Y returned to Nkambe. He took immediate action and contacted the higher judicial authority, namely the *procureur général* of the Appeal Court in Bamenda, to intervene against the imprisonment of his men. Three days later, the legal department at Nkambe received the instruction to release the suspects on bail. While the herdsmen were bailed the same day, their Bessa guide remained in custody for ten more days until he, too, was bailed by his Mbororo acquaintances. After the release of Alhaji Y's herdsmen on bail, the gendarmes suspended their prosecution.

Phase 2: Bessa Counteraction

By the time Alhaji Y and his herdsmen were settled once again in their homes, the atmosphere in the village was loaded with suspicion and fear, and with rumours about Alhaji Y's involvement in the 'cut-head' business. According to different accounts, Alhaji Y allegedly had a contract with a white partner to supply a total of twenty-eight heads, for which he was paid an enormous sum of money. Purportedly, Mr X's head was already the twenty-sixth. Other rumours indicated that Mr X's head was the seventh and was to be sent to Alhaji Y's wife in Europe. That was also the reason for Alhaji Y's journey to Yaoundé. These and similar rumours circulated among the Bessa community and were spread throughout Misaje Sub-Division. While many Grassfields interlocutors told these stories with conviction, Mbororo and Hausa informants were more reluctant to believe that a Mbororo man should participate in the 'cut-head' business. Yet, ultimately, they left the question open while hinting at Alhaji Y's allegedly ruthless character.

The Bessa community was apprehensive about further attacks, and potential strategies of defence and retribution were discussed at the level of BECUDA. On 25 August 2001, members of the BECUDA home chapter (the association's branch in the Bessa home area) convened a meeting at which they came up with a number of resolutions to guide the future approach of the Bessa population towards Alhaji Y and the Mbororo community. They recorded their resolutions in an official document and communicated them to the Bessa population at home and in the coastal areas, to representatives of the Mbororo community and to the sub-divisional administration. The document included a total of twelve resolutions, which I will discuss by focusing on three crucial issues: the demand of the return of the missing head, the appeal to trust in traditional and legal prosecution, and the plea for a boycott on all socio-economic relations with their Mbororo neighbours.

In the view of local Grassfielders, it was a crucial requirement that the crime against Mr X should be expiated and the head returned so as to enable a proper burial. The murderer was expected to acknowledge the deed and to apologize to the deceased's family. By denying his involvement and by refusing to produce the victim's head, Alhaji Y was seen to offend Mr X's relatives and, more importantly, to endanger the Bessa community, as the deceased might turn into a haunting spirit if not given a proper burial. To counteract this possible consequence, Bessa specialists performed so-called traditional rites that were intended to affect the family of Alhaji Y and make them leave the Bessa area. Following Bessa informants' accounts, similar measures had been taken before, but disloyal Bessa individuals had rendered them ineffective by providing Alhaji Y with counter-medicine. To avoid a similar outcome, the BECUDA home chapter emphasized the urgency of collaborative action and solidarity among members of the Bessa community.

In a second cluster of resolutions, the BECUDA home chapter pleaded to the Bessa population to refrain from violence and trust in ritual and legal prosecution. Many Bessa resented Alhaji Y for his immediate intervention in the legal investigation. They assumed that he would try to further obfuscate the matter by using his political influence and wealth. The BECUDA home chapter appealed to the external elite to counteract Alhaji Y's attempts by tabling protests to higher judicial authorities. Furthermore, it was alleged that Alhaji Y was lobbying for the transfer of two Bessa individuals who were instrumental in the murder investigation; one was a police officer, the other was Mr Z, who worked with the legal department. Members of the external Bessa elite were thus encouraged to exploit their political connections and oppose the transfer of their fellows.

Thirdly, the BECUDA home chapter proposed a boycott on all social and economic interaction between Bessa and Mbororo in order to reinforce their claim for the return of the victim's head and to reassert Bessa customary rights to land and land-based resources. They validated the resolution by referring to previous violent encounters between Bessa and Mbororo, and to long-standing grievances over crop destruction and rival land claims. While Alhaji Y was accused of monopolizing Bessa land, other Mbororo were blamed for selling Bessa land to a third party.

By initiating a boycott on all interaction with Mbororo, the BECUDA home chapter attempted to ethnicize the conflict. They justified extending the ban to the entire Mbororo community with the argument that some Mbororo leaders had morally and financially supported Alhaji Y and thus needed to be reprimanded. Furthermore, BECUDA officials had identified a lack of common initiative and solidarity among Bessa as a major obstacle to successfully counteracting Alhaji Y. They aimed at fostering a sense of unity by framing the conflict in ethnic terms.

The resolution was endorsed by two of the three Bessa communities. The third kept a neutral stance on the grounds that their territory was distant to the location of the murder and their Mbororo neighbours had no relations with Mbororo of that area. In order to reinforce the agreement, the representatives of the two Bessa communities performed traditional rites with the effect that every person who collaborated with the Mbororo would be punished by the ancestors and afflicted by illness and death.

In the long run, however, BECUDA's attempts at ethnicizing the conflict by opposing the Bessa to the Mbororo failed. Many Bessa individuals were unwilling to relinquish their work relations and friendships with their Mbororo neighbours, as they constituted an important source of income and assistance. Moreover, they defused the danger of ritual sanctions by using protective medicine. BECUDA members blamed the failure of the boycott on the weakness of Bessa institutions of social control and the cowardly character of their people. The stereotypes of Bessa cowardice and passivity were a consistent theme in interviews with Bessa informants.

Three days after the BECUDA home chapter had made its resolutions, it invited Alhaji Y for a meeting. Alhaji Y first paid a visit to the local *fon* before he proceeded to the meeting place. On the way there, he was blocked by a tree lying across the road and was threatened by Bessa attackers. He immediately turned back to the *fon*'s palace, where he left his motorcycle and went home on horseback. A few hours later, Mbororo youths entered the village armed with bows and arrows and intimidated Bessa villagers. As similar incidents had happened before, Bessa villagers were aware of Mbororo herders' fighting skills. Eventually, a cohort of gendarmes descended on the village and arrested some Mbororo youths.

As Alhaji Y later explained to me, he was frightened by the Bessa roadblock, which he perceived as a deliberate threat to his life instigated by Mr Z. In a meeting with the senior DO, which took place a few days after the incident, Alhaji Y attributed the mutilation of Mr X's corpse to the two elite Bessa: Mr Z and his colleague, the policeman. He suggested that the two men had found the corpse, cut off the head and buried it with the aim of aggravating the charge against him from a case of theft and self-defence to a case of calculated occult murder. The complaint was registered, but due to lack of evidence no further action was taken.

On 2 September 2001, the DO of Misaje Sub-Division, in whose constituency the murder had occurred, organized a meeting to which he invited the heads of the gendarmerie, the police and the rural council of Misaje, as well as the local *fon*, his notables and representatives of BECUDA. The DO expressed his sympathy for the family of the deceased and the Bessa community. He instructed them to trust in legal procedure and to abstain from further acts of violence. Furthermore, he urged them to desist from generalizing their sanctions to the entire Mbororo community, as many Mbororo were themselves critical of Alhaji Y's comportment. Finally, he insisted on being informed immediately of all incidents in order to enable a fair prosecution of the matter. The meeting was documented and the minutes distributed to the participants. As the DO confided to me in a personal interview, he actually sympathized with the Bessa population, as he himself had come to know Alhaji Y as a difficult person with considerable economic and political influence. However, in his position as administrator he could not officially take sides, since he primarily had to maintain peace and guarantee fair treatment to all.

On the day of the meeting with the DO, BECUDA elite members filed a petition with the Ministry of Justice, demanding the protection of their rights as an indigenous minority, as stipulated by the national constitution. They urged the government to ensure there was a trial for the murder of Mr X, and to clarify land-rights issues between Bessa and Mbororo residents. They never received an answer and filed a second petition in spring 2002. As a qualified lawyer and staff member of Ballotiral explained to me, the Bessa side lacked a decisive individual to follow up legal action against Alhaji Y. Because the deceased's relatives were unwilling to file charges and hire a lawyer, the prosecuting party in the case would have to be the state, which had little incentive to pursue it. Meanwhile, BECUDA's strategy of writing petitions and effecting collective action against its opponent was of no consequence.

Phase 3: Further Developments

The months of September and October were relatively quiet, but the social climate between Bessa and Mbororo remained tense.

On 18 and 19 November 2001, BECUDA held its annual conference. It was a major event which was well attended by BECUDA delegations from the coastal areas, the local Bessa population, members of neighbouring groups (including Mbororo), as well as representatives of the sub-divisional administration, the gendarmerie, the police and the education department. The meeting was inaugurated by the BECUDA president, an external elite living in the South West Region. In his opening speech he addressed the murder conflict. He requested a minute of silence in commemoration of Mr X and confirmed the measures against the Mbororo population that had been instituted in August 2001. After the president's introduction, the representative of the BECUDA elite circle addressed the Bessa population's most urgent problems, including infrastructural deficiencies and farmer–herder conflicts. He linked the murder of Mr X to ongoing disputes over crop damage and land. Next, the resolutions of the August meeting were read out. Then the floor was handed over to the new DO, who had replaced his predecessor in late October 2001. He expressed his sympathy with the Bessa community because of the death of the Mr X, of which he had read in a local newspaper. He assured the Bessa community of his support in hunting down the murderer, but advised them 'to keep a cool head' and only pursue legal avenues. He also affirmed his intention to resolve land disputes and farmer–herder conflicts in accordance with administrative regulations. The DO's speech was received with appreciation by the Bessa population, and BECUDA officials who saw him as supporting their cause.

The occasion was attended by a number of Mbororo, mainly youths, who were attracted by the cultural performances. Some Mbororo girls had come to the village to grind corn and were curious to hear what the conference organizers had to say about the murder case. From conversations with Mbororo interlocutors it became clear that they disapproved of the generalized sanctions BECUDA had instituted against the Mbororo community. They thought it unfair to hold all Mbororo responsible for the alleged fault of an individual. Yet, as I observed during the conference, they largely kept their objections to themselves and interacted with their Bessa neighbours on normal terms. Alhaji Y and his close relatives stayed away from the event.

During the BECUDA conference, the social atmosphere in the village was noticeably tense. Bessa individuals repeatedly and publicly expressed their contempt for their Mbororo neighbours, pointing accusing fingers at Mbororo passers-by and denying them the right to stay on Bessa land. Yet these eruptions were contingent on the occasion. Once the conference had passed, Bessa individuals were far less outspoken about the Mbororo.

In an interview in December 2001, a BECUDA official stated that the boycott on interaction with Mbororo herders had been lifted and ritual sanctions against the collaborators neutralized. He explained that Mbororo individuals had eventually apologized for the death of Mr X and pleaded that the matter should not be generalized. Moreover, the DO encouraged reconciliation between the two groups.

When I left Cameroon in January 2002, legal proceedings were stagnating. Via e-mail I was informed that legal proceedings had continued until 2003. Several court hearings took place at Nkambe, and Alhaji Y was required to bring forward all suspects released on bail. One of them absconded to Nigeria and it took some time to bring him back. Due to repeated adjournments, the local *fon* pleaded to the judge to be exempted from attending the court hearings on the grounds of health problems. This move was interpreted both as a sign of the *fon*'s unwillingness to testify against Alhaji Y and of his corruption. As the Bessa witnesses refused to give evidence, the case was dismissed eventually.

The same year, Mr Z was transferred to Bamenda, a development he welcomed as a way of evading witchcraft attacks from within his family. His elite colleague who worked with the police was also transferred to a distant location in north Cameroon. Thanks to the intervention of BECUDA elite members, it was possible to revoke his transfer and get him back to the divisional capital Nkambe.

In early 2004 the father of Alhaji Y died. One week later, Alhaji Y was installed as the new leader (*arDo*) of the Mbororo community. While he initially faced some opposition from among his own people, he soon became firmly established in his new position.

Analysis of the Murder Conflict

The case study includes a number of issues, such as farmer–herder disputes, cattle theft and discourses on occult aggression. Furthermore, it depicts actors' deployment of procedural strategies of conflict resolution within Cameroon's plural legal framework.

In the following I will develop two issues that are of particular relevance to the theme of my study, namely the incident's framing as an ethnic conflict, and the actors' exploration of plural legal avenues. Both subjects relate to secondary issues that will be further substantiated in the ensuing analysis of individual perspectives on the murder conflict.

From Occult Aggression to Ethnic Conflict

The murder conflict arose from an incident of occult aggression which was attributed to an economically and politically influential individual who was ell known for his assertiveness and difficult character. The accusations levelled against Alhaji Y were based on his declared enmity towards Mr X and expressed Bessa resentment concerning his apparent wealth accumulation.

In the initial phase of the murder conflict, the ethnic backgrounds of the victim and the indicted murderer were of secondary importance. As many Bessa informants argued, Alhaji Y was seen as 'a son of the soil' and a member of the local elite. They expected him to comply with Bessa conventions, which include apologizing to the victim's relatives and undergoing ritual cleansing. Alhaji Y, on the other hand, portrayed himself as a member of the local community who was temporarily ostracized on the basis of false allegations.

In identifying the source of the enmity between Mr X and Alhaji Y, interlocutors increasingly perceived and framed the conflict in economic and ethnic terms. From a Bessa perspective, the incident was grounded in long-standing farmer–herder problems and land disputes between Bessa and Mbororo. In the view of Mbororo informants, Mr X's death was the result of Bessa farmers' envy for the wealth of Mbororo graziers and the involvement of Bessa farmers in cattle theft.

By attributing the origin of the murder conflict to underlying disagreements between the two population groups, the conflict was elevated from an individual to an ethnic conflict. Although BECUDA ultimately failed in its attempt to mobilize the Bessa against the Mbororo, the murder conflict continued to be perceived in ethnic terms as an argument between the Bessa community and a Mbororo individual, Alhaji Y.

If we compare the murder conflict to the investiture conflict discussed in Chapter 1, we notice variation in the emotive and mobilizing capacity of claims to ethnic and cultural difference. In explaining this, we may draw on the argument of Geschiere (2009) who, in an attempt to delineate the seeming naturalness and emotional quality of autochthony discourses, compares two sets of rituals of belonging, namely rituals of nation-building and funerals. He concludes that the postcolonial emphasis on social engineering has lent the national celebration an artificial profile, leading to its eventual disappearance. Conversely, contemporary funerals allow for the creative involvement of all participants and entail an aesthetic concentration that engenders a shared experience. A similar interpretation may apply to the two conflict scenarios. Royal investiture ceremonies have a visceral quality, as exemplified by the masquerade performances, and require all participants' contributions. Conversely, the conferences organized by urban-based elite associations are characterized by an educational, top-down approach. This may account for BECUDA's failure to mobilize ethnic resistance.

Legal Avenues Explored by Individual and Collective Actors

The main opposing parties in the murder conflict were BECUDA (representing the Bessa community) and Alhaji Y. Both pursued legal strategies in resolving the conflict, which differed in their character and efficacy.

Alhaji Y was an educated and influential individual. By skilfully navigating the state legal system, he was able to defy the charge of premeditated murder. Conversely, the Bessa side opted for political lobbying and collective strategies within the local and state legal systems. They were less successful in their forum shopping, as they lacked the socio-political and economic means of their opponent.

The following illustration (Table 7.3) gives an overview of the normative and legal institutions that in one way or another were involved in negotiating, mediating and adjudicating the murder conflict.

The murder was classified as a criminal offence against the Cameroonian state and was prosecuted by the divisional judiciary, which provided the final judgement. The legal institutions addressed by BECUDA and the Bessa community included the traditional council, the sub-divisional administration, the gendarmerie and the Ministry of Justice. They supported the Bessa cause to varying degrees, but were unwilling or lacked the competence to intervene in the state legal proceedings. Thus, while BECUDA's strategy of mobilizing personal connections was effective in revoking the transfer of their elite colleague (the Bessa policeman), their political lobbying did not produce the desired results.

Alhaji Y focused his forum shopping on higher legal institutions. He intervened at the level of the divisional administration as well as the provincial and divisional judiciaries. Furthermore, he invested in preserving good relations with the local *fon* so as to have a supporter within the traditional council. The decisive factor leading to the acquittal of Alhaji Y and his herdsmen, however, was his

Table 7.3: Forum shopping in the murder conflict (in chronological order).

legal forum	approached by BECUDA/Bessa community	approached by Alhaji Y
gendarmerie	investigated the murder, after they were informed of the discovery of the corpse	
procureur général, Appeal Court, Bamenda		effected the release on bail of the detained herdsmen
traditional council	performed traditional rites to drive away Alhaji Y and to reinforce the boycott on interaction with Mbororo	
senior DO, Nkambe		called both parties for a reconciliatory meeting
outgoing DO, Misaje	demanded being informed and advised on legal strategies	
Ministry of Justice	solicited by BECUDA to ensure the Bessa people's civil and land rights; no reply	
incoming DO, Misaje	attended BECUDA annual conference and assured audience that state legal proceedings would continue	
High Court, Nkambe		eventually dismissed the case because witnesses refused to testify

ability to induce the relevant forums to decide in his and his herdsmen's favour. It is generally assumed that Alhaji Y used his socio-political and economic influence to corrupt local and state legal institutions as well as Bessa witnesses.

Individual Perspectives

The following statements are extracted from interviews with four key informants, namely Alhaji Y, the Bessa elite member Mr Z, and two local journalists (one Bessa, one Nchaney) who both investigated the matter in detail. I have arranged informants' assessments thematically, starting with the relevance of land disputes and cattle theft to the murder conflict, followed by informants' assessment of the case's legal prosecution and a final review of the social status of Alhaji Y within the local community.

Land Disputes, Cattle Theft and the Murder of Mr X
One of my prime informants on the murder conflict was a Bessa journalist who at the same time was secretary of the BECUDA home chapter, and who

meticulously investigated and documented all events of the conflict. He had a personal interest in the matter due to his affinal relationship with the deceased Mr X, whose sister was his wife. In his view, the present crisis had its origin in competing land claims by Mbororo graziers and Bessa farmers. Numerous incidents of crop damage and farmers' exclusion from grazing land caused growing dissatisfaction among the Bessa population who, on the basis of their anteriority, considered themselves the 'owners of the land'. A major farmer–herder conflict occurred in 1996 and required the intervention of the army to prevent violence. Consequently, some farmers began to retaliate by injuring or stealing cattle.

> [Bessa] women were farming about 5 kilometres from the village. But Alhaji Y came and claimed the land as his grazing area, producing a map from the Ministry of Territorial Administration. We refused that map since our fathers have lived in this area for more than 150 years, while Alhaji Y's father came only fifty years ago. So we believe, if somebody has stayed for more than 100 years in a place before another person followed, the latter has no right to claim the land [...] Cattle theft was actually caused by farmer–herder problems. Alhaji Y's father compensated people whose farms were damaged, but Alhaji Y told him that he was a stupid man. Since they had a land certificate there was no reason to compensate anybody. So people became angry and began to injure cows found on their farms. Wounded animals can easily die and people are interested in the meat. Others began to steal animals. That is how cattle theft started in the area.[4]

The Bessa journalist pointed to a pertinent issue that came up as a consistent theme in Bessa informants' assessments of the murder conflict, namely, Alhaji Y's claims to exclusive property rights over his grazing land. The extent of Alhaji Y's alleged control over Bessa territory became intelligible in my conversation with a Nchaney journalist who had interviewed Alhaji Y on this issue:

> From the documents I saw, they [the family of Alhaji Y] have an authorization to run a ranch.[5] Now, you know what a ranch is! That ranch is estimated at 1,600 square metres or something like that, if my brain does not fail me. Imagine that estimated area, which means they have almost three-quarters of the village land. Now, all this has been through the arrangements of the *fon*s who, once in a while, gave them land in exchange for money, gifts of cows and all the like. It would appear, after some time the *fon* regretted being exploited in that way. Sometimes he, too, encouraged villagers to encroach on that ranch land. So that is the whole secret. The whole secret is the farmer–herder problem, or rather the encroachment onto the ranch.[6]

This statement should not be taken at face value, as 1,600 square metres is the size of a small farm rather than a village. The journalist was obviously mistaken in his estimate, and his argument was primarily rhetorical. Nonetheless, as we learn from his statement, the land dispute between the Bessa community and Alhaji Y needs to be seen in the context of conflicting legal frameworks. Members of the Bessa community derived their claims from the customary land tenure system, which defines land and landed resources as communal property and attributes use rights according to the principle of anteriority.[7] Alhaji Y, on the other hand, claimed exclusive property rights over his grazing area on the basis of a land certificate that was obtained in accordance with state legislation.

Both state and customary land tenure systems are operative in Cameroon. The state claims all lands as national property and provides the option of converting parts of national lands into private property. As the respective administrative procedures are relatively complicated, costly and time consuming, the majority of the population relies on customary land tenure arrangements. Nonetheless, well-to-do individuals involved in profitable agricultural and pastoral business ventures have increasingly invested in land. Consequently, land has become a major subject and resource of economic and political power struggles, both within and between communities (Dafinger and Pelican 2006; Diduk 1992; Fisiy 1992; Goheen 1988, 1992; Mimche 2014; Mimche and Pelican 2012).

In the view of Alhaji Y, the murder conflict was not so much rooted in competing land claims as in the occurrence of cattle theft, which had increased since the mid 1990s. In his opinion, farmer–herder problems could be resolved amicably by showing good will and following administrative guidelines. Cattle theft, however, was an illicit and intolerable measure of retribution that had to be counteracted effectively. That is also the context in which Alhaji Y placed the killing of Mr X:

> Mr X used to steal cows, butcher them in the bush and eat the meat. He has stolen more than fifty of my cattle and almost finished a whole herd of sheep [...] When my herdsmen went to find out about the missing cow, they met Mr X in his hut drying the meat over the fire. He had a gun and a cutlass. The herdsmen saw the danger and started a fight. They wounded him seriously and left. He died afterwards from the injuries. When the village people came, they cut the head and buried it somewhere. They showed the decapitated body to the gendarmes and said it was us who removed the head to sell it. But this is not true. It was only a plan to incriminate my family so that it should look like a different story and not like a theft or a case of self-defence [...] Since the villagers had a grudge against my family, they decided to use the incident. The real claim is that they accuse us of appropriating their land. Mr X was only used as a pretext.[8]

Alhaji Y deliberately distanced himself from the allegations of occult murder. He denied his involvement in occult aggression on the grounds of his Muslim and Mbororo identity, while attributing the deed to his Bessa opponents.

Furthermore, by portraying himself as the victim of Bessa villagers' malice, he deployed a strategy common among Mbororo of depicting themselves as a vulnerable and exploited minority group. However, Alhaji Y framed this argument in a particular way, stressing his outstanding educational background as the reason for his social marginalization. In his view, it was his knowledge of his land and citizenship rights and his position as a government employee that rendered him a crucial opponent in the eyes of Bessa villagers.

The (In)Effectiveness of State and Local Legal Prosecution
All parties involved in the murder conflict insisted on involving the state legal system, each trusting in the validity of their claims and the effectiveness of their individual and collective strategies.

From a Bessa viewpoint, Alhaji Y offended the Bessa community twice: by allegedly murdering their member, and by undermining legal proceedings by resorting to corruption. As the Bessa journalist pointed out, many Bessa considered Alhaji Y's intervention at the Appeal Court in Bamenda as untimely and insolent. In their view, Alhaji Y intended not only to effect the release of his followers, but to demonstrate his power and thwart Bessa opposition. If he had waited with his intervention until the suspects were taken to Bamenda, the situation would have been interpreted differently.

Moreover, the Bessa journalist was concerned about the interference of the *procureur général*, as BECUDA lacked access to the crucial network to counteract Alhaji Y's influence:

> I hold the judiciary responsible. I do not hold the gendarmes or the state counsel [divisional judicial authority] in Nkambe responsible. I hold the authority of the Court of Appeal in Bamenda, the *procureur général*, responsible [...] The *procureur général*, who does not even know [the village where the incident occurred], instructed that those people who had committed the murder were [to be] released barely four days after they had been arrested. How did the *procureur général* even know that the land is Alhaji Y's grazing land? I believe that he was corrupted. Until today I know people who are boasting that they have corrupted justice. We will see the end.[9]

The venality not only of the judiciary but also of Bessa individuals was another crucial weakness consistently pointed out by Bessa and non-Bessa interlocutors. Accusing fingers pointed at the local *fon*, who was seen as profiting from conflicting land claims and whose stance in the murder conflict appeared to vacillate. A second person denounced for his alleged venality and deceit was the Bessa man who had guided the Mbororo herdsmen to the farm of Mr X. He purportedly witnessed the murder but kept quiet. When his participation was proven by ritual specialists, he was officially exiled from the village. He refused to obey the judgement and declared himself no longer a Bessa but a Mbororo. For many Bessa and BECUDA members, this man was a traitor and represented the enemy within.

Alhaji Y's Social Status within the Local Community

Alhaji Y was distressed by the social atmosphere that ensued after Mr X's murder. He felt threatened by the Bessa faction that demanded the boycott on interaction with Mbororo. Concurrently, he felt attached to the village where his family had been residing for more than sixty years and where he had lived and worked as a government employee and successful agro-pastoralist, and where he was the prospective leader (*arDo*) of the Mbororo community.

> Yes, I feel very insecure. My life is threatened. I cannot leave the area. I do not know where to go elsewhere. I have a lot of cattle, I have improved my compound, and I cannot go anywhere […] I have been born here and grew up with them [the Bessa]. So I feel like part of them. The only problem is that they should not steal my cows. I am very ready to be with them. They should not feel that I am a threat just because I am educated.[10]

Alhaji Y stressed that many Bessa individuals were on his side and ignored the boycott. Furthermore, he pointed out that he was willing to support his Bessa neighbours and to participate in the development of the area.

Shortly before the emergence of the murder conflict, Alhaji Y had agreed to collaborate in a school project initiated by Ballotiral. The project entailed the construction and running of a new primary school that was open to both Mbororo and Bessa children living in the surroundings of Alhaji Y's compound. Despite the tense atmosphere between Bessa and Mbororo during the murder conflict, the school project evolved successfully. Parents on both sides agreed that their children's education should not be affected by communal and individual differences. The Ballotiral staff corroborated the parents' views and cautiously avoided any involvement in the conflict and legal proceedings.

Finally, some Bessa informants argued that even though not everyone observed or agreed with the boycott, Alhaji Y's social status within the local community was no longer the same as it had been. In the long run, Bessa and Mbororo opted for tacitly ignoring the matter, thus adopting a strategy of functional indifference, as occurred during the investiture conflict (see Chapter 1).

Informants' assessments of Alhaji Y's social standing thus indicate that, while he succeeded in ensuring his liberty and rights by exploiting the state legal system, he inadvertently manoeuvred himself into a situation of temporary social isolation. This finding is relevant to the theme of this chapter, as it illustrates the potentially adverse effects of legal procedural strategies on social coexistence.

The Impact of Legal Procedural Strategies on Interethnic Relations

The murder conflict constituted a complex social situation in which multiple layers of individual and collective conflict converged, and which the participants attempted to resolve via procedural strategies, namely political lobbying and litigation. We could describe the murder conflict as an argument about land and cattle, expressed through occult murder, perceived as an offence committed by one community on another, and complicated by the ambiguities of Cameroon's plural legal framework.

In concluding, I will focus on two subjects relevant to the overall theme of this study, namely the role of ethnicity in the framing of local-level conflict, and the possible long-term impact of legal procedural strategies on interethnic relations in the Grassfields.

As I argued above, individuals and groups increasingly employ discourses of human, minority and civil rights to provoke and ensure legal action. The analysis of the murder conflict, however, has shown that the successful exploration of legal avenues ultimately depends on actors' socio-political and economic influence. Against this background it is striking that the murder conflict and related issues, such as conflicts over land and landed resources, are rarely expressed in terms of socio-economic difference, but tend to be framed in the idiom of ethnic conflict. I contend that the reason lies in the divergent validity of respective discourses. In the context of Cameroon's political liberalization and international emphasis on human and minority rights, ethnicity has become a respectable and popular idiom for framing local-level conflict. Conversely, class and elite discourses tend to be associated with witchcraft and other forms of occult economy and are largely excluded from official discourse (cf. Rowlands and Warnier 1988).

The second subject concerns the potential impact of procedural strategies on interethnic relations. Considering Cameroon's plural legal framework and the widespread practice of corruption, the question emerges of the degree to which procedural strategies, such as political lobbying and litigation, promote the reconciliation and social integration of opponents. As we have seen in the murder conflict, they may reinforce ethnic and social divides, as the attempts of individuals and groups to secure their rights are often frustrated.

In applying Elwert's conflict theory to the murder conflict, it becomes clear that litigation in Cameroon frequently evolves into pending rather than conclusive procedure. As Elwert (2005: 28–34) elaborates, conclusive procedure is defined by six indispensable criteria: an ordered sequence of action; the suspension of power differentials; autonomy in time; the indeterminacy of its outcome; a conclusive decision; and meaningful consequences for action. In the Cameroonian case, the suspension of power differentials, the indeterminacy of the procedure's outcome and the meaningful consequences for action are often impeded by the practice of corruption. In considering the judiciary in Benin, Bierschenk (2004) argues that, because the legal sector is generally understaffed and under-equipped, corruption constitutes a necessary strategy for upholding the system. Yet at the same time, it rescinds elementary principles of justice and thus undermines the legitimacy of the state. The same applies to Cameroon, with the effect that litigation often does not result in the desired resolution of the initial conflict, but increases frustration and mutual resentment between the conflicting parties.

Similarly, successful political lobbying is closely tied to exploiting critical socio-political and economic networks. Thus, while in the murder conflict BECUDA largely failed to mobilize respective networks, Ballotiral and MBOSCUDA have generally been more successful in effecting legal action against state functionaries; firstly, because they took advantage of the government's campaign against corruption; and secondly, because they enjoyed international backing. Moreover, while at the local level the Mboro are an ethnic minority, at the national level they constitute a sizeable population group, which substantiates MBOSCUDA's standing vis-à-vis the government. The different rates of success of ethnic elite associations in realizing their political and legal claims may thus endorse a perception of conflict in ethnic terms and reinforce interethnic tension.

I conclude that the promotion and pursuit of legal procedural methods inadvertently undermines interpersonal communication, joint decision making and compromise, all of which are strategies that contribute to the bolstering of multi-stranded relations and that ultimately endorse social cohesion. Thus, as the murder conflict and similar incidents suggest, state recognition of citizenship, land and minority rights has tended to discourage integration at the local level and to promote the polarization and politicization of interethnic relations.

Notes

1 A comprehensive discussion of procedure is provided in Elwert (2005: 23–35).
2 Law no. 97/9 of 10 January 1997, section 132(a) of the Cameroonian Penal Code.
3 The facts and opinions stated in this chapter are confined to those in the public domain.
4 Bessa journalist, Misaje, 22 December 2001.
5 The term 'ranch' here refers to the administrative category of a pastoral enterprise that supposedly operates according to the principles of market production. Ranching

is seen as opposed to the extensive grazing system commonly practised by Mbororo agro-pastoralists.
6   Nchaney journalist, Misaje, 13 November 2001.
7   On the customary land tenure system of Grassfields societies, see Fisiy (1997) and Kaberry (1950, 1960).
8   Alhaji Y, Nkambe, 20 November 2001.
9   Bessa journalist, Misaje, 3 October 2001.
10 Alhaji Y, Nkambe, 20 November 2001.

Epilogue

Sabga, August 2007. Government representatives forcefully intervene in a case of Mbororo leadership succession in Sabga, the main Mbororo settlement in northwest Cameroon. Through the influence of a wealthy and well-connected entrepreneur, the community-elected leader is administratively deposed and replaced by a Mbororo ruler of his choosing. Large parts of the Sabga community resent this interference, as they are fearful of the entrepreneur's attempt to gain control over their leadership and property. They stage a public protest to which the government reacts with military intervention.

The Mbororo elite in Sabga decides to use their international connections to pressurize the government. In fear for their lives, the deposed leader and his supporters seek refuge at the American Embassy in Yaoundé. Mbororo women picket the Prime Minister's Office and demand the reinstatement of their legitimate community leader. Moreover, with the help of MBOSCUDA they report the issue to national and international human rights organizations as well as to the Human Rights Council of the United Nations. For a short while, the Cameroonian government seems willing to reconsider the case. On the initiative of the prime minister, an official investigation team is sent to Sabga. They report their findings to the presidency, but no action is taken. Mbororo human rights activists further publicize the case and solicit national and international bodies to issue official letters of concern. The Cameroonian government, however, fails to respond to these appeals. Concurrently, discord emerges within the Sabga community, pitting neighbours and even relatives against each other. After many months of dissent, the argument gradually dies down. The community resigns itself to coming to terms with its new leader.

This incident took place when I returned to Cameroon to start a new project. While out to study migrant transnationalism and South–South mobility, I could not do otherwise than follow up the conflict in Sabga, as it tied in with my previous research (Pelican 2009a, 2010, 2013). What new insights can we derive from this case?

Firstly, it illustrates that conflicts over identity, belonging and entitlement continue to arise, taking ever new forms and dimensions. Secondly, it provides an example of how actors change their strategies and adopt new ones, which may or may not produce desired outcomes. In this particular case, Mbororo men and women explored rather novel and unwonted avenues, such as public protest, diplomatic refuge and recourse to international justice. Obviously, their choice of action has been influenced by examples from both neighbouring population groups and the international media, as well as by their connections with national and international agencies. Thirdly, the case corroborates my earlier argument that while participation in global networks may enhance the status of a group or individual, it does not necessarily provide viable solutions to local conflict.

Among the three groups under study, the most striking transformations in self-understanding and collective strategies have been evident with regard to Mbororo ethnicity. While renowned for their social aloofness and evasiveness in the face of conflict, Mbororo actors have come to adopt a notable voice in the local and national political arena. Situating their case against the background of globalization theory, we may draw on the argument of Meyer and Geschiere (1999), who emphasize the simultaneity of 'global flows' and 'cultural closure', and the growing preoccupation with identity and difference.

While much of my research was conducted in the relatively remote and rural setting of Misaje, globalization's impact has been felt more strongly in the country's urban centres and their fringes. In recent years, there has been a growing tendency among both educated and impoverished Mbororo youths to move into town in search of work (Keja 2009). Thus the major cities of Bamenda, Bafoussam, Douala and Yaoundé now host a considerable number of Mbororo who engage in a variety of occupations, including trading, driving, NGO work and, increasingly, government employment. Some have ventured beyond the boundaries of Cameroon and have gone south to Gabon or South Africa, others to Europe and the US, and a few to the United Arab Emirates (Pelican 2011a, 2011b, 2014; Pelican and Tatah 2009). Women have equally been involved in these new trends, and, for many, marriage has been the pathway to an alternative future. While girls' marriage with a non-Mbororo or non-Muslim partner is rare in remote areas like Misaje, it has become more frequent in urban settings, such as Bamenda. These and similar developments – including the actions of the Sabga community in the above conflict – reflect global flows and, more specifically, Mbororo individuals' involvement in them.

On the other hand, we also notice signs of cultural closure and an enduring preoccupation with identity. MBOSCUDA's recent claims that Mbororo are an 'indigenous people' exemplifies such tendencies. While for many the concept of indigenous peoples is far from lived realities, the question of whether they can or should be identified as such has engendered much debate among the very sections of Mbororo society that partake in global flows. Controversies centre on the continued portrayal of the Mbororo as a marginalized and backward people, as well as on the issues of Mbororo development and their integration into mainstream society. Obviously, Mbororo identity remains a discursive space of ever widening radius.

Yet issues of identity continue to be relevant not only to Mbororo but most population groups, albeit expressed in different idioms. As Geschiere (2009) outlines for southern Cameroon, here it is the idiom of 'autochthony' in which struggles over belonging and entitlement are framed. Conversely, in the anglophone northwest, the term 'indigenous' has gained currency and has been appropriated by different population groups. Confusion may arise over its divergent interpretations. On the one hand, 'indigenous' may be read as a substitute for 'native', the colonial classification applied to all Grassfields societies. On the other, according to the definition adopted by the United Nations, those groups may count as 'indigenous' that are set apart from the dominant majority by cultural difference and political marginalization. Consequently, both Grassfielders and Mbororo qualify as 'indigenous' according to one or other definition. The two, however, are mutually incompatible and produce paradoxical, if not antagonistic results (Pelican 2009a).

In comparing the divergent ways in which Mbororo, Grassfielders and Hausa have engaged with recent discourses of identity and belonging, we may wonder if all ethnicities entail the same potential for political mobilization. This question firstly came to my mind upon reading Burnham's conclusion to his seminal study *The Politics of Cultural Difference in Northern Cameroon*. He writes:

> It follows from my emphasis upon the cultural specificity of ethnic identities that I conceive of there being many kinds of ethnic projects. Ethnic discourses are based on different cultural logics, each with different implications for actors' practices and each displaying its own mode of articulation with the state and other more global processes. Some ethnic discourses are exclusivist; some are inclusivist. And some are more effective for political mobilisation than others. (Burnham 1996: 168)

While I largely agree with Burnham, I take issue with his concluding remark. In his reading, the Mbororo ethnic project cannot sustain political mobilization because of its inherently evasive nature. Yet, the Sabga conflict and many of the earlier developments described in this book undermine his claim. As Burnham's analysis is limited to the early 1990s, he could not take into account the emergence of MBOSCUDA and its political ascendancy in the late 1990s and 2000s. Moreover, we must acknowledge that there are regional differences which lead to different conclusions (Pelican 2008). Similar differences also apply to the Hausa case. As Cohen (1969: 190–94) shows with regard to the 1960s, the Hausa migrant community in Ibadan stood out for its politicized ethnicity, geared at securing economic and political privileges. By contrast, Hausa in northwest Cameroon have not responded to the country's democratization with ethnic mobilization, but continue to pursue their interests via good relations with their Grassfields and Mbororo neighbours.

Hence, as the examples of Mbororo and Hausa in different regions reveal, both ethnic projects may or may not sustain political mobilization, depending on the context. I thus contend that there is no correlation between the kind of ethnicity – be it more inclusivist or exclusivist – and its potential for political mobilization. Rather, it is historical, material and political factors that account for differences in the politicization of ethnic identities. Regarding the contrasting strategies of Grassfielders, Mbororo and Hausa, I have suggested a number of contributing factors, including differences in group size and socio-economic influence, the differential treatment of groups by colonial and postcolonial administrations, and the presence or absence of an educated elite with international connections

Finally, I wish to take up a question raised at the very outset of this book. How can we account for the relative absence of extreme ethnic violence in northwest Cameroon as compared to the large-scale massacres in other parts of Africa and the somewhat smaller incidents that Burnham described for Meiganga in the early 1990s?

Much anthropological literature has been concerned with explaining the emergence of ethnic violence and its extreme forms, fewer with its absence. Yet, as detailed analyses of specific conflicts suggest, there is no easy answer to this question. However, I wish to draw attention to a common feature of the conflict situations studied in this book. While collective and individual actors tend to view themselves and phrase their claims in the idiom of ethnicity, most often they perceive as their common adversary not the ethnic 'other' but the Cameroonian state and its representatives. Considering the investiture conflict, farmer–herder disputes or the murder conflict, in each case a moment emerged in which public anger turned against the government and its officials, who have been accused of partiality, corruption and ineffectiveness. Similarly, in the Sabga conflict, Mbororo claims were primarily directed against the government for violating their entitlement to self-determination. They enjoyed the support of many non-Mbororo, including Grassfields journalists and human rights associations. The specific colonial heritage and political history of anglophone Cameroon are among the factors that account for this general discontent with the Cameroonian government and the emergence of an implicit regional unity that eschews ethnic boundaries.

At the same time, the Sabga conflict illustrates another tendency, away from ethnic rivalry to conflict between interest groups that are separated by criteria of education, wealth and power. We may witness an incipient shift from one discourse to another, as well as the emergence of new or parallel idioms in which disagreement and rivalry may be framed. Ultimately, providing a comprehensive explanation for the existence or absence of ethnic conflict defies generalization, and remains as complex and variable as the histories and the local, national and global contexts that nurture it.

Glossary

akuji	Fulfulde: white zebu, literally 'Aku cattle'
alhaji (masc.), *hajja* (fem.)	Fulfulde/Hausa (from Arabic): courtesy title for a man (*alhaji*) or woman (*hajja*) who has accomplished the pilgrimage to Mecca (*hajj*)
alkali	Fulfulde/Hausa (from Arabic): Muslim judge
arDo (sing.), *arDo'en* (pl.)	Fulfulde: Mbororo leader, especially of a migratory group
ardorate	administrative English: territory under the control of an *arDo* (Mbororo leader)
bahaushe (sing.), *hausawa* (pl.)	Hausa: Hausa man, Hausa people
ballotiral	Fulfulde: working together; here, name of a non-governmental organization/partnership programme
bi	Fulfulde: child/son of
boDeeji	Fulfulde: red zebu
bordel	Pidgin English: prostitute, prostitution
boyjo, boy na'i	Pidgin English (adapted from Fulfulde): Grassfields herdsman
Bugaje, Buzaye	Hausa: ethnonym for Hausa of Tuareg slave descent
chombu ju-ju	Ncane/Pidgin English: mask of the palace, acting as messenger and local police
coBBal/fura	Fulfulde/Hausa: maize or millet dumplings, normally consumed with milk
'country-fashion'	Pidgin English: custom, socio-cultural practices
'country-man'	Pidgin English: ethnic fellow, Grassfielder
'country-people'	Pidgin English: local Grassfielders, 'natives' (colonial term)
'cut-head'	Pidgin English: trade in human body parts, in particular human heads; category of occult economy
daneeji	Fulfulde: white zebu

fembene	Ncane: home or palace of Mbene, historical settlement site of the Nchaney
fewong	Ncane: head of the village, our country; here, the sacrificial site of Nkanchi
fon (also spelt *foyn* or *mfon*)	Grassfields languages: Grassfields chief
gaynaako (sing.), *waynaaBe* (pl.)	Fulfulde: herdsman
gudaali	Fulfulde: cattle breed from northern Cameroon; stocky, short-legged zebu
imam	Fulfulde/Hausa (from Arabic): Muslim cleric, religious leader of Muslim community
jagora, kollitowo	Hausa/Fulfulde: guide, helper; here, social guide for Muslim convert
jangali	Hausa: cattle tax
jihad	Arabic: Islamic holy war
ju-ju	Pidgin English: individual mask, medicine
juulDo (sing.), *juulBe* (pl.)	Fulfulde: Muslim converts, lit. 'those who pray'
kaaDo (sing.), *haaBe* (pl.)	Fulfulde: non-FulBe, black African
kafala	Arabic: foster parenting, sponsorship
kaigamma	Fulfulde/Hausa: chief of slaves or serfs
Kamerun	German: name of the German protectorate, 1884–1916
kanwa	Pidgin English: potash, also locally known as 'lime stone'
kariya	Hausa: protection; here, staff-hurling performance of Aku herders
karuwa (sing.), *karuwai* (pl.)	Hausa: 'free woman', woman between marriages
kawtal pulaaku	Fulfulde: FulBe meeting; name of a Mbororo women's group
kibalaki	Ncane/Pidgin English: name of a quarter of Misaje town, 'the (German) barracks'
kilah	Ncane: mask in charge of protection, owned by the Yahdo family of the Nchaney
kollitowo, jagora	Fulfulde/Hausa: guide, helper; here, social guide for Muslim convert
kwifon	Kom (Grassfields language): regulatory society
lamidate	administrative English: territory under control of a *laamiiDo* (FulBe superior chief)

Glossary

laamiiDo (sing.), *laamiiBe* (pl.)	Fulfulde: FulBe superior chief
lenyol (sing.), *lenyi* (pl.)	Fulfulde: lineage, descent group, ethnic group
mai saje	Hausa: master of the beard; origin of the toponym Misaje
makala	Hausa: maize-banana snack
mallam (sing.), *mallum'en/mallamai* (pl.)	Fulfulde/Hausa (from Arabic): Muslim scholar, person who has completed reading the Koran
maquisards	French: rebels in the Bamiléké area, early 1960s
masa	Hausa: maize snack
mbororoji	Fulfulde: red zebu, literally 'Mbororo (Jaafun) cattle'
Mbororojo (sing.), *Mbororo'en* (pl.)	Fulfulde: a Mbororo person, Mbororo people
mimbo	Pidgin English: alcohol
murshid	Arabic: Muslim spiritual and legal guide
nchan	Ncane: original ethnonym of the Nchaney
Nchanti	administrative English: British colonial ethnonym for Nchaney
ngambe	Pidgin English: soothsaying
nggumba	Grassfields languages/Pidgin English: regulatory society
nggumba ju-ju	Ncane/Pidgin English: mask of the regulatory society
ngwerong	Lamnso (Grassfields language): regulatory society
nji	Grassfields languages: Grassfields sub-chief, advisor
pettoowu	Fulfulde: rinderpest
pulaaku	Fulfulde: FulBe complex of moral values and social practices, FulBe code of conduct
pullo (sing.), *fulBe* (pl.)	Fulfulde: FulBe man/woman, FulBe people
sadaka	Fulfulde/Hausa (from Arabic): charity, alms
salla	Hausa: praying
sarki	Hausa: leader, chief
sarkin hausawa	Hausa: head of a Hausa settlement, Hausa chief
sarkin pawa	Hausa: chief of the butchers
sawru	Fulfulde: herding staff
shah	Grassfields languages/Pidgin English: maize beer
shey	Ncane: title for an ex-chief
soro	Fulfulde: competitive stick-beating contests between Jaafun youths

suudu (sing.), *suudi* (pl.)	Fulfulde: house, hut; also section of a lineage
'tie heart'	Pidgin English: persevere, take courage
unguwa rogo	Hausa: cassava quarter (name of a quarter in Misaje)
wakiili	Fulfulde/Hausa: assistant of FulBe or Hausa chief
zakka/jakka	Hausa/Fulfulde (from Arabic): religious tax, alms

References

Abu-Manga, A.-A. 1986. *Fulfulde in the Sudan: Process of Adaptation to Arabic*. Berlin: Dietrich Reimer.
——— 1999. *Hausa in the Sudan: Process of Adaptation to Arabic*. Cologne: Rüdiger Köppe.
Adamu, M. 1976. 'The Spread of Hausa Culture in West Africa, 1700–1900', *Savannah* 5: 3–13.
——— 1978. *The Hausa Factor in West African History*. Zaria, Ibadan: Ahmadu Bello University Press and Oxford University Press Nigeria.
Alber, E. 2005. 'Georg Elwert (1947–2005): Ein Nachruf', *Sociologus* 55(1): 1–8.
——— 2013. 'The Transfer of Belonging: Theories on Child Fostering in West Africa Reviewed', in E. Alber, J. Martin and C. Notermans (eds), *Child Fostering in West Africa: New Perspectives on Theories and Practices*. Leiden: Brill, pp.79–107.
Amselle, J.-L. 1998. *Mestizo Logics: The Anthropology of Identity in Africa and Elsewhere*. Stanford: Stanford University Press.
Anderson, B. 1983. *Imagined Communities: Reflections on the Origin and Spread of Nationalism*. London: Verso.
Angwafo, F. 2009. *Royalty and Politics: The Story of My Life*. Bamenda: Langaa.
Ardener, E. 1970. 'Witchcraft, Economics and the Continuity of Belief', in M. Douglas (ed.), *Witchcraft Confessions and Accusations*. London: Tavistock, pp.141–60.
Ardener, E., S. Ardener and W.A. Warmington. 1960. *Plantation and Village in the Cameroons: Some Economic and Social Studies*. London: Oxford University Press.
Ardener, S. 1964. 'The Comparative Study of Rotating Credit Associations', *Journal of the Royal Anthropological Institute* 94(2): 201–29.
Ardener, S., and S. Burman (eds). 1995. *Money-Go-Rounds: The Importance of Rotating Saving and Credit Associations for Women*. Oxford: Berg.
Argenti, N. 2001. 'Ephemeral Monuments, Memory and Royal Sempiternity in a Grassfields Kingdom', in A. Forty and S. Küchler (eds), *The Art of Forgetting*. Oxford: Berg, pp.21–52.
——— 2006. 'Remembering the Future: Slavery, Youth and Masking in the Cameroon Grassfields', *Social Anthropology* 14(1): 49–69.
——— 2007. *The Intestines of the State: Youth, Violence and Belated Histories in the Cameroon Grassfields*. Chicago: University of Chicago Press.
Awasom, N. 1984. 'The Hausa and Fulani in the Bamenda Grasslands 1903–1960', PhD diss. Yaoundé: University of Yaoundé.
——— 2003a. 'From Migrants to Nationals, and from Nationals to Undesirable Elements: The Case of the Fulani (Mbororo) Muslim Graziers in Cameroon's North West

Province', in C. Coquet Vidrovitch, O. Georg, I. Mande and F. Rajaonah (eds), *Etre étranger et migrant en Afrique du XXe siècle: Enjeux identitaires et modes d'insertion*. Paris: L'Harmattan, pp.403–14.

―― 2003b. 'The Vicissitudes of Twentieth-century Mankon *Fons* in Cameroon's Changing Social Order', in W. van Binsbergen (ed.), *The Dynamics of Power and the Rule of Law*. Münster: Lit, pp.101–20.

Awde, N. 1996. *Hausa–English, English–Hausa Dictionary*. New York: Hippocrene Books.

Bailey, F.G. 1996. *The Civility of Indifference: On Domesticating Ethnicity*. Ithaca, NY: Cornell University Press.

Barkow, J. 1972. 'Hausa Women and Islam', *Canadian Journal of African Studies*, special issue, 6(2): 317–28.

―― 1976. 'The Generation of an Incipient Ethnic Split: A Hausa Case (Nigeria)', *Anthropos* 71: 857–67.

Barth, F. 1969. 'Introduction', in F. Barth (ed.), *Ethnic Groups and Boundaries: The Social Organisation of Culture Difference*. London: Allen and Unwin, pp.9–38.

―― 1994. 'Enduring and Emerging Issues in the Analysis of Ethnicity', in H. Vermeulen and C. Govers (eds), *The Anthropology of Ethnicity: Beyond 'Ethnic Groups and Boundaries'*. Amsterdam: Het Spinhuis, pp.11–32.

Bassett, T. 1988. 'The Political Ecology of Peasant–Herder Conflicts in the Northern Ivory Coast', *Annals of the Association of American Geographers* 78(3): 453–72.

Bayart, J.-F. 1979. *L'état au Cameroun*. Paris: Presses de la Fondation Nationale des Sciences Politiques.

―― 1993. *The State in Africa: The Politics of the Belly*. London: Longman.

Bayart, J.-F., S. Ellis and B. Hibou. 1999. *The Criminalization of the State*. Bloomington: University of Indiana Press.

Beeler-Stücklin, S. 2009. *Institutioneller Wandel und Ressourcenkonflikte: Fischerei, Viehzucht und Landwirtschaft im Nigerbinnendelta von Mali*. Cologne: Rüdiger Köppe.

Bierschenk, T. 2004. 'Die Informalisierung und Privatisierung von Konfliktregelung in der Beniner Justiz', in J. Eckert (ed.), *Anthropologie der Konflikte: Georg Elwerts konflikttheoretische Thesen in der Diskussion*. Bielefeld: Transcript, pp.186–216.

Blench, R. 1994. 'The Expansion and Adaptation of Fulbe Pastoralism to Subhumid and Humid Conditions in Nigeria', *Cahiers d'Etudes Africaines* 34(133–135): 197–212.

Blundo, G., and J.-P. Olivier de Sardan (eds). 2001. 'La corruption au quotidien', *Politique Africaine*, special issue, 83.

Bocquené, H. 2002. *Memoirs of a Mbororo: The Life of Ndudi Umaru, Fulani Nomad of Cameroon*. Oxford: Berghahn.

Boesen, E. 1989. *Der Weg der Fulbe: Ethnischer Konservatismus in einer pluralen Gesellschaft (VR Benin)*. Berlin: Das Arabische Buch.

―― 1994. 'Kultureller Eigensinn und gesellschaftliche Dependenz', *Anthropos* 89: 421–31.

―― 1996. 'Fulbe und Arbeit', in K. Beck and G. Spittler (eds), *Arbeit in Afrika*. Hamburg: Lit, pp.193–208.

―― 1997. 'Identité et démarcation: les pasteurs peuls et leurs voisins paysans', in T. Bierschenk and P.-Y. Le Meur (eds), *Trajectoires peuls au Bénin: Six études anthropologiques*. Paris: Karthala, pp.21–47.

―――― 1998. 'Identité culturelle et espace culturé: Les FulBe entre brousse et village', in E. Boesen, C. Hardung and R. Kuba (eds), *Regards sur le Borgou: Pouvoir et altérité dans une région ouest-africaine*. Paris: L'Harmattan, pp.221–42.

―――― 1999a. *Scham und Schönheit: Über Identität und Selbstvergewisserung bei den Fulbe Nordbenins*. Hamburg: Lit.

―――― 1999b. 'Pulaaku: Sur la Foulanité', in R. Botte, J. Boutrais and J. Schmitz (eds), *Figures peules*. Paris: Karthala, pp.83–97.

Bourdieu, P. 1990. *The Logic of Practice*. Cambridge: Polity.

Boutrais, J. 1990. 'Derrière les clôtures … Essai d'histoire comparée des ranchs africains', *Cahiers des Sciences Humaines* 26(1/2): 73–95.

―――― 1994. 'Pour une nouvelle cartographie des Peuls', *Cahiers d'Etudes Africaines* 34(133–135): 137–46.

―――― 1996. *Hautes terres d'élevage au Cameroun*. Paris: Orstom. 2 vol. + cart.

―――― 1998. 'Les taurins de l'ouest du Cameroon', in C. Seignobos and E. Thys (eds), *Des taurins et des hommes*. Paris: Orstom, pp.313–26.

Bovin, M. 1974/1975. 'Ethnic Performances in Rural Niger: An Aspect of Ethnic Boundary Maintenance', *Folk* 16/17: 459–74.

Brackenbury, E.A. 1923a. 'Notes on the "Bororo Fulbe" or Nomad "Cattle Fulani", Part I', *Journal of the Royal African Society* 23(91): 208–17.

―――― 1923b. 'Notes on the "Bororo Fulbe" or Nomad "Cattle Fulani", Part II', *Journal of the Royal African Society* 23(92): 271–77.

Breedveld, A., and M. de Bruijn. 1996. 'L'image des Fulbe: Analyse critique de la construction du concept de *pulaaku*', *Cahiers d'Etudes Africaines* 36(144): 791–821.

Breusers, M., S. Nederlof and T. van Rheenen. 1998. 'Conflict or Symbiosis? Disentangling Farmer–Herdsman Relations: The Mossi and Fulbe of the Central Plateau, Burkina Faso', *Journal of Modern African Studies* 36(3): 357–80.

Bridges, W.M. 1933. 'Intelligence Report on the Bum Area', unpublished manuscript. Buea: National Archives of Cameroon, Ad. 6.

Brubaker, R. 2002. 'Ethnicity without Groups', *European Journal of Sociology* 43: 163–89.

―――― 2004. *Ethnicity without Groups*. Cambridge, MA: Harvard University Press.

Brye, E., and E. Brye. 2001. *Rapid Appraisal and Intelligibility: Testing Surveys of the Eastern Beboid Group of Languages (Northwest Province)*. Yaoundé: Summer Institute of Linguistics International/Ministry of Scientific and Technical Research.

Burnham, P. 1972. 'Racial Classification and Ideology in the Meiganga Region: North Cameroon', in P. Baxter and B. Sansom (eds), *Race and Social Difference: Selected Readings*. London: Penguin, pp.301–18.

―――― 1991. 'L'ethnie, la religion et l'état: Le rôle des Peuls dans la vie politique et sociale du Nord-Cameroun', *Journal des Africanistes* 61(1): 73–102.

―――― 1996. *The Politics of Cultural Difference in Northern Cameroon*. Edinburgh: Edinburgh University Press.

Butake, B. 1999. *Lake God and Other Plays*. Yaoundé: Editions Clé.

Callaway, B.J. 1984. 'Ambiguous Consequences of the Socialization and Seclusion of Hausa Women', *Journal of Modern African Studies* 22(3): 429–50.

Chabal, P., and J.-P. Daloz. 2002. *Africa Works: Disorder as Political Instrument*. Oxford/Bloomington: James Currey/Indiana University Press.

Chilver, E. 1977. 'Nineteenth-century Trade in the Bamenda Grassfields, Southern Cameroons', in Z.A. Konczacki and J.M. Konczacki (eds), *An Economic History of Tropical Africa: The Precolonial Period*. London: Frank Cass, pp.147–65.

––––––– 1989. 'Women Cultivators, Cows and Cash-crops: Phyllis Kaberry's Women of the Grassfields Revisited', in P. Geschiere and P. Konings (eds), *Proceedings/Contributions of a Conference on the Historical Economy of Cameroon: Historical Perspectives*. Leiden/Yaoundé: Centre of African Studies/MESIRES, pp.383–421.

Chilver, E., and P. Kaberry. 1967. *Traditional Bamenda: The Pre-colonial History and Ethnography of the Bamenda Grassfields*. Buea: Government Printer.

––––––– 1970. 'Chronology of the Bamenda Grassfields', *Journal of African History* 11(2): 249–57.

––––––– 1971. 'The Tikar Problem: A Non-problem', *Journal of African Languages* 10(2): 13–14.

Cohen, A. 1965. 'The Social Organization of Credit in a West African Cattle Market', *Africa* 35(1): 8–20.

––––––– 1966. 'Politics of the Kola Trade', *Africa* 36(1): 18–36.

––––––– 1969. *Custom and Politics in Urban Africa: A Study of Hausa Migrants in Yoruba Towns*. London: Routledge and Kegan Paul.

––––––– 1974. 'Introduction: The Lesson of Ethnicity', in A. Cohen (ed.), *Urban Ethnicity*. London: Tavistock, pp.ix–xxiv.

––––––– 1981. 'Variables in Ethnicity', in C. Keyes (ed.), *Ethnic Change*. Seattle: University of Washington Press, pp.307–31.

Cohen, D.W., and E.S.A. Odhiambo. 1992. *Burying SM: The Politics of Knowledge and the Sociology of Power in Africa*. London: Heinemann/James Currey.

Comaroff, J. 1995. 'Ethnicity, Nationalism and the Politics of Difference in an Age of Revolution', in J. Comaroff and P. Stern (eds), *Perspectives on Nationalism and War*. New York: Gordon and Breach, pp.243–76.

Dafinger, A. 2013. *The Economics of Ethnic Conflict: The Case of Burkina Faso*. Oxford: James Currey.

Dafinger, A., and M. Pelican. 2006. 'Sharing or Dividing the Land? Land Rights and Herder–Farmer Relations in a Comparative Perspective', *Canadian Journal of African Studies* 40(1): 127–51.

Davis, L. 1995. 'Opening Political Space in Cameroon: The Ambiguous Response of the Mbororo', *Review of African Political Economy* 22(64): 213–28.

De Rosny, E. 1985. *Healers in the Night*. Maryknoll, NY: Orbis Books.

Diallo, Y. 1996. 'Bauern, Viehzüchter und Staatliche Intervention im Norden der Elfenbeinküste', in G. Schlee and K. Werner (eds), *Inklusion und Exklusion: Die Dynamik von Grenzziehungen im Spannungsfeld von Markt, Staat und Ethnizität*. Cologne: Rüdiger Köppe, pp.87–106.

––––––– 2001. 'Abgrenzung- und Assimilierungsprozesse bei den Fulbe in der Elfenbeinküste und Burkina Faso', in A. Horstmann and G. Schlee (eds), *Integration durch Verschiedenheit: Lokale und globale Formen interkultureller Kommunikation*. Bielefeld: Transcript, pp.333–66.

––––––– 2005. 'Beitrag zur Geschichte der Fulbe-Forschung', in K. Geisenhainer and K. Lange (eds), *Bewegliche Horizonte*. Leipzig: Leipziger Universitätsverlag, pp.471–88.

––––––– 2008. *Nomades des espaces interstitiels:Pastoralisme, identité, migrations (Burkina Faso – Côte-d'Ivoire)*. Cologne: Rüdiger Köppe.

Diallo, Y., and G. Schlee (eds). 2000. *L'ethnicité peule dans des contextes nouveaux*. Paris: Karthala.

Diduk, S. 1992. 'The Paradoxes of Changing Land Tenure in Kedjom Chiefdoms, North West Province, Cameroon', *Paideuma* 38: 195–217.

Django, S., W. Shei and J. Duni. 2011. *Legal Framework for the Regulation of Access to, and Management of Pastoral Resources in Cameroon*. Bamenda: MBOSCUDA/PASOC.

Dognin, R. 1981. 'L'installation des Djafoun dans l'Adamaoua camerounais: La djakka chez les Peul de l'Adamaoua', in C. Tardits (ed.), *Contribution de la recherche ethnologique à l'histoire des civilisations du Cameroun*. Paris: CNRScientifique, pp.139–57.

Duni, J., R. Fon, S. Hickey and N. Salihu. 2009. 'Exploring a Political Approach to Rights-based Development in North-West Cameroon: From Rights and Marginality to Citizenship and Justice', *Brooks World Poverty Institute Working Paper No. 104*. Manchester: Brooks World Poverty Institute.

Dupire, M. 1970. *Organisation sociale des Peuls*. Paris: Plon.

Eboussi Boulaga, F., and V.S. Zinga. 2002. *Fight Against Corruption: Is there Anything Impossible with Cameroonians?* Yaoundé: Presses Universitaires d'Afrique.

Eckert, J. 2004. 'Einleitung: Gewalt, Meidung und Verfahren: zur Konflikttheorie Georg Elwerts', in J. Eckert (ed.), *Anthropologie der Konflikte*. Bielefeld: Transcript, pp.7–25.

Eguchi, M.J. 1973. 'Aspects of the Lifestyle and Culture of Women in the Fulbe Districts of Maroua', *Kyoto University African Studies* 8: 14–92.

Elwert, G. 1997. 'Gewaltmärkte: Beobachtungen zur Zweckrationalität der Gewalt', in T. von Trotha (ed.), *Soziologie der Gewalt*. Opladen: Westdeutscher Verlag, pp.86–101.

——— 2001. 'Conflict, Anthropological Perspectives', in N. Smelser and P. Baltes (eds), *International Encyclopedia of the Social and Behavioral Sciences*. Amsterdam: Elsevier, pp.2542–47.

——— 2002. 'Switching Identity Discourses: Primordial Emotions and the Social Construction of We-Groups', in G. Schlee (ed.), *Imagined Differences:Hatred and the Construction of Social Identities*. Münster: Lit, pp.33–54.

——— 2004. 'Anthropologische Perspektiven auf Konflikt', in J. Eckert (ed.), *Anthropologie der Konflikte*. Bielefeld: Transcript, pp.26–38.

——— 2005. 'Fragmente zu einer Konflikttheorie als Instrument des Gesellschaftsvergleiches', *Sociologus* 55(1): 9–37.

Engard, R. 1989. 'Dance and Power in Bafut (Cameroon)', in W. Arens and I. Karp (eds), *Creativity of Power: Cosmology and Action in African Societies*. Washington: Smithsonian Institution Press, pp.129–62.

Eriksen, T.H. 1998. *Common Denominators: Ethnicity, Nation-building and Compromise in Mauritius*. New York: Berg.

Evans-Pritchard, E.E. 1940. *The Nuer: A Description of the Modes of Livelihood and Political Institutions of a Nilotic People*. Oxford: Oxford University Press.

Fardon, R. 2006. *Lela in Bali: History through Ceremony in Cameroon*. Oxford: Berghahn.

Feyissa, D. 2011. *Playing Different Games: Paradoxes of Anywaa and Nuer Identification Strategies in Gambella, Ethiopia*. Oxford: Berghahn.

Feyissa, D. and M. Zeleke. 2015. 'The Contestation over the Indigenous in Africa: The Ethiopian Example', in University of Cologne Forum 'Ethnicity as a Political Resource' (ed.), *Ethnicity as a Political Resource – Conceptualizations across Disciplines, Regions, and Periods*. Bielefeld: Transcript.

Fisiy, C. 1992. 'Power and Privilege in the Administration of Law: Land Law Reforms and Social Differentiation in Cameroon', PhD diss. Yaoundé: University of Yaoundé.

——— 1997. 'State Dislocation of Customary Management Systems: Land Colonization on the Slopes of Mount Oku, North West Province of Cameroon', in R. Kuppe and R. Potz (eds), *Law and Anthropology*. The Hague: Martinus Nijhoff, pp.124–45.

Fisiy, C., and P. Geschiere. 2001. 'Witchcraft, Development and Paranoia in Cameroon: Interactions between Popular, Academic and State Discourse', in H. Moore and T. Sanders (eds.), *Magical Interpretations, Material Realities: Modernity, Witchcraft and the Occult in Postcolonial Africa*. London: Routledge, pp.226–46.

Fokwang, J. 2009. *Mediating Legitimacy: Chieftaincy and Democratisation in Two African Chiefdoms*. Bamenda: Langaa.

Fombad, C.M. 2000. 'Endemic Corruption in Cameroon: Insights on Consequences and Control', in K.R. Hope and B.C. Chikulo (eds), *Corruption and Development in Africa: Lessons from Country Case Studies*. Houndsmill: Macmillan, pp.234–60.

Fowler, I., and D. Zeitlyn. 1996. 'Introduction: The Grassfields and the Tikar', in I. Fowler and D. Zeitlyn (eds), *African Crossroads: Intersections between History and Anthropology in Cameroon*. Oxford: Berghahn, pp.1–16.

Frantz, C. 1981. 'Development without Communities: Social Fields, Networks, and Action in the Mambila Grassland of Nigeria'. *Human Organization* 40(3): 211–20.

——— 1986. 'Fulani Continuity and Change under Five Flags', in M. Adamu and A.H.M. Kirk-Greene (eds), *Pastoralists of the West African Savanna*. Manchester: Manchester University Press, pp.16–39.

Galanter, M. 1981. 'Justice in Many Rooms: Courts, Private Ordering and Indigenous Law', *Journal of Legal Pluralism* 19: 1–47.

Gausset, Q. 1998. 'Historical Account or Discourse on Identity? A Re-examination of Fulbe Hegemony and Autochthonous Submission in Banyo', *History in Africa* 25: 93–110.

——— 1999. 'Islam or Christianity? The Choices of the Wawa and the Kwanja of Cameroon', *Africa* 69(2): 257–78.

Geary, C. 1976. *Die Genese eines Häuptlingtums im Grasland von Kamerun*. Wiesbaden: Franz Steiner.

Geertz, C. 1973. *The Interpretation of Cultures*. New York: Basic Books.

——— 1985. 'Centers, Kings, and Charisma: Reflexions on the Symbolics of Power', in W. Sean (ed.), *Rites of Power*. Philadelphia: University of Pennsylvania Press, pp.13–38.

GERDDES. 1999. 'Corruption in Cameroon'. Yaoundé: Friedrich Ebert Stiftung/SAAGRAPH.

Geschiere, P. 1993. 'Chiefs and Colonial Rule in Cameroon: Inventing Chieftaincy, French and British Style', *Africa* 63(2): 151–75.

——— 1997. *The Modernity of Witchcraft: Politics and the Occult in Postcolonial Africa*. Charlottesville: University Press of Virginia.

——— 2005. 'Funerals and Belonging: Different Patterns in South Cameroon', *African Studies Review* 48(2): 45–64.

——— 2009. *The Perils of Belonging: Autochthony, Citizenship, and Exclusion in Europe and Africa*. Chicago: University of Chicago Press.

——— 2013. *Witchcraft, Intimacy and Trust: Africa in Comparison*. Chicago: University of Chicago Press.

Geschiere, P., and J. Gugler. 1998. 'The Urban–Rural Connection: Changing Issues of Belonging and Identification', *Africa* 68(3): 309–19.

Geschiere, P., and F. Nyamnjoh. 1998. 'Witchcraft as an Issue in the "Politics of Belonging": Democratisation and Urban Migrants' Involvement with the Home Village', *African Studies Review* 41(3): 69–91.

——— 2000. 'Capitalism and Autochthony: The Seesaw of Mobility and Belonging', *Public Culture* 12(2): 423–52.

Gluckman, M. 1955. *Custom and Conflict in Africa*. Oxford: Blackwell.

——— 1963. *Order and Rebellion in Tribal Africa*. London: Cohen and West.

Goheen, M. 1988. 'Land Accumulation and Local Control: The Manipulation of Symbols and Power in Nso, Cameroon', in R.E. Downs and S.P. Reyna (eds), *Land and Society in Contemporary Africa*. Hanover: University Press of New England, pp.280–308.

——— 1992. 'Chiefs, Sub-chiefs and Local Control: Negotiations over Land, Struggles over Meaning', *Africa* 62(3): 389–412.

——— 1996. *Men Own the Fields, Women Own the Crops: Gender and Power in the Cameroon Grassfields*. Madison: University of Wisconsin Press.

Goody, E.N. 1971. 'Forms of Pro-parenthood: The Sharing and Substitution of Parental Roles', in J. Goody (ed.), *Kinship: Selected Readings*. London: Penguin, pp.331–45.

Greenblatt, S. 1994. 'Zur Zirkulation sozialer Energie', in C. Conrad and M. Kessel (eds), *Geschichte schreiben in der Postmoderne*. Stuttgart: Reclam, pp.219–50.

Greiner, C. 2013. 'Guns, Land, and Votes: Cattle Rustling and the Politics of Boundary (Re)Making in Northern Kenya', *African Affairs* 112(447): 216–37.

Griffiths, J. 1986. 'What is Legal Pluralism?' *Journal of Legal Pluralism* 24: 1–50.

Guichard, M. 1996. 'So nah und doch so fremd: Über die Beziehungen zwischen Fulbe und Bariba im Borgou (Nordbenin)', in G. Schlee and K. Werner (eds), *Inklusion und Exklusion: Die Dynamik von Grenzziehungen im Spannungsfeld von Markt, Staat und Ethnizität*. Cologne: Rüdiger Köppe, pp.107–32.

——— 1998. 'Du discours sur la faiblesse du pouvoir Fulbe', in E. Boesen, C. Hardung and R. Kuba (eds), *Regards sur le Bourgou*. Paris: L'Harmattan, pp.185–202.

——— 2000. 'L'étrangeté comme code de communication interethnique: les relations entre agropasteurs peuls et paysans bariba du Borgou (Nord-Bénin)', in Y. Diallo and G. Schlee (eds), *L'ethnicité peule dans des contextes nouveaux*. Paris: Karthala, pp.93–127.

Haaf, E., and M. Fondö. 1992. *Die Meta: Eine ethno-medizinische Studie über eine Ethnie im Grasland von Westkamerun*. Giessen: Tropeninstitut Giessen.

Hagberg, S. 1998. *Between Peace and Justice: Dispute Settlement between Karaboro Agriculturalists and Fulbe Agro-pastoralists in Burkina Faso*. Uppsala: Acta Universitatis Upsaliensis.

——— 2004. 'Ethnic Identification in Voluntary Associations: The Politics of Development and Culture in Burkina Faso', in H. Englund and F. Nyamnjoh (eds), *Rights and the Politics of Recognition in Africa*. London: Zed Books, pp.195–218.

——— 2005. 'Dealing with Dilemmas: Violent Farmer–Pastoralist Conflicts in Burkina Faso', in P. Richards (ed.), *No Peace, No War: An Anthropology of Contemporary Armed Conflict*. Athens/Oxford: Ohio University Press/James Currey, pp.40–56.

Hallpike, C.R. 1977. *Bloodshed and Vengeance in the Papuan Mountains: The Generation of Conflict in Tauade Society*. Oxford: Clarendon Press.

Harshbarger, C. 1995. 'Farmer–Herder Conflict and State Legitimacy in Cameroon', PhD diss. Gainesville: University of Florida.

Hassan, M., and M. Shuaibu. 1952. *A Chronicle of Abuja*. Ibadan: Ibadan University Press.

Hassert, K. 1917. 'Pflanzengeographische Übersichtskarte der Grashochländer Nordwest-Kameruns', unpublished manuscript. Oxford: Bodleian Library, E 16: 6 (2).

Herms, I. 1987. *Wörterbuch Hausa–Deutsch*. Leipzig: VEB Verlag Enzyklopädie.

Hickey, S. 2002. 'Transnational NGDOs and Participatory Forms of Rights-based Development: Converging with the Local Politics of Citizenship in Cameroon', *Journal of International Development* 14: 841–57.

——— 2007. 'Caught at the Crossroads: Citizenship, Marginality and the Mbororo Fulani in Northwest Cameroon', in D. Hammet, P. Nugent and S. Rich-Dorman (eds), *Citizenship in Africa*. Leiden: Brill, pp.81–104.

Hill, P. 1969. 'Hidden Trade in Hausaland', *Man* 4(3): 392–409.

——— 1972. *Rural Hausa: A Village and a Setting*. Cambridge: Cambridge University Press.

Hobsbawm, E., and T. Ranger (eds). 1983. *The Invention of Tradition*. Cambridge: Cambridge University Press.

Hodgson, D. 2011. *Being Maasai, Becoming Indigenous: Postcolonial Politics in a Neoliberal World*. Bloomington: Indiana University Press.

Hussein, K. 1998. *Conflict between Farmers and Herders in the Semi-arid Sahel and East Africa*. London: International Institute for Environment and Development.

Jeffreys, M.D.W. 1946. 'Mythical Origin of Cattle in Africa', *Man* 46: 140–41.

——— 1951. 'List of Tribal Notes Sent to Professor Forde on 10.12.1951', unpublished manuscript. Oxford: Private collection of Sally Chilver.

——— 1964. 'Who are the Tikar?' *African Studies* 23(3/4): 141–53.

——— 1966. 'Some Notes on the Fulani of Bamenda, in West-Cameroon', *Abbia* (Nigeria) 14/15: 127–34.

Jones, N. 2010. 'Battle to Degas Deadly Lakes Continues', *Nature* 466: 1033.

Jua, N. 1991. 'Cameroon: Jump-starting an Economic Crisis', *Africa Insight* (Pretoria) 21(3): 162–70.

Kaberry, P. 1950. 'Land Tenure among the Nsaw of the British Cameroons', *Africa* 20(4): 307–23.

——— 1952. *Women of the Grassfields: A Study of the Economic Position of Women in Bamenda, British Cameroons*. London: Her Majesty's Stationery Office.

——— 1960. 'Some Problems of Land Tenure in Nsaw, Southern Cameroons', *Journal of African Administration* 12: 21–28.

Kaberry, P., and E. Chilver. 1961. 'An Outline of the Traditional Political System of Bali-Nyonga, Southern Cameroons', *Africa* 31(4): 355–71.

Kapfer, R. 2005. *Die Frauen von Maroua: Liebe, Sexualität und Heirat in Nordkamerun*. Wuppertal: P. Hammer.

Keja, R. 2009. 'Moving in and into the Urban: Mbororo Generations Finding and Creating a Place in Bamenda, Cameroon', MA diss. Leiden: African Studies Centre, Leiden University.

Kintz, D. 1985. 'Archétypes politiques peuls', *Journal des Africanistes* 55: 93–104.

Kirby, J., and G. Shu. 2005. 'Culture-Drama: A New Enactment Genre for Peacebuilding', in D. Millar, S. Bugu Kendie, A. Atia Apusigah and B. Haverkort (eds), *African Knowledges and Sciences: Understanding and Supporting the Ways of Knowing in Sub-Saharan Africa*. Leusden: Compas, pp.149–61.

——— 2010. 'Re-reconciling Culture-based Conflicts with "Culture-Drama"', in E. Leveton (ed.), *Healing Collective Trauma Using Sociodrama and Drama Therapy*. New York: Springer, pp.207–33.

Koloss, H.-J. 1977. *Kamerun: Könige, Masken, Feste.* Stuttgart: Institut für Auslandsbeziehungen.

——— 1980. 'Götter und Ahnen, Hexen und Medizin: Zum Weltbild in Oku (Kameruner Grasland)', in W. Raunig (ed.), *Schwarz-Afrikaner.* Innsbruck/Frankfurt am Main: Pinguin/Umschau, pp.69–82.

——— 2000. *World-view and Society in Oku (Cameroon).* Berlin: Dietrich Reimer.

Konings, P. 1996. 'The Post-colonial State and Economic and Political Reforms in Cameroon', in A.F. Jilberto and A. Mommon (eds), *Liberalisation in the Developing World: Institutional and Economic Changes in Latin America, Africa and Asia.* London: Routledge, pp.244–65.

——— 2001. 'Mobility and Exclusion: Conflicts between Autochthons and Allochthones during Political Liberalization in Cameroon', in M. de Bruijn, R. van Dijk and D. Foeken (eds), *Mobile Africa: Changing Patterns of Movement in Africa and Beyond.* Leiden: Brill, pp.169–94.

Konings, P., and F. Nyamnjoh. 2003. *Negotiating an Anglophone Identity: A Study in the Politics of Recognition and Representation in Cameroon.* Leiden: Brill.

Kopytoff, I. 1981. 'Aghem Ethnogenesis and the Grassfields Ecumene', in C. Tardits (ed.), *Contribution de la recherche ethnologique a l'histoire des civilisations du Cameroun*, Vol. 2. Paris: Centre National de la Recherche Scientifique, pp.371–81.

——— 1987. 'The Internal African Frontier: The Making of African Political Culture', in I. Kopytoff (ed.), *The African Frontier: The Reproduction of Traditional African Societies.* Bloomington: Indiana University Press, pp.3–84.

Kourouma, A. 2001. *Waiting for the Vote of the Wild Animals.* Charlottesville: University Press of Virginia.

Kremling, V. 2004. *Zu kalt zum Aufstehen? Einflüsse von Identität und Weltbild auf die Entwicklungszusammenarbeit mit Fulbe-Viehhaltern im Liptako (Burkina Faso).* Herbolzheim: Centaurus Verlag.

Kuper, A. 2003. 'The Return of the Native', *Current Anthropology* 44(3): 389–402.

——— 2005. *The Reinvention of Primitive Society: Transformations of a Myth.* London: Routledge.

Leenhardt, O. 1995. *La catastrophe du lac Nyos au Cameroun: Des mœurs scientifiques et sociales.* Paris: L'Harmattan.

Lentz, C. 1998. *Die Konstruktion von Ethnizität: eine politische Geschichte Nord-West Ghanas 1870–1990.* Cologne: Rüdiger Köppe.

——— 2002. 'Ahnenland oder Staatsdomäne? Kontroversen über Boden in Westafrika', *Department of Anthropology and African Studies Working Paper No. 9.* Mainz: Johannes Gutenberg Universität.

——— 2013. *Land, Mobility, and Belonging in West Africa.* Bloomington: Indiana University Press.

Little, K. 1973. *African Women in Town.* Cambridge: Cambridge University Press.

Luhmann, N. 1969. *Legitimation durch Verfahren.* Frankfurt am Main: Suhrkamp.

MacMillan School Atlas of Cameroon. 1985. London, Basingstoke: Macmillan Education Ltd.

Maruyama, J. 2010. *Bushmen Living in a Changing World: Between Development Program and Indigenous Peoples' Movement.* Kyoto: Sekaishisosha Publishing (in Japanese).

Maruyama, J. and M. Pelican (eds). 2015. 'Indigenous Identities and Ethnic Coexistence in Africa', *African Study Monographs* (special Issue) 36(1).

Mbembe, A. 1992. 'Provisional Notes on the Postcolony', *Africa* 62(1): 3–37.
Mebenga, M., M.O. Nguini and P. Zibi. 2007. *National Integrity Systems. Transparency International Country Study Report: Cameroon 2007*. Berlin: Transparency International.
Mercer, C., B. Page and M. Evans. 2008. *Development and the African Diaspora: Place and the Politics of Home*. London: Zed Books.
Meyer, B., and P. Geschiere. 1999. 'Globalization and Identity: Dialectics of Flow and Closure', in P. Geschiere and B. Meyer (eds), *Globalization and Identity: Dialectics of Flow and Closure*. Oxford: Blackwell, pp.1–16.
MdlC. 2002. 'Culture Infos 2000'. Yaoundé: Ministère de la Culture.
Mimche, H. 2014. *Le temps de la sédentarisation immigration et enjeux familiaux et sociodémographiques chez les Mbororo des Grassfields du Cameroun*. Sarrebruck: Presses Académique Francophones.
Mimche, H. and M. Pelican. 2012. 'Quand les immigrants se font "autochtones": dynamiques d'insertion des Mbororo et insécurité foncière à l'ouest-Cameroun', in P. Kamdem and M. Kuete (eds), *L'"in"sécurité au Cameroun: mythe ou réalité?* Paris: Iresma, pp. 145–67.
Mitchell, J.C. 1983. 'Case and Situation Analysis', *Sociological Review* 31: 187–211.
Monga, C. 1995. 'Trade Reform and Exchange Rate Issues in the CFA Zone', *Working Papers in African Studies No. 195*. Boston: African Studies Centre, Boston University.
Moritz, M. 2006. 'Introduction: Changing Contests and Dynamics of Herder–Farmer Conflicts across West Africa', *Canadian Journal of African Studies* 40(1): 1–40.
Moritz, M., K. Ritchey and S. Kari. 2011. 'The Social Context of Herding Contracts in the Far North Region of Cameroon', *Journal of Modern African Studies* 49(2): 263–85.
Moritz, M., P. Scholte and S. Kari. 2002. 'The Demise of the Nomadic Contract: Arrangements and Rangelands under Pressure in the Far North of Cameroon', *Nomadic Peoples* 6(1): 124–43.
Mouiche, I. 2011. 'Democratisation and Political Participation of Mbororo in Western Cameroun', *Africa Spectrum* 46(2): 71–97.
Mutie, P.M. 2013. *The Art of Interethnic Coexistence: Some Evidence from Kenya*. Saarbrücken: Lambert Academic Publishing.
Ndze, Y.E. 1998. 'Islam and its Effects on the Nso Society', BA diss. Buea: University of Buea.
Newton, R. 1935. 'Intelligence Report on Mbembe and Nchanti Areas in the Bamenda Division of the Cameroons Province', unpublished manuscript. Buea: National Archives of Cameroon, 1428, Ac. 12a.
Nicolas, G. 1975. 'Les categories d'ethnie et de fraction ethnique au sein du système social Hausa', *Cahiers d'Etudes Africaines* 16(59): 399–441.
Njeuma, M. 1987. *The Record Club, 1953–58*. Yaoundé: Centre d'Edition et de Production pour l'Enseignement et la Recherche.
Njeuma, M., and N. Awasom. 1989. 'The Fulani in Bamenda Grasslands: Opportunity and Conflict 1940–1960', in P. Geschiere and P. Konings (eds), *Proceedings of the Conference on the Historical Economy of Cameroon: Historical Perspectives*. Leiden: Centre of African Studies, pp.459–71.
——— 1990. 'The Fulani and the Political Economy of the Bamenda Grasslands, 1940–1960', *Paideuma* 36: 217–233.

Nkwi, P.N. 1987. *Traditional Diplomacy: A Study of Inter-chiefdom Relations in the Western Grassfields, North West Province of Cameroon*. Yaoundé: Department of Sociology, University of Yaoundé.

Nkwi, P.N., and J.-P. Warnier. 1982. *Elements for a History of the Western Grassfields*. Yaoundé: University of Yaoundé Press.

Noye, D. 1989. *Dictionnaire Foulfouldé–Français: Dialecte peul du Diamaré Nord-Cameroun*. Paris: Geuthner Dictionnaires.

Ntoban V. n.d. [late 1990s]. 'Coffee Production in Misaje: From Arabica to Robusta', MSc diss. Buea: University of Buea.

Nyamnjoh, F. 1999. 'Cameroon: A Country United by Ethnic Ambition and Difference', *African Affairs* 98: 101–18.

——— 2001. 'Delusions of Development and the Enrichment of Witchcraft Discourses in Cameroon', in H. Moore and T. Sanders (eds), *Magical Interpretations, Material Realities: Modernity, Witchcraft and the Occult in Postcolonial Africa*. London: Routledge, pp.28–49.

——— 2002a. 'Cameroon: Over Twelve Years of Cosmetic Democracy', *News from the Nordic Africa Institute* 3: 5–8.

——— 2002b. '"A Child Is One Person's Only in the Womb": Domestication, Agency and Subjectivity in the Cameroonian Grassfields', in R. Werbner (ed.), *Postcolonial Subjectivities in Africa*. London: Zed Books, pp.111–38.

——— 2003. 'Might and Right: Chieftaincy and Democracy in Cameroon and Botswana', in W. van Binsbergen (ed.), *The Dymanics of Power and the Rule of Law*. Münster: Lit, pp.121–49.

——— 2005. *Africa's Media, Democracy and the Politics of Belonging*. London: Zed Books.

Nyamnjoh, F., and M. Rowlands. 1998. 'Elite Associations and the Politics of Belonging in Cameroon', *Africa* 68(3): 320–37.

Ogawa, R. 1993. 'Ethnic Identity and Social Interaction: A Reflection on Fulbe Identity', *Senri Ethnological Studies* 35: 119–37.

Ogunbiyi, I.A. 1996. 'The Position of Muslim Women as Stated by Uthman B. Fudi', *Odu: A Journal of West African Studies* (Ife) 2: 43–60.

Oppong, Y. 2002. *Moving through and Passing on: Fulani Mobility, Survival and Identity in Ghana*. New Brunswick, NJ: Transaction Publishers.

Ottiger, N. 1996. *Die Ökonomie der Geschlechter: Kooperation und Konflikte bei den Mmen im Kameruner Grasland*. Zurich: Argonaut Verlag.

Paden, J.N. 1970. 'Urban Pluralism, Integration, and Adaptation of Communal Identity in Kano, Nigeria', in R. Cohen and J. Middleton (eds), *From Tribe to Nation in Africa*. Scranton, PA: Chandler, pp.242–70.

Pandey, G. 1991. 'In Defence of the Fragment: Writing about Hindu–Muslim Riots in India Today', *Economical and Political Weekly* 26(11/12): 559–72.

Pelican, M. 1999. 'Die Arbeit der Mbororo-Frauen früher und heute: Eine Studie zum Wandel der sozio-ökonomischen Situation semi-nomadischer Fulbe-Frauen im nordwestlichen Grasland Kameruns', MA diss. Bayreuth: University of Bayreuth.

——— 2004a. 'Frauen- und Männerfreundschaften im Kameruner Grasland: ein komparativer Ansatz', *Africa Spectrum* 39(1): 63–93.

——— 2004b. 'Im Schatten der Schlachtviehmärkte: Milchwirtschaft der Mbororo in Nordwestkamerun', in G. Schlee (ed.), *Ethnizität und Markt: Zur ethnischen Struktur von Viehmärkten in Westafrika*. Cologne: Rüdiger Köppe, pp.131–58.

——— 2006. 'Getting along in the Grassfields: Interethnic Relations and Identity Politics in Northwest Cameroon', PhD diss. Halle/Saale: Martin Luther University Halle-Wittenberg.

——— 2008. 'Mbororo Claims to Regional Citizenship and Minority Status in Northwest Cameroon', *Africa* 78(4): 540–60.

——— 2009a. 'Complexities of Indigeneity and Autochthony: An African Example', *American Ethnologist* 36(1): 52–65.

——— 2009b. 'Customary, State and Human Rights Approaches to Containing Witchcraft in Cameroon', in B. Turner and T. Kirsch (eds), *Permutations of Order: Religion and Law as Contested Sovereignties*. Aldershot: Ashgate, pp.149–64.

——— 2010. 'Umstrittene Rechte indigener Völker: das Beispiel der Mbororo in Kamerun', *Zeitschrift für Ethnologie* 135: 39–60.

——— 2011a. 'Researching South–South/South–East Migration: Transnational Relations of Cameroonian Muslim Migrants', *Tsantsa* (Zurich) 16: 169–73.

——— 2011b. 'Mbororo on the Move: From Pastoral Mobility to International Travel', *Journal of Contemporary African Studies* 29(4): 521–34.

——— 2012a. 'From Cultural Property to Market Goods: Changes in Economic Strategies and Herd Management Rationales of Fulbe in NW Cameroon', in A. Khazanov and G. Schlee (eds), *Who Owns the Stock? Collective and Multiple Property Rights in Animals*. Oxford: Berghahn, pp.213–30.

——— 2012b. 'Friendship among Pastoral Fulbe in Northwest Cameroon', *African Study Monographs* 33(3): 165–88.

——— 2013. 'Insights from Cameroon: Five Years after the Declaration on the Rights of Indigenous Peoples', *Anthropology Today* 29(3): 13–16.

——— 2014. 'Urban Life-worlds of Cameroonian Migrants in Dubai', *Urban Anthropology and Studies of Cultural Systems and World Economic Development*, special issue, 43(1–3): 255–309.

——— 2015. 'Ethnicity as a Political Resource: Indigenous Rights Movements in Africa', in University of Cologne Forum 'Ethnicity as a Political Resource' (ed.), *Ethnicity as a Political Resource – Conceptualizations across Disciplines, Regions, and Periods*. Bielefeld: Transcript.

Pelican, M., and P. Tatah. 2009. 'Migration to the Gulf States and China: Local Perspectives from Cameroon', *African Diaspora* 2(2): 229–45.

Pfeffer, G. 1936. 'Die Djaafun-Bororo, ihre Gesellschaft, Wirtschaft und Sesshaftwerdung auf dem Hochland von Ngaoundere', *Zeitschrift für Ethnologie* 68: 150–96.

Price, D. 1979. 'Who Are the Tikar Now?' *Paideuma* 25: 88–98.

Ranger, T. 1983. 'The Invention of Tradition in Colonial Africa', in E. Hobsbawm and T. Ranger (eds), *The Invention of Tradition*. Cambridge: Cambridge University Press, pp.211–62.

——— 1993. 'The Invention of Tradition Revisited: The Case of Colonial Africa', in T. Ranger and O. Vaughan (eds), *Legitimacy and the State in Twentieth-century Africa*. Oxford: Macmillan, pp.62–111.

Regis, H. 2003. *Fulbe Voices: Marriage, Islam, and Medicine in Northern Cameroon*. Boulder, CO: Westview Press.

Ritzenthaler, R. 1960. 'Anlu: A Women's Uprising in the British Cameroons', *African Studies* 18(3): 151–56.

Ritzenthaler, R., and P. Ritzenthaler. 1962. *Cameroons Village: An Ethnography of the Bafut*. Milwaukee: Milwaukee Public Museum Publications in Anthropology.

Röschenthaler, U. 2011. *Purchasing Culture: The Dissemination of Associations in the Cross River Region of Cameroon and Nigeria*. Trenton, NJ: Africa World Press.

Rowlands, M. 1979. 'Local and Long Distance Trade and Incipient State Formation on the Bamenda Plateau in the Late 19th Century', *Paideuma* 25: 1–19.

——— 2002. 'Cultural Heritage and the Role of Traditional Intellectuals in Mali and Cameroon', in C. Shore and P. Nugent (eds), *Elite Cultures: Anthropological Perspectives*. London: Routledge, pp.145–57.

Rowlands, M., and J.-P. Warnier. 1988. 'Sorcery, Power and the Modern State in Cameroon', *Man* 23(1): 118–32.

Salihu, N.J. 1999. 'The Idea of MBOSCUDA: The Augments of 10 Years Ago', unpublished document. Bamenda: Mbororo Social and Cultural Development Association Archives.

Salomone, F. 1975a. 'A Hausa Bibliography', *Africana Journal* 6: 99–163.

——— 1975b. 'Becoming Hausa: Ethnic Identity Change and its Implications for the Study of Ethnic Pluralism and Stratification', *Africa* 45(4): 410–25.

——— 1975c. 'The Serkawa of Yauri: Class, Status or Party?' *African Studies Review* 18(1): 88–101.

——— 1980. 'Indirect Rule and the Reinterpretation of Tradition: Abdullahi of Yauri', *African Studies Review* 23(1): 1–14.

Sanjek, R. 1977. 'Cognitive Maps of the Ethnic Domain in Urban Ghana: Reflections on Variability and Change', *American Ethnologist* 4(4): 603–22.

Schilder, K. 1993. 'Local Rulers in North Cameroon: The Interplay of Politics and Conversion', *Afrika Focus*, special issue, 9(1/2): 43–72.

——— 1994. *Quest for Self-esteem: State, Islam, and Mundang Ethnicity in Northern Cameroon*. Leiden: African Studies Centre.

Schildkrout, E. 1982. 'Dependence and Autonomy: The Economic Activities of Secluded Hausa Women in Kano, Nigeria', in E.G. Bay (ed.), *Women and Work in Africa*. Boulder, CO: Westview Press, pp.55–81.

Schlee, G. 1994. 'Ethnicity Emblems, Diacritical Features, Identity Markers: Some East African Examples', in D. Brokensha (ed.), *A River of Blessing*. New York: Syracuse University Press, pp.129–43.

——— 1997. 'Cross-cutting Ties and Interethnic Conflict: The Example of the Gabbra, Oromo and Rendille', in K. Fukui, E. Kurimoto and M. Shigeta (eds), *Ethiopia in Broader Perspective*, Vol. 2. Kyoto: Shokado Book Sellers, pp.577–96.

——— 2000. 'Identitätskonstruktion und Parteinahme: Überlegungen zur Konflikttheorie', *Sociologus* 10(1): 64–89.

——— 2001. 'Einleitung', in A. Horstmann and G. Schlee (eds), *Integration durch Verschiedenheit: Lokale und globale Formen interkultureller Kommunikation*. Bielefeld: Transcript, pp.17–46.

——— 2003. 'Integration und Konflikt: Integration and Conflict', *Entwicklungsethnologie* 12(1/2): 74–95.

——— 2004. 'Taking Sides and Constructing Identities: Reflections on Conflict Theory', *Journal of the Royal Anthropological Institute* 10(1): 135–56.

——— 2008. *How Enemies Are Made: Towards a Theory of Ethnic and Religious Conflict*. Oxford: Berghahn.

——— 2012. 'Feedback and Cross-fertilization: The "Declaration of Indigenous Communities of Moyale District"', in G. Schlee and A. Shongolo (eds), *Pastoralism & Politics in Northern Kenya & Southern Ethiopia*. Woodbridge: James Currey, pp.137–44.

Schnepel, B. 1998. 'Der Raub der Göttin: Rituelle Inszenierungen von Macht und Autorität in Orissa, Indien', in B. Schmidt and M. Münzel (eds), *Ethnologie und Inszenierung: Ansätze zur Theaterethnologie*. Marburg: Curupira, pp.459–85.

Schultz, E. 1979. 'Ethnic Identity and Cultural Commitment: A Study of the Process of FulBeization in Guider, Northern Cameroon', PhD diss. Bloomington: Indiana University.

——— 1980. 'Perceptions of Ethnicity in Guider Town', in E. Schultz (ed.), *Image and Reality in African Interethnic Relations: The FulBe and their Neighbours*. Williamsburg, VA: College of William and Mary, pp.127–49.

——— 1984. 'From Pagan to Pullo: Ethnic Identity Change in Northern Cameroon', *Africa* 54(1): 46–64.

Shack, W. 1979. 'Open Systems and Closed Boundaries: The Ritual Process of Stranger Relations in New African States', in W. Shack and E.P. Skinner (eds), *Strangers in African Societies*. Berkeley: University of California Press, pp.37–47.

Shanklin, E. 1988. 'Beautiful Deadly Lake Nyos', *Anthropology Today* 4(1): 12–14.

Simmel, G. 1908. *Soziologie: Untersuchungen über die Formen der Vergesellschaftung*. Frankfurt am Main: Otthein Rammstedt.

Skinner, E.P. 1963. 'Strangers in West African Societies', *Africa* 33(4): 307–20.

Smith, M. 1952. 'A Study of Hausa Domestic Economy in Northern Zaria', *Africa* 22(4): 333–47.

——— 1959. 'The Hausa System of Social Status', *Africa* 29(3): 239–51.

——— 1961. 'Field Histories among the Hausa', *Journal of African History* 2(1): 87–101.

——— 1965. *Baba of Karo: A Woman of the Muslim Hausa*. London: Faber.

Socpa, A. 2002. *Democratisation et autochtonie au Cameroun: Trajectoires regionales divergentes*. Leiden: Leiden University Press.

Stenning, D. 1959. *Savannah Nomads: A Study of the WoDaaBe Pastoral Fulani of Western Bornu Province Northern Region, Nigeria*. London: Oxford University Press.

Sutton, J.E.G. 1979. 'Towards a Less Orthodox History of Hausaland', *Journal of African History* 20: 179–201.

Takougang, J., and M. Krieger. 1998. *African State and Society in the 1990s: Cameroon's Political Crossroads*. Boulder, CO: Westview Press.

Tardits. C. 1980. *Le royaume bamoum*. Paris: Armand Colin.

Tonah, S. 2002. 'Fulani Pastoralists, Indigenous Farmers and the Contest for Land in Northern Ghana', *Africa Spectrum* 37(1): 43–59.

Topographical Map of Cameroon, Nkambe, 1:500,000. 1972. Paris, Yaoundé: Institut Géographique National.

Tourneux, H., and Y. Dairou. 1999. *Vocabulaire peul du monde rural: Maroua-Garoua (Cameroun)*. Paris: Karthala.

Turner, V. 1957. *Schism and Continuity in an African Society: A Study of Ndembu Village Life*. Manchester: Manchester University Press.

——— 1967. *The Forest of Symbols: Aspects of Ndembu Ritual*. Ithaca, NY: Cornell University Press.

——— 1974. *Dramas, Fields and Metaphors: Symbolic Action in Human Society*. Ithaca, NY: Cornell University Press.
Vabi, M.B. 1991. 'Social Relationships between Indigeneous Cultivators and Fulani Graziers in the Derived Savannah of Southwestern Nigeria and the Northwestern Province of Cameroon', PhD diss. Ibadan: University of Ibadan.
van Santen, J. 1993. 'They Leave their Jars behind: The Conversion of Mafa Women to Islam (North Cameroon)', PhD diss. Utrecht: Rijksuniversiteit
——— 1995. 'Women and the Spread of Islam in West Africa: Their Changing Role in a North Cameroonian Town', in C. van Dijk and A.H. de Groot (eds), *State and Islam*. Leiden: School of Asian, African, and Amerindian Studies, pp.178–203.
——— 1998. 'Islam, Gender and Urbanisation among the Mafa of North Cameroon: The Differing Commitment to "Home" among Muslims and non-Muslims', *Africa* 68(3): 403–24.
VerEecke, C. 1993. 'Traditions of Exclusiveness and Ethnic Identity in a Changing African Pastoral Society: The Fulbe of Adamawa, Nigeria', *Ethnic Groups* 10: 301–21.
——— 1996. 'Pulaaku, Adamwa Fulbe Identity and its Transformations', PhD diss. Philadelphia: University of Pennsylvania.
Virtanen, T. 2003. 'Performance and Performativity in Pastoral Fulbe Culture', PhD diss. Helsinki: Helsinki University.
von Benda-Beckmann, F. 1994. 'Rechtspluralismus: Analytische Begriffsbildung oder politisch-ideologisches Programm', *Zeitschrift für Ethnologie* 119: 1–16.
von Benda-Beckmann, F., K. von Benda-Beckmann and A. Griffiths (eds). 2009. *The Power of Law in a Transnational World: Anthropological Enquiries*. Oxford: Berghahn.
von Benda-Beckmann, K. 1981. 'Forum Shopping and Shopping Forums: Dispute Processing in a Minangkabau Village in West Sumatra', *Journal of Legal Pluralism* 19: 117–59.
Walker, S. 1980. 'From Cattle Camp to City: Changing Roles of Fulbe Women in Northern Cameroon', *Journal of African Studies* 7(1): 54–63.
Wall, L. 1988. *Hausa Medicine. Illness and Well-being in a West African Culture*. Durham, NC: Duke University Press.
Warnier, J.-P. 1985. *Échanges, développement et hierarchies dans le Bamenda pré-colonial (Cameroun)*. Stuttgart: Franz Steiner.
——— 1993. *L'esprit d'entreprise au Cameroun*. Paris: Karthala.
——— 1995. 'Slave-trading without Slave-raiding in Cameroon', *Paideuma* 41: 251–72.
——— 2007. *The Pot-King: The Body and Technologies of Power*. Leiden: Brill.
Waters-Bayer, A., and W. Bayer. 1994. 'Coming to Terms: Interactions between Immigrant Fulani Cattle-keepers and Indigenous Farmers in Nigeria's Subhumid Zone', *Cahiers d'Etudes Africaines* 34(133–135): 213–29.
Wazaki, H. 1992. 'The Political Structure of the Bamoun Kingdom in Cameroon and the Urban–Rural Relationship', *Senri Ethnological Studies* 31: 303–71.
Weber, M. 1949. *The Methodology of the Social Sciences*, trans. and ed. E.A. Shils and H.A. Finch. New York: Free Press.
Werthmann, K. 1997. *Nachbarinnen: Die Alltagswelt muslimischer Frauen in einer nigerianischen Großstadt*. Frankfurt am Main: Brandes and Apsel.
Westermann, V. 1992. *Women's Disturbances: Der Anlu-Aufstand bei den Kom (Kamerun) 1958–1960*. Münster: Lit.
Whitting, C.C.J. 1955. 'Fulani Floggings', *West African Review* 26(328): 10–12.

Winchester, N.B. 1976. 'Strangers and Politics in Urban Africa: A Study of the Hausa in Kumasi, Ghana', PhD diss. Bloomington: Indiana University.

Works, J.A. 1976. *Pilgrims in a Strange Land: Hausa Communities in Chad*. New York: Columbia University Press.

Yamani, M. 1998. 'Cross-cultural Marriage within Islam: Ideals and Reality', in R. Breger and R. Hill (eds), *Cross-cultural Marriage: Identity and Choice*. Oxford: Berg, pp.153–69.

Yenshu, V.E., and G.A. Ngwa. 2001. 'Changing Intercommunity Relations and the Politics of Identity in the Northern Mezam Area, Cameroon', *Cahiers d'Etudes Africaines* 41(161): 163–90.

Index

A

acceptance
  of political hierarchies, 29, 104
  of socio-cultural differences, 29
access to
  natural and state resources, 1, 4, 31, 43, 66, 74n11, 82–83, 95, 120–22, 132, 177
  Adamaoua Highlands/Plateau, 52, 79, 80, 82, 83, 141–42, 146, 177
administration
  (colonial and) postcolonial, 58, 61–62, 71, 112, 114, 133, 156, 158, 185, 213
Afrique en miniature, 32
agency, 6, 49–50
Aku, 13, 47n20, 63– 66, 74nn20–21, 76, 78–94, 96, 101, 105, 107n6, 107n10, 111, 114, 115, 117, 140. *See also* Mbororo
akuji (white cattle breed), 87
Alber, Erdmute, 42, 168
allegiances, 38
  cross-cutting, 9, 37, 41
  individual and group, 8, 39, 151
  religious and social, 39, 64
alliances
  ancestor/s, 28, 43, 52–55, 66, 78, 89, 99, 175, 196
  interethnic, 112
  political, 59, 150
anecdotes, 54, 62
arDo (Mbororo leader), 65, 83, 88, 89, 90, 91, 94, 96, 107n8, 107n11, 118, 124–26, 192, 199, 206
Ardos Union, 100
Argenti, Nicolas, 3, 29, 30, 34, 53, 74n18, 172

army intervention, 25, 32. *See also* violence
assistance, 37, 41, 66, 68, 71, 78, 118, 131, 140, 154, 155, 168, 187, 197
associations, 67–70, 99–100, 103, 108n27, 195, 213
  social and cultural, 34, 49, 61, 66, 67, 74n27, 89, 116, 120, 130, 154–56, 159, 160n12, 184, 186, 201, 208
Association pour la Promotion de l'Elevage au Sahel et en Savane (APESS), 95–96
authorities
  'native authorities', 'native authority areas', 17–18, 20n7, 50, 65
  'traditional authorities', 45n1, 49, 71
authority
  government, 1, 44
  legal, judicial, 98, 125, 188, 194, 205
  political, 4, 27, 41, 59, 62, 72, 74n11, 104
  ritual, 27, 34, 36, 58
  royal, 29–30, 36, 37, 57, 68, 83
  territorial, 59, 62, 95
autochthony, 2, 30, 50, 103, 201, 212
autonomy, 27, 40, 53, 208
avoidance, 2, 8, 9–10, 169. *See also* conflict model
  functional indifference, 42
  strategy of, 9–10, 42, 44, 45, 184–86
Awasom, Nicodemus, 31, 74n26, 76, 80, 84, 85, 95, 100, 135, 139, 140, 144, 145, 159n1, 169

B

Babanki, 83, 94, 95, 98
Bafut, 74n24, 140
Bali, 47n19, 50, 74n24, 74n26, 140
Ballotiral, 102, 108n30, 121, 123–27, 155, 156, 186–87, 188, 198, 206, 208

Bamenda, 26, 62, 64, 73n8, 211
  Highlands/Plateau, 78, 82–84, 92, 110, 121–22, 140, 143, 180
  Town, 79, 94, 95, 97, 134n7, 147, 166, 175, 194, 199, 202, 205
Bamoun kingdom, 45n5, 180
Barth, Frederik, 5, 52
Bayart, Jean-François, 31, 53, 68, 190
belonging, 211, 212
  ethnic and regional, 2, 3, 30, 48, 50, 53, 67, 73, 151, 162
  notions of, 4, 69, 152, 175
  politics of, 2, 3, 11, 18, 61
  rituals of, 182n4, 201
Benin, 42, 105, 107n25, 134n12, 191, 208
Bessa Cultural and Development Association (BECUDA), 61, 69–70, 75n30, 167, 192, 195–202, 205–6, 208
Bierschenk, Thomas, 185, 190, 191, 208
boDeeji (red cattle breed), 80, 86–87
Boutrais, Jean, 16, 18, 76–80, 83, 87, 91, 93, 104, 107n9, 113, 116, 133n3, 135, 139, 141, 143, 144, 145, 159n1
bridewealth, 165, 176, 183n6
Bridge Five, 20n7, 90
British colonial administration, 17, 74n24, 83, 93, 99, 187, 189
Brubaker, Roger, 6, 138, 152, 159
Buea, 147
Bum, 55, 59, 61, 74n10, 74n24, 75n29, 90, 141
burial rites, 163, 164, 175, 182n1, 182n4
Burkina Faso, 95, 107n25, 112, 132–33, 134n4
Burnham, Philip, 2, 8, 78, 105, 161, 176, 178, 179, 180, 183n12, 212–13

C
Cameroon
  northwest, 1, 2, 11–12, 73n2, 76, 78–79, 81, 83, 94, 97, 101–3, 105, 112–19, 121, 123, 139, 153, 162–64, 177, 187–91, 210, 213
  Grassfields, 1, 3–10, 12–13, 19, 20n5, 28, 36, 43, 61, 76, 77, 79, 80, 82–89, 91, 103, 105, 109, 121–22, 125, 132, 138, 140, 143, 158, 161, 174, 178, 179, 184
Cameroon People's Democratic Movement (CPDM), 32, 46n10, 70, 99, 192

Cameroonian
  constitution, 31, 85, 102, 186, 198
  Penal Code, 208n2
categories, 138
  ethnic and cultural, 2, 5, 13, 16, 19, 28, 69, 76–78, 80, 82, 84, 105, 135–39, 149, 152, 153, 158, 178, 180, 181
  of identification, 77–79, 94, 105, 106n5
  'neo-colonial', 6
cattle husbandry, 76, 111, 114, 116–19, 121
  theft, 19, 64, 66, 109, 114, 118–33, 134n9, 186, 194, 200, 202–4
ceremony
  ceremonial ground, 24–25, 30, 34, 35, 38, 39, 45
  investiture ceremonies, 1, 19, 23–25, 29, 30, 35–39, 157, 201
  national ceremonies, 28, 46n14, 69
CFA (*Communauté Financière Africaine*), French Central African Currency Union, 1, 31, 46n9, 70, 85, 129, 131, 134n5, 165, 183n6
Chako, 20n2, 90
charity, 147, 152, 167, 168
chiefdom/s, 67
  Bessa, 16, 59, 70, 192
  Bum, 55, 59, 61, 74n24, 141
  Grassfields, 4, 12, 20n5, 24, 28–30, 40, 45n5, 48, 53, 57, 59, 62, 83, 94, 95, 104, 125, 150, 171, 188
  inter-chiefdom war, 37, 43, 54
  Mankon, 4, 46n7, 74n11, 74n24
  Nchaney, 16, 19, 23–25, 29, 33–34, 41, 43, 48, 51, 52–66, 70–72, 153, 156
  Nso, 40, 45n5, 55, 61, 74n24, 141, 180
Chilver, Elizabeth, 50, 51, 54, 58, 61, 73n5, 76, 113, 116, 121, 125, 141, 143, 172
Christianity, *see* religion
citizenship, 31, 85, 208
  Cameroonian, 85, 102
  national, 2, 33
  regional, 50, 67
civil servants, 31, 123, 125–26, 128, 131
clan/s, 8, 49–50, 59, 61, 62, 66, 67, 69, 72
  clan territory, 50, 58, 62, 66, 68, 71–72
classification, colonial, 49, 72, 74n24, 212
coexistence, 10, 61, 187
  ethnic and social, 1, 3, 5, 7– 9, 19, 23, 25, 28, 42–45, 105, 181, 182, 207
  of farmers and herders, 113, 119, 121

Cohen, Abner, 6, 135, 137, 138, 144, 152, 153, 182n4, 213
collaboration, 94, 101–3, 123, 131, 186
colonial rule/powers, 6, 19, 29, 43, 50, 52, 66, 72, 83, 146, 156, 158, 213
  British, 12, 17, 49, 73n2, 74n24, 83, 84, 93, 99, 113, 133, 144, 145, 147, 187, 189
  French, 12, 42, 113, 140, 144
  German, 12, 58, 73n8, 82, 96, 140, 144
colonialism, 49
Commission Nationale Anti-Corruption (CONAC), 191
community
  formation, 20n4, 138–40, 146–53
  'moral community', 135, 153–54, 161, 163–70
  Muslim community, *see* Muslim
competition, 7, 61, 114, 129, 187–88
  economic, 119–20, 132
  over natural resources/access to land, 1, 10, 112, 121–22, 132–33
compromise, 10–11, 24, 30, 38, 40–45, 126–27, 208
conflict
  escalation, 8, 29, 32
  ethnic conflict, 1, 2, 7, 10, 11, 37, 45n3, 121, 132, 196, 200, 207, 208, 214
  farmer–herder conflict, 3, 19, 20n2, 66, 70, 109–34, 185, 198, 203
  investiture conflict, 3, 8, 10, 23, 27–45, 48, 63, 73, 157, 181, 182, 184, 185, 186, 200, 206, 213
  management, 9, 11, 19, 42, 45, 184–209
  model, 8, 9, 42, 44, 184, 185, 191, 207. *See also* Elwert; violence
  murder conflict, 2, 9, 20, 184, 186, 187, 191–94, 198, 200–8, 213
  over religious and cultural difference, 1, 45, 103, 179
  resolution, 10, 20, 41–42, 124, 126, 133, 184, 185, 186, 187, 191, 192, 200, 201
  violent conflict, 8, 29, 43, 59, 127
confrontation, 3, 8, 10, 95, 113, 125, 186
  open, 25, 39
  ritual, 34–36
Congo-Kinshasa, 2
constructionist approaches/perspective, 5, 6, 138, 160n16

conversion, *see also* marriage; religion: Islam
  religious and ethnic, 5, 9, 19, 45n5, 64, 136–37, 150–53, 159, 161–83
corruption, 113, 122, 126, 189–91, 199, 205, 207, 208, 213
Côte d'Ivoire, 2, 42, 112, 133n3, 134n4
cross-cutting ties, 8–9, 20, 43, 61, 162, 181, 182
cultural heritage/politics, 32, 33
custom, 49, 73n1, 80, 90, 153, 166, 179
customary land tenure system, 204, 209n7
'cut-head', 193, 195. *See also* occult; witchcraft

D

Daneeji, 79, 89–92, 94, 107n6, 107n10
Dafinger, Andreas, 107n25, 112, 113, 122, 133, 134n4, 204
decentralization, 2, 20n3
decision making, 37, 38, 208
democratic freedoms, 30
democratization, 1, 2, 11, 30, 31, 66, 213
descent, descendants, 43, 52, 61, 72, 78, 89, 104, 135–37, 145, 147, 150, 179
diacritical markers/features, 28, 45n4
dichotomy, 36
  between 'citizens' and 'aliens', 29
  between 'farmers' and 'herders', 114–19
  between Grassfielders and Muslims, 36
  between 'host' and 'stranger', 29
difference
  ethnic and cultural, 1–3, 5, 19, 23–48, 62, 89, 124, 171, 179, 201, 212
  integration through difference, 7, 8, 10, 43, 112
discourses
  of autochthony, 2, 30, 103, 201
  of belonging, 30, 212
  frontstage and backstage, 132–33
  global/international rights discourse, 2, 3, 4, 6, 19, 103, 186
  of human and minority rights, 11, 101, 184, 186, 207
distinction, 10, 11, 16, 28, 50, 64, 65, 78, 100, 105, 117, 128, 132, 138, 178, 185
  between rebellion and revolution, 44
Divisional Officer (DO), 24, 25, 27, 30, 32, 33, 35, 37, 38, 40, 41, 46n11, 69, 70, 128, 131, 189, 192, 197–99, 202
Donga Mantung Division, 13, 16
Douala, 69, 145, 166, 167, 211

drama, 123
    culture-drama, 127
    social, 8, 27, 41, 43
dramatis personae, 23, 192
Dumbo, 16, 18, 20n7, 55, 57, 59, 64, 88, 90, 110, 136, 147–49, 159n7

E
Economic and Social Council (ECOSOC), 102. *See also* United Nations
economy, 18, 55, 83, 88, 93, 113, 116, 139, 207
    decline, 1, 31
    economic competition, 132
    economic depression, 18
    economic diversification, 3, 7, 19, 109, 113–14, 118–20, 132
education, 28, 68, 69–70, 88, 93–94, 100, 106, 107n22, 108n29, 116, 118, 124–26, 152, 154–55, 166, 174, 181, 198, 201, 205, 206, 214
elite, 62, 68, 103, 125, 163, 192, 196–200, 202, 207, 210, 213
    elite associations, 1, 11, 30, 49, 51, 61, 66–71, 74n11, 74n27, 116, 120, 154, 156, 158, 159, 184, 201, 208
    external elite, 58, 69, 71, 196, 198
Elwert, Georg, 7, 9–10, 42, 44–45, 162, 180, 184–85, 191, 207, 208n1. *See also* conflict model; violence
embedding, 9, 42, 44, 184–85, 191
embodiment
    of historical memory, 3
emotional, emotions, 3, 125, 163, 201
encounters, 19, 26, 28, 35, 40, 42, 52, 62, 96, 148, 158, 196
    contemporary, 5–6
    historical, 5–6
Enugu, 145
Eriksen, Thomas Hylland, 28, 42, 154
ethnic
    boundaries, 6, 8, 12, 19, 162, 213
    emblems, 45
    groups, 6, 20n4, 28, 49, 68, 70–71, 74nn20–21, 113, 114, 117, 121, 132, 136, 138, 158, 159n1, 179, 193
    minorities, 31, 208
    stereotypes, 3, 62, 109, 121, 122, 124, 126–27, 132–33
ethnicity, ethnicities, 3, 5, 10–11, 16, 37, 49, 59, 62, 69, 71, 89, 99, 104, 117, 132, 135, 138, 151, 153, 155, 158, 175, 180, 211
    concepts of ethnicity, 2, 4, 6–7, 19, 158, 160n16, 179
    models of ethnicity, 29, 138
    political and instrumental, 2, 4, 10, 20, 66, 137–38, 157, 212, 213
    role of ethnicity, 2, 207
ethnicization
    of competition, 7
    of conflict, 10, 128
    of national and local politics, 2
exchange networks, 48

F
Far North Region, 177, 180
farmers, 42, 53, 66, 76, 83–84, 93, 99, 110–16, 118–20, 122–27, 133, 134n8, 134n10, 138, 190, 192, 200, 203
farmer–grazier commission, 122, 189
farmer–herder conflict, 3, 19, 20n2, 66, 70, 109–34, 185, 198, 203
farmer–herder relations, 83, 93, 109, 111–14, 121, 126, 132–33, 134n4, 158
Festival National des Arts et de la Culture, 33
'fields of shared meaning', 28
first-comers, 88, 94, 103
folklore, folklorization, 33, 98
fon (Grassfields chief), 16, 20n5, 34, 38, 40, 41, 53–58, 61–72, 73n3, 74n24, 95, 98, 124–25, 130–31, 134n10, 154, 156–57, 180, 189, 192, 194, 197, 199, 201, 203, 205
Fonfuka, 147
forced labour, 3
forum shopping, 187–88, 201
foster parenting, 167–69, 178
Foumban, 140
'free women', 148–49, 159n8
friendship, 61, 115, 117, 118, 167, 197
Fulani Council, 84
FulBe
    hegemony, 77, 80, 178
    nomadic FulBe (WoDaaBe), 79–80
    pastoral FulBe (Mbororo), 76, 78–79, 100, 105, 112, 115, 149
    Town FulBe (Huya), 78–79, 92, 100, 105, 107n20, 136–37, 146–49, 178
Fulbeization, 178–80
Fulfulde, 35, 63, 74n21, 76–78, 80, 84, 90, 94–96, 101, 102, 107n6, 116–18, 144, 147, 155–56, 159n4, 174, 179–80

Index 239

functional indifference, 10, 28, 41–42, 45, 206
Fungom, 84

G
Garoua, 146
German Development Service (DED), 101
Geschiere, Peter, 2–3, 30, 31, 46n10, 68, 73n2, 74n10, 75n29, 171, 172, 182n4, 201, 211–12
Ghana, 42, 127, 133n3, 137
give-and-take, 9–10
   relationship, 42
'global flows', 211–212
globalization, 2, 211
Gluckman, Max, 8, 44, 162
godparent, 174
governmentality of containers, 4
Grassfields
   chiefdoms, 4, 20n5, 24, 28, 40, 45n5, 48, 53, 57, 59, 61–62, 104, 171, 188. *See also* chiefdoms
   chiefs, 4, 29, 31, 49, 53, 62, 67, 70, 74n11, 83, 116, 131, 134n10
   diplomacy, 61
   ethnicities, 59
   masks, 3, 33, 36, 45n2
   polities, 4, 29
   societies (organization of), 4–5, 16, 19, 34
   traders, 18
graziers, 65, 77, 89, 113, 116–17, 120, 126
   Mbororo graziers, 82, 85, 89, 92, 106n2, 118–19, 122–23, 126, 128, 143–45, 147, 200, 203
   'native graziers', 116–20, 126, 128–33
   Nchaney graziers, 118
group size, 6, 158, 213
Groupe d'Etudes et de Recherche en Démocratie, Développement Economique et Sociale (GERDDES), 190–91
'groupism', 6
'groupness', 7, 138, 152, 157, 159
gudaali, 87, 90, 111

H
Hausaization, 178–80
Hausaland, 137–38, 141–42
headscarf, 33
hegemony, cultural, 40, 80, 178
Helvetas, 154

herders, 25, 39, 64–65, 76, 82, 86, 106n2, 110–33, 134n10, 145, 148, 180, 190, 197, 199
hierarchy, hierarchies, 4, 29, 157, 158, 175
   lineage hierarchy, 78, 96
   palace hierarchy, 23–25, 29–30, 33–34, 37, 40, 46n17, 48, 51, 62, 73, 83, 128
historical
   memory, 3, 10–11, 79, 145–52
   reconstruction, 54, 80, 97
history
   collective, 51, 79, 94
   Hausa, 139–40, 145–46, 152, 153
   history-telling, 49, 80, 96
   Mbororo, 65, 79–80, 89, 96, 139
   migration, 71–72, 79
   Nchaney, 49–54, 67, 71, 73n3, 77, 98, 104, 106n5, 139
   oral histories, 54
   recent, 2, 64
   Sabga, 95–96
   shared, 53, 63
homicide, 45
host–guest relations, 99
host–stranger relations, 29
House of Chiefs, 66, 68
Human Rights Council, 103, 210
husband–wife relations, 169, 172
Huya, 13, 78, 92, 100, 105, 107n20, 136, 138, 145–50. *See also* Town FulBe

I
identity, identities
   collective, 32, 61
   cultural, 27, 32, 44, 46n6
   and difference, 5, 27, 211
   ethnic, 5–6, 33, 63, 71, 82, 149, 151, 155, 158, 162–63, 181, 212–13
   FulBe, 89, 178–80
   Hausa, 135, 137–39, 150, 152, 178, 180–81
   identity cards, 102
   identity markers, 45n4
   identity politics, 5, 20, 45, 76–108
   Mbororo, 4, 19–20, 35, 76–77, 89, 100–1, 103–6, 204, 212
   multiple identities, 19
   Muslim, 5, 76, 89, 93, 99, 171, 175, 177
   national, 2, 31, 68, 76
   Nchaney, 48, 53, 59, 71–72
   pastoral, 78, 105, 114
   religious, 155, 162–63, 167, 175, 178

Imam (Muslim prayer leader), 95–98, 107n21
immigration, immigrants, 6, 13, 73, 84, 87, 91, 116, 140, 146
inclusion and exclusion, 3, 6–7, 49, 52, 77
indigeneity, 2, 102, 108n32
indigenous
  minority, 102, 106, 198
  'indigenous people', 6, 11, 76, 102–3, 211. *See also* United Nations
  rights movement, 106
instrumentalist approach, 6
integration, 2, 4, 7–8, 10–11, 40, 59, 62–63, 65, 73, 76, 85, 102, 106, 113, 115, 122, 135, 152, 157–58, 163, 179, 183n14, 193, 207, 208, 212
  through difference, 7, 10, 43, 112
interdependency, 120
interethnic
  marriage, 150–52, 162, 181–82
  relations, 2, 8, 19, 27–29, 41, 45, 58, 76, 104, 118–19, 123, 139, 171, 187, 207–8
International Labour Organization (ILO), 102
International Monetary Fund (IMF), 30, 186
inter-village, 58
intra-ethnic relations, 19, 28, 76, 85, 128
'invention of tradition', 6, 49, 95
Islam, *see* religion
  Islamic Youth Association, 155, 168

J

Jaafun, 13, 47n20, 64–66, 74nn20–21, 76, 78–90, 92–93, 96, 101, 105, 107n10, 111, 114, 115, 140. *See also* Mbororo
jihad
  FulBe *jihad*, 53, 80, 140
Jos Plateau, 82, 84, 92

K

Kaberry, Phyllis, 50, 51, 54, 58, 61, 73n5, 84, 116, 121, 172, 209n7
Kamerun (German protectorate), 144
Kamine, 16, 61, 69–70
Kano, 59, 80, 82, 90–92, 137–38, 146
Katsina, 91, 92, 138
Kawtal Pulaaku, 155
Kemezung, 16, 59, 66, 69
Kenya (northern), 8, 42, 108n3
Kibbo, 16, 58–59, 72, 90
kingmakers, 52–53

Kopytoff, Igor, 4, 48, 53, 73n5
Kom, 47, 74n24
Koran, 63, 64, 144, 165, 166, 171, 174, 183n12, 183n14
Kumba, 147
Kumbo, 180–81
Kwei, 16

L

laamiiDo (FulBe paramount chief), 94–97, 103, 107n11, 148
labour
  division of, 112, 115, 133n2
Lake Nyos, 18, 21n8
Lassin, 147
Last, Murray, 138
latecomers, 28, 62, 66
legal pluralism, 187, 191
liberalization, 4, 19, 30–31, 45, 57, 68, 94, 98–99, 102, 128, 184, 207
Liberia, 2
litigation, 1, 9, 184, 186–87, 207–8
lobbying, 1, 9, 100, 108n27, 184, 186–87, 196, 201, 207–8
locality
  production of, 4, 53
Lompta, 82, 96, 107n20
loyalty, 4, 30, 181

M

Mafa, 177–78, 180, 182n5
Mafor University Women, 154–55
Mambila Plateau/Highlands, 90
Manchester School, 8, 9, 12
Mankon, 4, 46n7, 74n10, 74n24, 140, 150
marginalization, 3, 205, 212
Maroua, 146, 148, 179
marriage, 148–49, 168, 176, 177, 211. *See also* bridewealth; conversion; interethnic marriage
  intermarriage, 5, 9, 48, 59, 61, 104, 135, 146, 165–66
masks, 1, 3, 8, 27, 33, 45n2
  chombu ju-ju, 24–25, 34–35, 38. *See also* Nchaney
  nggumba ju-ju, 25–26, 34–40, 182. *See also* Nchaney
masquerade/s, 12, 24, 33, 46n17, 164, 171, 201
  Nchaney masquerade, 27, 32, 36
'master fiction', 26, 37
master narrative, 40
Mbembe, 39, 46n14, 50, 63, 150

Mbissa, 16, 59, 61, 69
Mbororo, *see also* FulBe; pastoralists
  (herding) staffs, 25, 33, 36
  lineages, 76, 78–80, 82–84, 88–92, 96, 100, 101, 105, 106n5, 107n6, 107n10, 114–15. *See also* Aku; Jaafun
  sedentarization, 5, 19, 84, 94, 104, 114
  staff-hurlers, 26, 27, 32, 35–36
Mbororo Social and Cultural Development Association (MBOSCUDA), 98–103, 108n27, 123, 156, 208, 210–12
mbororoji, 87
memory, 3, 10–11, 32, 59, 61, 79, 91, 145, 147
  collective recollections, 26, 43
  vestigial memories, 3
migration, 4–5, 48, 52, 54, 77, 90–91, 104, 140
  history, 71–72, 76, 78–80, 86, 106n5, 139, 146
  labour migration, 12–13, 75n29, 177
  Mbororo southward migration, 81–82, 85
  Muslim migrants, 5
  mythical migration, 52
  pastoral migration, 19, 84–85
minority, 6, 40, 84, 89, 104, 152, 179, 205. *See also* indigenous minority.
  representation, 32–33, 44
  rights, 2, 9, 11, 40, 101, 103, 184, 186, 207–8
Misaje
  Native Authority Area, 18
  Sub-Division, 13, 16, 18, 65, 69–70, 77, 79, 85–86, 88–89, 107n10, 110–11, 117, 127–30, 192, 195, 197
  town, 1, 13–19, 28, 40, 55, 61, 64, 70, 110, 153–55, 161
Misaje Area Elite Association (MELA), 69
mobility, 11, 12, 59, 80, 92–93, 177, 179, 210
mobilization, 2, 6, 20, 212–13
Mokolo, 180
Mossi, 133
multiparty politics, 30
multiple ethnic categories, 2
multivocality (of symbols), 33
Mundang, 180
Muslim/s, 34, 45n5, 151, 171
  caps, 1, 10, 24, 27, 30, 33–36, 46n15
  community, 23, 25, 28, 30, 33, 37–41, 136, 153–56, 159, 161, 163, 168, 170, 173–75, 177, 181–82
  conversion, 135, 138, 161–65, 167–69, 172, 174–78, 181, 183n14
  ideology and practice, 24, 39, 163, 165, 172–74, 179

N

name-list, 54, 65
nation-building, 201
national
  citizenship, 2, 31, 33, 50, 67, 85, 102, 106
  politics, 2, 6, 11, 32, 42, 44, 55, 67, 94
National Union for Democracy and Progress (NUDP), 99
Native Authorities, 83, 85
  Council, 84
'natives', 50, 66, 84, 103, 134n6
Ncane (language), 48, 58, 59
Nchaney
  clan territory, 58, 62, 66, 71–72
  masks, 34, 36, 39–40
  myth of origin, 52–54
  notables, 24–25, 27, 35, 37–40, 51, 52, 54–55, 57–58, 67
  polity, 52, 59–60, 62, 66, 71
  territory, 37, 39, 55, 58, 59–61, 63, 64, 70, 71, 79, 89, 156–57
Ndop, 140
Ndu, 65, 131, 143
negotiation, 10, 19, 27, 29, 33, 34, 36, 42, 51, 106, 125, 126, 127, 188, 189
'neo-colonial', 6
Newton, R., 50, 51, 52, 58, 61, 63, 73nn8–9, 139
Nfume, 16, 58–59, 62, 72, 89–91
Ngaoundal, 91, 93
Niger, 90, 137, 159n5
Nigeria, 4–5, 6, 13, 59, 62, 63, 64, 65, 73n8, 78, 80, 82, 84–85, 90, 91, 92, 105, 134n8, 136, 137, 139, 140–44, 146–47, 150, 151, 153, 159n4, 164, 167, 178, 182n2, 192, 199
Nkambe, 16, 31–32, 58, 64, 65, 88, 123, 124, 143, 147, 151, 163, 194, 199, 202, 205
Nkanchi, 16, 17–18, 20n7, 48, 52–55, 58, 63, 66, 71–72, 73n3, 73nn8–9, 74n24, 141, 146–48, 154, 156
non-governmental organizations (NGO), 94–95, 98, 101–2, 105, 121, 123, 125, 134n4, 154, 155, 184, 186, 188, 190, 211
Noni, 59

North West Fons'
  Association (NOWEFA), 67
  Conference (NOWEFCO), 67
  Union (NOWEFU), 68, 100
North West Lamidos Forum, 100
Nsari (Bessa language), 59, 69
Nso, 13, 37, 40, 43, 45n5, 47n19, 55, 61, 63, 64, 65, 74n24, 98, 140, 141, 143, 161, 178, 180–81
Nuer, 8, 160n16
Nyamnjoh, Francis, 30, 31, 46n10, 46n13, 58, 68, 74n10, 74n26, 75n29, 171

O

occult
  aggression, 20, 119, 169–72, 177, 193–94, 200, 204
  murder, 3, 184, 193, 197, 204, 207. *See also* conflict: murder conflict
  practices, 171–72, 193
Opération Epervier (Operation Sparrow Hawk), 191
Onitsha, 147
Orissa, 36
'otherness', 79, 105–6

P

palace
  fon's palace, 18, 38, 55–56, 58, 98, 116, 127, 197
  hierarchy, *see* hierarchy, hierarchies
party politics, 30, 67, 99
pastoralism, 76, 104, 114–16
pastoralists (Mbororo), 16, 17–18, 19, 55, 64–65, 76, 83, 134n8, 135, 144, 208n5
  agro-pastoralists, 13, 76, 78, 111, 114, 116
patron–client relations, 99, 101, 190
performance, 3, 24, 33, 46n6, 46n17, 123, 174, 199, 201
  kariya (staff hurling), 25–26, 35–36, 39, 47n20
  ritual, 3, 36
  staged, 121, 123
Pidgin English, 20n5, 45nn1–2, 47n19, 49–50, 68, 110, 116, 125, 143, 148, 159n8, 165, 170, 171, 173, 174, 176, 183n7
Pinyin, 13, 18, 62–64, 89, 116–17, 134n7, 145
policies, 5, 6, 33, 42, 44, 83, 105, 111–13
  colonial and postcolonial, 29, 84, 109

political
  hegemony, 61, 178
  hierarchy, 29, 157–58
  liberalization, 4, 19, 30, 45, 57, 68, 94, 99, 102, 128, 184, 207
  lobbying, 1, 100, 184, 186–87, 201, 207–8
  parties, 186
  representation, 52, 66–67, 71, 76, 92, 94, 98–102, 104, 139, 153–58
  rights, 31
politicization, 7, 19, 208, 213
politics, *see also* belonging, politics of
  cultural, 32–36, 46n13
  national, 2, 32, 55, 67
  politics of cultural performance, 36
  'politics of the belly', 190
polygyny, 173
power
  differences, 50
  distribution of, 29, 44
  mystical/spiritual powers, 34–35, 55
  relations, 29–31, 36, 43, 57, 58
  supernatural powers, 58
pre-colonial, 12, 53–54, 61, 112, 116, 140–41
Presbyterian Church, 165
primordialist approaches, 5, 160n16
procedural strategies, 184–87, 191, 200, 207
property rights, 203–4
pulaaku (FulBe code of conduct), 76–77, 88, 93, 101, 104–6, 106n3

R

reconciliation, 10, 38, 41, 127, 157, 199, 207
regime
  Ahidjo, 31, 66, 68, 99, 107n26, 177, 180
  Biya, 31
relations
  farmer–herder, *see* farmer–herder relations
  gender, 91, 169, 173, 177, 179
  host–guest, *see* host–guest relations
  interethnic, *see* interethnic relations
  inter-group, 6, 31, 36, 38, 43
  patron–client, 99, 101, 190
  socio-economic, 66, 109, 119, 133, 134n8, 134n12, 135, 153, 195
relationship
  Jaafun-Aku, 85–88
  Mbororo-Hausa, 64, 145–46, 156

religion, *see also* conversion
  Christianity, 9, 163, 168, 174
  Islam, 5, 9, 38, 45n5, 64, 88, 92–93, 105, 111, 115, 130, 144, 147, 152, 154–55, 161, 164, 168–69, 175, 177, 182n5, 183n9, 183n12, 187
  local African religions, 9, 12, 89, 161, 163
reunification, 57, 66, 85
Ring Road, 17, 18, 55, 64
ritual
  authority, 27, 36, 58
  performance, 3, 36
  of rebellion, 44
  violence, 33, 34, 36
rivalry,
  economic, 121
  personal, 33, 61
  political, 3, 31
royal
  authority, 36
  'royal excrement', 4
Rwanda, 2

S
Sabga, 79–80, 82–83, 94–98, 103–4, 106n5, 107n20, 107n26, 126, 163, 210–14
Sabongari, 140
Salomone, Frank, 137–38, 152, 159n2, 178
sarki, sarkin (Hausa chief), 145–48, 150–51, 154, 157, 160n14, 170, 181
Schilder, Kees, 51, 176, 178, 180
Schlee, Günther, 6–8, 10, 43, 45n4, 77, 108n32, 112, 134n9, 158, 162, 182
Schnepel, Burkhard, 33, 36
Schultz, Emily, 161, 176, 178–79, 180
secret societies, 34
sedentarization, 19, 84, 94, 104, 114
self-categorization, 49
self-understanding, 2, 5, 6, 19, 49, 52–53, 62, 71, 76, 92, 98, 100, 103, 105, 152, 158, 163, 211
slavery, 3, 53
social
  cohesion, 8, 20, 184, 208
  energy, 3, 26–27
  insecurity, 30–32, 42, 44
  integration, 7, 65, 207
  liabilities, 175–76, 180
  status, 33, 163, 177, 202, 206
  transformation, 4

Social Democratic Front (SDF), 32, 46n10, 70, 99
Société de Développement d'Elevage et du Commerce (SODELCO), 108n27
Société de Développement et d'Exploitation des Productions Animales (SODEPA), 18
Society for Initiatives in Rural Development and Environmental Protection (SIRDEP), 154
Sokoto, 53
solidarity, 78, 101, 128–29, 152, 167, 169, 170, 196
Somalia, 2
Sotramilk, 95
Southern Africa, 44
staff-hurlers, *see* Mbororo
state (the), 66–71, 99–100, 102, 104, 118, 156, 157, 187, 189–91, 198, 201, 204, 208, 212
  authority, 1
  law, 187
  officials, 24, 27, 29, 44, 104, 123, 126
strangers, 6, 28, 50, 84, 85, 99, 130, 167
strategies
  individual and collective, 20, 33, 101, 201, 205, 211
Sudan, 2, 159n4
symbolic stand-off, 1, 3, 25, 27, 44

T
Takum, 90
territoriality, 48, 62, 72
territorialization, 4, 53
theatre for development, 123
Tibati, 82
Tignère, 82
Tikar, 50, 52, 73n5
Tiko, 145
Tiv revolts, 85
tourism, 97
Town FulBe, *see* FulBe; Huya
trade
  cattle trade, 16, 18, 64, 90, 93, 94, 134n7, 144–45, 146, 147, 149
  in human heads, 171, 193–94
  long-distance, 4, 12, 135, 140–44
  salt, 140, 143, 146, 150
  textiles, 140, 141, 146
tradition, *also* 'country-fashion', 35, 49, 51, 58, 59, 68, 73n1, 139, 163, 164, 171, 176. *See also* 'invention of tradition'
'traditional authorities', 45n1, 49, 71

transhumance, 64, 83–84, 111, 147, 148
Transparency International, 190
tribe/s, 48, 49–50, 62, 66, 74n20, 153
Turner, Victor, 8, 27, 33, 41, 43

U
United Nations, 102, 210, 212
  concept of 'indigenous peoples', 6, 11
unity, 39, 53, 62, 213
  sense of unity, 196
  'unity through diversity', 32

V
van Santen, José, 161, 172, 176–77, 178, 180, 182n5
Viktoria (Limbe), 145
Village AiD, 101–2
Virtanen, Tea, 77, 79, 89, 105, 106n3, 107n7
visceral quality, 3, 201
violence, 2, 7, 8–9, 11, 32, 39, 42–44, 83, 173, 184–85, 193, 196, 197, 213. *See also* conflict model; Elwert; ritual
  army intervention, 32, 203
  militancy and violence, 1, 31
  physical, 32
  symbolic, 1, 3, 8, 19, 27, 28

visual and theatre anthropology, 12
von Benda-Beckman, Keebet, 187

W
Warnier, Jean-Pierre, 4, 12–13, 46n7, 48, 53, 56, 62, 74n11, 74n18, 116, 141, 150, 172, 207
Wawa, 164
We, 84
West Africa, 3, 43, 109, 112, 115, 141, 144, 152, 190
West Region, 12, 107n20
Widekum, 50
Wimbum, 13, 59, 64, 67, 74n18, 161, 181
witchcraft, 64, 70, 119, 131, 161, 164, 169, 170–72, 188, 190, 193, 199, 207
WoDaaBe (nomadic FulBe), 79, 80
World Bank, 30, 186
Wum, 84, 90

Y
Yaoundé, 69, 99, 154, 194, 195, 210, 211
Yola, 80, 82, 148

Z
Zambia, 43

Integration and Conflict Studies

Published in association with the Max Planck Institute for Social Anthropology, Halle/Saale

Volume 1
How Enemies are Made: Towards a Theory of Ethnic and Religious Conflicts
Günther Schlee

Volume 2
Changing Identifications and Alliances in North-East Africa
Vol.I: Ethiopia and Kenya
Edited by Günther Schlee and Elizabeth E. Watson

Volume 3
Changing Identifications and Alliances in North-East Africa
Vol.II: Sudan, Uganda and the Ethiopia-Sudan Borderlands
Edited by Günther Schlee and Elizabeth E. Watson

Volume 4
Playing Different Games: The Paradox of Anywaa and Nuer Identification Strategies in the Gambella Region, Ethiopia
Dereje Feyissa

Volume 5
Who Owns the Stock? Collective and Multiple Property Rights in Animals
Edited by Anatoly M. Khazanov and Günther Schlee

Volume 6
Irish/ness is All Around Us: Language Revivalism and the Culture of Ethnic Identity in Northern Ireland
Olaf Zenker

Volume 7
Variations on Uzbek Identity: Strategic Choices, Cognitive Schemas and Political Constraints in Identification Processes
Peter Finke

Volume 8
Domesticating Youth: The Youth Bulge and its Socio-Political Implications in Tajikistan
Sophie Roche

Volume 9
Creole Identity in Postcolonial Indonesia
Jacqueline Knörr

Volume 10
Friendship, Descent and Alliance in Africa: Anthropological Perspectives
Edited by Martine Guichard, Tilo Grätz and Youssouf Diallo

Volume 11
Masks and Staffs: Identity Politics in the Cameroon Grassfields
Michaela Pelican

Volume 12
The Upper Guinea Coast in Global Perspective
Edited by Jacqueline Knörr and Christoph Kohl

Volume 13
Staying at Home: Identities, Memories and Social Networks of Kazakhstani Germans
Rita Sanders

Volume 14
'City of the Future': Built Space, Modernity and Urban Change in Astana
Mateusz Laszczkowski

Volume 15
On Retaliation: Towards an Interdisciplinary Understanding of a Basic Human Condition
Edited by Bertram Turner and Günther Schlee

www.ingramcontent.com/pod-product-compliance
Lightning Source LLC
Chambersburg PA
CBHW072149100526
44589CB00015B/2153